Springer Business Cases

Springer Business Cases is a book series featuring the latest case studies in all areas of business, management, and finance, from around the world. The well-curated case collections in each of the books represent insights and lessons that can be used both in the classroom as well as in professional contexts. The books also place a focus on regional and topical diversity as well as encouraging alternative viewpoints which bring the knowledge forward. Both teaching cases as well as research cases are welcome.

Mohammad Moshref-Javadi • Sridhar Seshadri
Editors

Impacts of COVID-19 on Supply Chains

Disruptions, Technologies, and Solutions

Springer

Editors
Mohammad Moshref-Javadi
Department of Business Administration
University of Illinois Urbana-Champaign
Champaign, IL, USA

Sridhar Seshadri
Alan J and Joyce D Professor, Department of Business Administration, Gies College of Business
University of Illinois at Urbana Champaign
Champaign, IL, USA

Health Innovation Professor, Biomedical and Translational Medicine, Carle Illinois College of Medicine
University of Illinois at Urbana-Champaign
Champaign, IL, USA

ISSN 2662-5431 ISSN 2662-544X (electronic)
Springer Business Cases
ISBN 978-3-031-47736-2 ISBN 978-3-031-47734-8 (eBook)
https://doi.org/10.1007/978-3-031-47734-8

This Springer imprint is published by the registered company Springer Nature Switzerland AG
The registered company address is: Gewerbestrasse 11, 6330 Cham, Switzerland

Paper in this product is recyclable

Preface

Since the beginning of 2020, many companies' supply chains have been affected due to the disruptions caused by the pandemic. From production stoppages in facilities to shortages of supplies, logistical problems, and shortages of labor, the problems persist even to date. Many companies made adjustments to their supply chains to cope with the impacts of supply chain disruptions. These adjustments include changes in product offerings and production schedules, changes in sourcing and distribution strategies, and changes in scheduling work and outsourcing. Supply chains that were once simply taken for granted continued to operate and supply not just vital parts and products but also day-to-day goods. Many heroic actions of firms prevented a pandemic from interrupting the activities of the global economy. During this period, the word "supply chain" became almost as well known as COVID-19 due to its use by everyone and every day to diagnose failures as well as laud successes.

We started writing this book to record these actions and draw lessons. Soon it became obvious to us that several major themes were emerging and also that we did not have the data or insight to record what was happening in several areas. The main themes were that the impact flowed from the retail end that quickly adjusted, and the supply chains accommodated these changes, albeit slowly. Understanding the ebbs and flows of the pandemic was essential to create forward-looking strategies; therefore, forecasting became extremely important to stay ahead of the changes in demand, fulfillment, supplies, and availability of resources. Several supply chains were quickly created to operate at the highest levels of efficiencies and massive scale of operations, including testing and provision of PPE and vaccines. Finally, new technologies were used to plan, manage, monitor, and control. We recruited subject matter experts to write about each of these four areas; thus, the book became a compendium.

In chapter "Adjustments to Supply Chains in Response to the COVID-19 Pandemic: A Survey", we begin with a survey of the effects of the pandemic on supply chains and the consequent adjustments made by companies to cope with these effects. The survey includes long-term and short-term adjustments in different industries such as automotive, semiconductor, pharmaceutical, food and beverage, transportation, and retail. We also present lessons learned from such disruptions and identify the factors for companies and industries to consider in making their supply chains resilient to similar disruptions.

In chapter "Post-Pandemic Online Grocery Delivery Services: Trends, Challenges, and Empirical Evidence from Germany", the authors, Jakob Schmidt and Konstantinos Nikolopoulos, focus on online grocery delivery in Germany. The chapter analyzes the operational challenges to online grocery delivery in Germany before and during the COVID-19 pandemic. The analysis is based on surveying several resources, such as news and research articles. The analysis is complemented by semi-structured interviews with industry experts. They also compare the challenges and characteristics of online grocery delivery with deliveries in retailing. The main lessons learnt are that the majority of the respondents are confident that they will order groceries online in the future. The top chosen reasons for this are comfort, time saving, and impulse buying, while personal safety was not a major reason.

Chapter "Forecasting and Planning with Auxiliary Data During a Pandemic: Evidence from UK Google Trends" aims to develop reliable methods to predict excess demand during the COVID-19 and similar pandemics. The authors, Maryam Mojdehi, Konstantinos Nikolopoulos, and Vasileios Bougioukos, are experts in the science of forecasting. Weekly Google Trend data is gathered for nine retail products in three different categories: electronics, toiletries, and groceries. Forward Stepwise Selection is used to investigate the relationship between excess demand and multiple other variables at once. Finally, various models based on regression, decision trees, and neural networks are developed for demand prediction. The findings are that forecasting during a pandemic was less challenging for electronics than that for toiletries and groceries. Consumer demand is affected by the public health environment of a pandemic, and consumers' panic buying and hoarding had a serious impact on demand for those products for which they had most immediate need, such as toiletries and groceries.

Chapter "Supply Chain and SARS-CoV-2 Mitigation: Adjustments Made to Administer Six Million SARS-CoV-2 Tests in a Large Public Testing Program" describes SHIELD Illinois's approach to managing millions of COVID-19 tests. The challenges along with developments and mitigation plans to tackle the challenges are explained by Len Musielak and Ronald S. Watkins. The lessons learned are presented to elaborate on the successful expansion of this program to other cities in the state of Illinois. SHIELD Illinois established an integrated supply chain and technology system that enabled PcR testing results within 13 h from sample collection to individual results from anywhere in a 400 by 200 miles state. The logistics established can provide insights into future emergency responses.

Finally, chapter "The Role of Technologies in Supply Chain Efficiency and Resiliency" reviews the role of digitization and various technologies, such as blockchain, artificial intelligence, digital twin, augmented reality, and autonomous driving in the supply chain. Each technology is introduced along with various real-world use examples from companies to mitigate the risks during the COVID-19 pandemic. The authors conclude that IoT, blockchain and similar technologies can be significantly helpful to enhance supply chain transparency during the disruptions and therefore improve inventory availability.

The accumulated knowledge of supply chain management has served us well in managing through the COVID-19 pandemic. Firms that were already well along in using systems, technologies, and people in the best possible ways were benefitted during these disruptions. We will perhaps be unable to predict when the next disruption will occur but the knowledge, questions, and preparations necessary to handle massive disruptions are available for all to study.

Champaign, IL

Mohammad Moshref-Javadi
Sridhar Seshadri

Acknowledgments

Mohammad and Sridhar are grateful for the generous support from the Collaboratory Initiative in the Information, Operations, Supply Chain, and Analytics (IOSA) Area in the Department of Business Administration at the Gies College of Business. We also express our appreciation to the generous research support from the Department of Business Administration, Gies College of Business, and Carle Illinois College of Medicine at the University of Illinois. We thank all the students in the Fall 2020 and 2021 Supply Chain Management graduate classes for collecting information that was used to create the plan for the book. We deeply appreciate Harish Reddy and Mayank Tripathi, graduate students at Gies College of Business, for their assistance in preparing the chapters. We are very grateful to Jialin Yan, Editor, and Sneha Arunagiri, Project Coordinator, for their encouragement and guidance throughout the process.

Contents

About the Editors

Mohammad Moshref-Javadi is Assistant Teaching Professor at the Department of Business Administration at the University of Illinois at Urbana-Champaign. He is currently the Illinois Director of Supply Chain Management Corporate Affiliates Program. Dr. Moshref-Javadi earned his PhD degree in Industrial Engineering from Purdue University in 2017. His research focuses on supply chain analytics, logistics, and process improvement using data-driven optimization and simulation methods. Dr. Moshref-Javadi has published in various journals, such as *European Journal of Operational Research, International Journal of Production Research, Computers & Operations Research*, and *Transportation Research Part E.*

Sridhar Seshadri obtained his PhD at the University of California, Berkeley, after graduating from the Indian Institute of Technology, Madras, India, with a Bachelor of Technology and the Indian Institute of Management, Ahmedabad, India, with a Post-Graduate Diploma in Management. He is currently the Alan J and Joyce D Baltz Professor in the Gies College of Business and Health Innovation Professor, Biomedical and Translational Medicine, Carle Illinois College of Medicine. His current research projects focus on applications of analytics to different policy questions. These include Healthcare as part of the Heartgroup (https://heartanalytics.github.io/), the Development of Micro, Small and Medium Manufacturing Enterprises in India, and Sourcing and Risk Management in Global Supply Networks. His professional service includes serving as the Associate Editor, *Naval Research Logistics*; Associate Editor, *Management Science*; and Department Editor (Operations and Finance Interface), *Production and Operations Management Journal.* He is a founding board member of the Supply Chain Analytics Institute.

Adjustments to Supply Chains in Response to the COVID-19 Pandemic: A Survey

Mohammad Moshref-Javadi and Sridhar Seshadri

1 Introduction

The World Health Organization (WHO) declared COVID-19 to be an epidemic disease in March 2020 and recommended that all countries take preparatory actions to cope with its spread (World Health Organization, 2020). As predicted, the pandemic has had considerable effects on global economies. In 2020, the global economy and trade reduced by approximately 3.2% and 5.3%, respectively (Jackson et al., 2021). In September 2021, the number of deaths surpassed that of the Spanish flu of 1918 (Jackson et al., 2021). Furthermore, consumer prices and the inflation rate increased unexpectedly (O'Brien, 2022). The United States also lost billions of jobs with an unemployment rate of nearly 25% in 2020 (Lambert, 2020). Later in 2022, workers started quitting, changing, and switching their jobs, leading to big raises in salary and therefore higher inflation (Guilford & Cambon, 2022). In addition, because of the shift in demand for products, supply chain disruption, and increased prices, the inflation rate increased from approximately 2% in 2020 to more than 8% in March 2022 (Bernstein & Tedeschi, 2021; U.S. Department of Statistics, 2022) and a 40-year high of 8.3% in May 2022 (Guilford, 2022a, 2022b) and 9.1% in June 2022 (Bureau of Labor Statistics, 2022). Since November 2020, consumer prices rose by over 6.8%, food prices by 6.1%, and energy prices by 33.3% in November 2021

M. Moshref-Javadi (✉)
Department of Business Administration, Gies College of Business, University of Illinois at Urbana Champaign, Champaign, IL, USA
e-mail: moshref@illinois.edu

S. Seshadri
Alan J and Joyce D Professor, Department of Business Administration, Gies College of Business, University of Illinois at Urbana Champaign, Champaign, IL, USA

Health Innovation Professor, Biomedical and Translational Medicine, Carle Illinois College of Medicine, University of Illinois at Urbana-Champaign, Champaign, IL, USA

M. Moshref-Javadi, S. Seshadri (eds.), *Impacts of COVID-19 on Supply Chains*, Springer Business Cases, https://doi.org/10.1007/978-3-031-47734-8_1

(Bureau of Labor Statistics, 2021). Several of these effects were caused by supply chain disruptions and inefficiencies, which have been the topic of discussion in almost every forum, from shortages to bottlenecks and from local to national and global issues that affect every firm, in almost every industry and region.

During the pandemic, many companies in various industries were affected, primarily because of supply chain disruptions and slowness in response due to the pandemic. Studies show that 94% of Fortune 1000 companies experienced supply chain disruptions caused by COVID-19 (Accenture, 2021). Due to the halt of production operations in East Asia, the sourcing of many parts and products from that region stopped for several weeks (Ting-Fang & Li, 2021). For instance, the lack of sufficient semiconductor chips sourced from Asia heavily impacted a variety of industries such as electronics, automotive, data processing, and networking and communication industries around the world (Harris, 2022; Lepcha, 2022). The chip shortage also affected manufacturing and production operations in the United States, primarily the electronics and automotive industries. The precautionary actions and regulations at factories to prevent the spread of the virus further slowed the production process (Eisenstein, 2020; Mutikani, 2020). Likewise, the trucking industry was also heavily affected, and many trucking companies sidelined thousands of trucks, while other truckers had to make empty backhaul trips. In India, for example, 80% of the 10 million trucks were sidelined (Plume, 2020). Similarly, the International Road Transport Union (IRU) in Geneva indicated that new freight contracts declined by 60–90% due to COVID-19, and empty runs increased by up to 40% (Plume, 2020).

Many companies adjusted their supply chain operations to cope with the impacts of supply chain disruptions. For instance, due to the sheer number of online orders, Amazon prioritized fulfillment of essential items such as baby products, health and household items, groceries, and pet supplies (Hu & Dastin, 2020). Several companies resumed their manufacturing operations after a few weeks of stoppage while abiding by safety measures such as daily symptom screenings, ensuring six-foot distance guidelines between workers, mask mandates, and staggering shifts to avoid over-crowding (Beggin, 2020; Heilweil, 2020). Similarly, due to the changes in demand and consumers' shopping preferences, some companies adjusted their operations to produce high-demand products such as ventilators and masks (Koenig & Miller, 2020; Wayland, 2020). Due to a surge in online orders, retailers and grocery stores invested in new distribution channels such as in-store and curbside pickup (Corral, 2020). Curbside pickup increased by 208% during the pandemic, driven by consumer preference and rapid response by retailers, department stores, and grocery stores (Thomas, 2020). Although many of these adjustments were applied as short-term solutions, some companies also considered long-term solutions to their supply chain inefficiencies. Samsung and Intel, for instance, announced new chip plants in the U.S. in 2021 to tackle chip shortages (Leonard & Kim, 2021; Nellis, 2021).

In this survey, we present a review of the impacts of supply chain disruption in six industries, automotive, food and beverage, retailers, pharmaceutical, semiconductors, and logistics industries. Further, we review what actions several companies took to cope with these impacts. Adjustments are focused on several aspects of supply chain operations such as manufacturing, transportation, warehousing, sourcing and procurement, product offering, and more. We present the supply chain issues and companies' adjustments based on available secondary data. Finally, we summarize lessons learned and propose recommendations for designing resilient and responsive supply chains to effectively deal with potential future disasters.

The organization of the paper is as follows. Section 2 presents a review of the impacts of COVID on supply chains, adjustments made by companies to tackle them, and lessons learned for different industries. Section 3 discusses the trends and adjustments made, and conclusions and future research directions are presented in Sect. 4.

2 Impacts of COVID-19 and Companies' Adjustments to the Supply Chain: The Six Industries

In this section, we evaluate the effects of COVID-19 on different industries, as well as the adjustments made by companies in response, and elaborate on the lessons learned for each industry.

2.1 The Automotive Industry

Impacts of COVID-19

Both the production and sales operations in the automotive industry were affected considerably by the pandemic. Many automakers in Europe and the United States such as BMW, Renault, Volkswagen, Honda, Toyota, Nissan, and Ford suspended production operations immediately because of supply chain disruptions and stay-at-home orders (Beredo et al., 2020). When the COVID-19 pandemic began spreading globally in the first quarter of 2020, many global supply chains were halted due to lockdowns, border restrictions, and local government emergency policies. In anticipation of this chaos, many manufacturers in the auto industry placed oversized orders of semiconductors, which was a major factor causing the global chip shortage. This shortage led Ford to halt production or reduce the hours scheduled at a total of eight production plants. These actions led to an estimated loss of more than 1.1 million units of production (50%) in 2021 because of chip shortages (Leonard, 2021b). Ford completed the 2020 fiscal year with a net loss of $1.3 billion and GM reported approximately $2 billion lost in 2021 (Grzelewski, 2021). Chip shortage also heavily affected the truck production industry, reducing the General Motors truck production volume by more than 3000 trucks in the first quarter of 2021 (Stinson, 2021). Shortage of supplies, port delays, and container shortages also impacted Tesla's production, with Elon Musk indicating "insane difficulties" with its supply chain (Kay, 2021b).

The disruption effect of COVID-19 on the auto supply chain started in 2020 and has continued to 2022, even though the impacts of the pandemic have reduced in terms of disease spread and death rates. For example, used and new car and truck prices are up in 2022 due to the increased demand and supply shortages (Giusti, 2022; Guilford, 2022a). Also, Mercedes Benz's sales dropped by 16% in April and July 2022 with a major reduction in sales in China (Bellwood, 2022). Overall new vehicles sales fell by 17% during the first six months of 2022 (Elliott & Bobrowsky, 2022). On the other hand, the pandemic has considerably increased electric vehicle (EV) sales. Mercedes Benz EV sales increased by 134% in the first half of 2022, and Ford EV sales increased by 77% in 2022 compared to the year before, mostly impacted by the sales of the Mustang Mach-E and the F-150. However, EV production is also highly dependent on batteries. With 90% of synthetic graphite anodes and 60% of natural graphite production based in China, it is also a risky industry highly vulnerable to disruption (Cuevas, 2022).

Figure 1 shows the summary of automotive industry performance since the fourth quarter of 2019. The top left chart plots the gross margin. Mercedes Benz and Ford increased gross margin, suggesting a price increase. Tesla's gross margin has considerably increased compared to other companies due to significant receipts of regulatory credits (Kolodny, 2020). The top right chart shows the return on assets. The increase for Ford and Mercedes could be related to an increase in margins. The return on assets for Volkswagen reduced mainly due to a major car recall during the pandemic. The bottom left chart shows the effect on inventories. The accumulation of inventory also increased for many companies due to the chip shortage and,

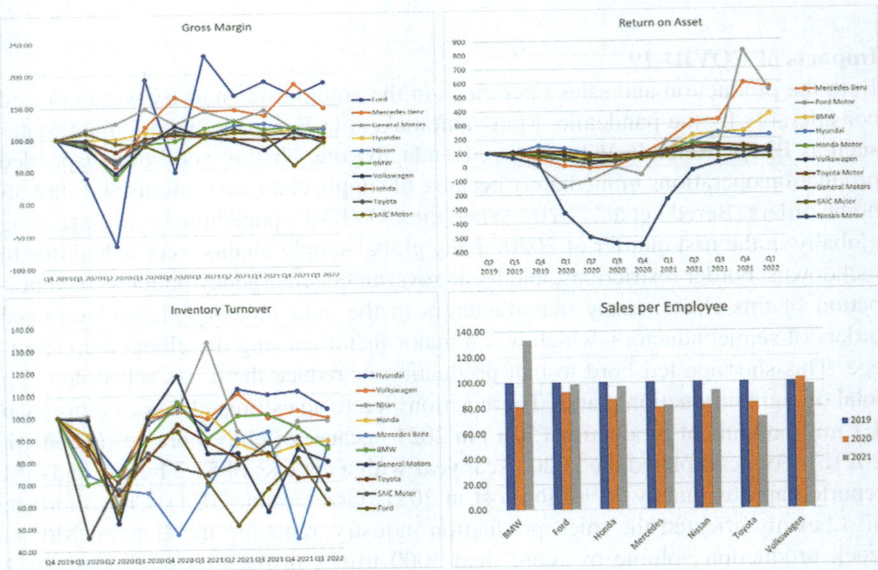

Fig. 1 Summary of the performance of the major companies in the automotive industry. Note: Data is collected from Bloomberg. Return on asset = (net income + (1 − tax rate) × interest expenses)/(total assets), gross margin = (net income + (1 − tax rate) × interest expenses)/(total revenue), sales per employee = (revenue)/(number of employees), and inventory turnover = (cost of goods sold)/inventory. The tax rate is assumed to be 35%

therefore, the increase in work-in-process inventory. The bottom right chart plots sales per employee as a proxy for labor shortages. The sales per employee has increased for many companies. We believe this is primarily due to a shortage of labor rather than an actual increase in productivity.

Adjustments Made

Due to chip shortages, many automakers started to temporarily drop some add-on features such as blind-spot detection, fuel consumption management software, and Apple CarPlay and Android Auto (Colias & Foldy, 2021; Nadelle, 2022). On a broader scale, due to supply shortages, auto manufacturers decided to optimize the mix of cars based on supply availability and profit margin as well as customers' preferences and demand for popular cars (Colias & Foldy, 2021). Tesla also decided to focus on car production rather than on Powerwall due to a shortage of supplies (Garland, 2021c).

Some automakers decided to follow new paths for sourcing parts. Ford used dual-sourcing and aimed for design interchangeability for single-sourced parts (Garland, 2021a). Ford uses several suppliers spread across the globe, with many of its suppliers in Western Europe and a few in East Asia. Most of Ford's European suppliers ship components from Western Europe, across the Atlantic Ocean, through the Erie Canal, and into the Great Lakes for delivery to Ford's Midwestern production plants. This network of suppliers and available routes has allowed Ford to circumvent some of the huge delays in global logistics.

Because of supply chain disruptions, auto manufacturers such as Ford and GM had to rethink their supply chains comprehensively to be able to have better control and perhaps move toward a more vertically integrated supply chain. Ford plans on designing its semiconductors, which are tailored specifically to optimize Ford vehicles' performance, help automate self-driving capabilities, and improve internal battery systems (Sorkin et al., 2021). Particularly, they plan to work on designing and developing their chips domestically (Colias & Foldy, 2021). The Biden administration supported this by prioritizing domestic chip production with a $50 billion research and development fund. Although this support and all the actions made by car manufacturers could be promising in the long term, in the short term many companies had to reduce production or adjust car features because of chip shortages (Colias & Foldy, 2021). Some car manufacturers such as Volkswagen, Ford, and GM plan to enter battery production in addition to semiconductor businesses. Entering these new businesses can help these companies improve car features based on their needs and do so in an agile approach (Colias & Foldy, 2021). This is a long-term solution, however, which will take several years for Ford and GM to develop and master. In addition to the insourcing of chips, some companies such as GM also plan to redesign these chips, aiming to reduce the number of unique chips to reduce the complexity of the automotive supply chain (Colias & Foldy, 2021).

Tesla also suffered from supply chain issues during the pandemic, particularly related to the shortage of raw materials such as nickel, cobalt, and lithium for electric car batteries. Tesla had to order many materials from multiple origins, increasing procurement and transportation costs for Tesla and, consequently, increasing prices for customers (Denton, 2021; Elliott & Bobrowsky, 2022). However, because of several reasons, Tesla's supply chain was considerably less affected by the pandemic. First, Tesla used substitute chips, which helped considerably to cope with the effect of chip shortages. Second, Tesla produces a smaller variety of cars compared to other car manufacturers. This low variety reduces the types of chips and parts needed for cars and, therefore, reduces the risk of shortage. Third, Tesla produces 500,000 cars per year while BMW produces more than 2.5 million cars per year. The smaller scale of production by Tesla perhaps reduces the effect of supply chain disruptions as well, as long as Tesla can compensate suppliers adequately to keep supplies flowing. Tesla's sales increased nearly 36% to 499,550 cars in 2020 (Boudette, 2021), and Tesla delivered more than 200,000 vehicles in Q2 of 2021 amid the peak pandemic. Fourth, Tesla produces only electric cars while other companies produce several types such as electric, hybrid, and gas vehicles. This significantly reduces the variety of raw materials, production facilities, and processes for Tesla. Tesla also uses vertical integration, which allows for manufacturing flexibility, process control, and increased supply chain coordination (Elliott & Bobrowsky, 2022; UKEssays, 2020). Finally, Tesla primarily uses direct shipping to customers without using dealerships, enabling Tesla to reliably deliver its cars to customers. However, Tesla restructured the corporation and laid off 9% of workers to reduce future human resource costs. The layoff did not include the workers in the production line, and the production line worked almost at full capacity during the pandemic.

Having effective inventory management policies played an important role during the pandemic. Toward implementing postponements and delayed differentiation strategies, for example, Ford planned on stockpiling critical parts (Garland, 2021a) while it leaned toward a leaner purchasing and inventory management approach for finished vehicles. Ford planned this by revamping the purchasing process to allow dealerships to hold a smaller number of vehicles in inventory (Leonard, 2021a). This also allowed automotive companies to cope with potential future risks such as further waves of the pandemic by using a safety stock of parts in combination with the postponement strategy. As a counterpoint to this strategy, however, when asked about empty lots, a dealer said that "customers are looking around the lot and ordering exactly what they want on the internet!"

To mitigate the effects of this global shortage, Ford has recently shifted its supply chain strategy from a "build-to-stock" strategy to a "build-to-order" strategy (Garland, 2021a). This shift helps Ford ensure that all precious semiconductors are used to produce vehicles that can be sold to customers rather than remain unsold in a dealership lot. Additionally, Ford continues production of parts such that once the chips become available, they finalize the assembly of the vehicles, followed by extensive quality checks to reduce customer wait times (Grzelewski, 2021). This is becoming known as the build-shy strategy. Using this strategy, companies continue to produce cars although they do not have all the chips available for the cars to avoid the extreme costs of turning off and on the assembly lines. Because of this strategy, some companies such as Ford and GM had more than 20,000 vehicles and 30,000 pick-up trucks waiting for final assembly by summer 2021 (Colias & Foldy, 2021).

Lessons Learned

- Among the several studied automakers, some of them performed more effectively during the pandemic. For instance, some companies were able to swiftly switch the mix and variety of products that are produced and offered to customers. Obtaining this level of flexibility to quickly switch between products and adjust their features, both in terms of the range of products and time to switch, can result in reducing lost sales and preventing potential inventory build-up. Nevertheless, in-advance preparation such as having technical and knowledge resources is a key criterion to achieving this flexibility and repurposeability. Some methods such as product modularization, combined with the postponement strategy, can make this possible.
- Learning from Tesla's supply chain, we notice that reducing the variety of products and even the variety of parts used in products can considerably simplify the extent and size of the supply chain, making the supply and production of parts more manageable. In addition, companies with a vertically integrated supply chain are more successful in managing supplies during disruptions because they have more control over the supply chain operations to react to product mix and volume changes.
- Changing the fulfillment strategy from assemble-to-order to make-to-order and also using the postponement and delayed differentiation strategies can also be an effective solution during the pandemic in response to the shortages of supplies and changes in consumers' demands and preferences.
- Many companies are rethinking their supply and sourcing strategies, bringing supplies and production close to the demand locations. Companies such as Ford and GM decided to insource the design and potentially the production of semiconductor chips. We hypothesize that when multiple companies rely on a single supplier, which becomes the bottleneck during disruption, it can considerably increase the risks of disruption in the supply chain. Predicting and preventing these bottlenecks can significantly reduce the risks in the supply chain. To this end, some companies have chosen to diversify suppliers geographically, for example having two or three suppliers in three different regions to mitigate the risks of disruptions, as a step toward regionalization.

2.2 *The Food and Beverage Industry*

Impacts of COVID-19

The shift in demand impacted the sales and operations of several companies. Changes in consumer demand for Nestlé led to nearly 5% growth in sales in 2020 powered by pet food and health nutrition (Dawson, 2020). Coca-Cola, for example, experienced low demand for immediate consumption supplies such as fountain drinks and single bottle purchases, while demand for future consumption supplies such as cases of cans increased. This caused a shortage of several supplies, including aluminum cans, due to limited national production capacity (CSCMP, 2021).

Coca-Cola's revenue decreased by 5% in the last quarter of 2020, losing 28% net income, and 13% lower profit compared to the previous year (Hays & Banerjee, 2021). Coca-Cola also experienced a shortage of labor during the pandemic, especially for merchandiser positions for stocking products at stores (CSCMP, 2021). Kellogg's increased sales by 7% in the first three months of 2020 as consumers considerably increased their shopping for long-lasting food products due to stay-at-home orders and an increase in remote work (McNeil, 2020; Silver, 2021).

Figure 2 shows the industry summary. The increased sales per employee across these companies indicate a labor shortage during the pandemic. JBS and Tyson achieved incredible performance due to price hikes and increased sales. Some companies such as JBS and Pepsi also carried more inventory during the pandemic to increase safety cushions to cope with the underlying uncertainties.

Adjustments Made

As demand for coffee grew in the later stages of the pandemic, Starbucks assisted its suppliers by extending a line of credit and providing in-farm assistance with labor training and inventory management to ensure the timely availability of supplies. Additionally, Starbucks began to consolidate the supply chain by going into long-term contracts with transportation companies, thus reducing its overall long-term costs. Since roasted coffee beans can retain freshness for 2–3 weeks on average, Starbucks adjusted its coffee bean purchasing policy to reduce production and minimize variable costs and wastes.

During the pandemic, due to the fear of potential lost sales, companies not only strove to cope with the impacts of the pandemic on their supply chains but also tried to rethink and improve their operations to optimize them. In an attempt to minimize

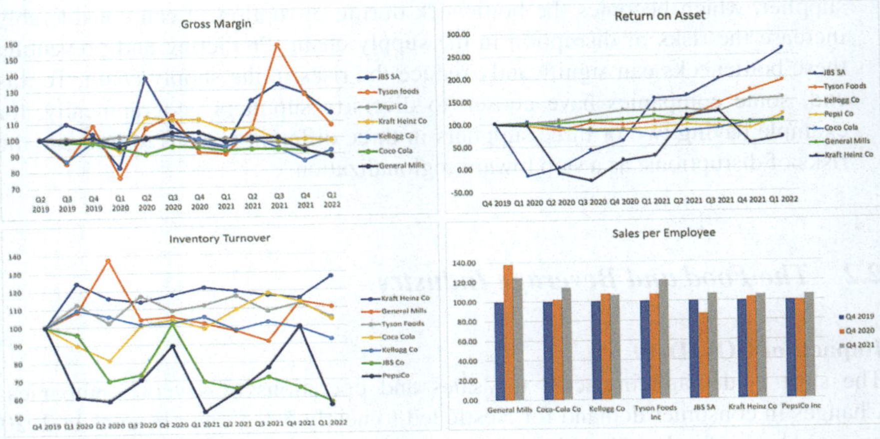

Fig. 2 Summary of the performance of the major companies in the food and beverage industry. Note: Data is collected from Bloomberg. Return on asset = (net income + (1 – tax rate) × interest expenses)/(total assets), gross margin = (net income + (1 – tax rate) × interest expenses)/(total revenue), sales per employee = (revenue)/(number of employees), and inventory turnover = (cost of goods sold)/inventory. The tax rate is assumed to be 35%

costs, Kraft Heinz evaluated that the same materials are purchased from different suppliers with a 2–30% price difference. To this end, it optimized sourcing and supply strategies based on suppliers, quality, materials, and prices (Nunes, 2020). As a part of a $2 billion saving plan for procurement, manufacturing, and logistics, Kraft Heinz reformed its supply chain. Among many different changes to the supply chain, it was able to reduce its SKU count by 20% to minimize procurement and inventory costs (Cosgrove, 2020; Nunes, 2020). Kraft Heinz also suffered from various inefficiencies due to the fragmented structure, lack of sufficient communication among departments and facilities, and lack of visibility. The company decided to reform the organization to a more automated and centralized system to be able to consolidate several decision-making processes. Using this approach, it hopes to achieve $350–$400 million in cost-saving through improved purchasing price savings, inventory management, and supply management integration (Nunes, 2020).

Several companies also improved their IT technologies to cope with the impact of disruptions. Starbucks successfully integrated the Elementum software that enhances visibility in its supply chain through risk management strategies to better prepare for potential future disruption (Mikhail, 2020). Similarly, Procter & Gamble uses a cloud-based real-time information system to monitor and control demand in supply chains, and Toyota uses a database visualization tool to identify and alert potential disasters in its supply chain (Schatteman et al., 2020).

To be able to serve customer demands, several companies such as Kellogg's increased inventory to more than several weeks of safety stock. This was possible due to a well-designed network of suppliers and warehouses to efficiently refill warehouses in Australia (Silver, 2021).

To resolve the can shortage problem due to limited domestic production capacity, Coca-Cola imported cans from Brazil and South Korea (CSCMP, 2021). Coca-Cola's supply and distribution network consisting of hundreds of local bottlers and distributors worldwide enables it to sell more than $1.9 billion in products every day. Coca-Cola uses a micro fulfillment strategy with more than 250 bottling partners worldwide, keeping control of the brand and downstream operations (Keller, 2021). To reduce the complexity of the supply chain and improve its efficiency, Coca-Cola announced that it cut 200 drink brands, an approximate 50% reduction from its previous number of drink brands, as an attempt to combat the impact of the pandemic. The remaining 50% are among the most profitable drink brands, accounting for more than 98% of revenues (Wiener-Bronner, 2020). Similarly, Kraft Heinz plans to reduce its SKU counts by 20% (Best, 2020).

Lessons Learned

- Compared to other industries, IT technologies and information systems play more significant roles in the food and beverage industry due to the effect of this industry on the health and wellness of consumers and the perishability of the products. Tracking and information integration systems can effectively help manage supplies and track and trace the origin and status of materials and ingredients used for the production of food and beverages (Jagt et al., 2020). Companies such as Coca-Cola and Starbucks improved their IT systems to be

able to track the movement of materials in their supply chain and enhance visibility. These investments paid off during the pandemic to match demand and supply.
- Having a capable and adaptable supply network has been a key factor in the success of companies in dealing with the pandemic. A supply network with a well-designed network structure, backup suppliers, and efficient communication among the organizations in the supply chain can improve the success of supplying the materials at the right time and location. Suppliers with innovative and collaborative operations can also support an increase or reduction in production capacity in case of a shift in demand. This can also support the goals to temporarily increase or reduce the safety stock inventory in response to the shift in demand, as Kellogg's approached the problem (Silver, 2021).
- Several companies increased their focus on operations to enhance performance. For instance, companies reduce SKU counts to reduce complexities in the supply chain, reducing various designs, ingredients, and inventory costs. Companies also focused on the centralization of decision-making processes using integrated information management systems. Several companies centralized decision-making processes to improve supply management and procurement operations in an attempt to monitor, optimize, and control their global supply chains comprehensively to minimize costs.

2.3 *The Retail Industry*

Impacts of COVID-19

Due to the lockdowns and stay-at-home orders during the first phases of COVID-19, many retailers had to close their stores, leading consumers to switch to online shopping rather than in-store. Due to this shift, online sales boomed, resulting in huge profits and increased market capitalization for those retailers with strong online sales platforms. From February 2020 until April 2021, for example, retail sector market capitalization increased by 35% because of consumers redecorating homes and exploring new hobbies, clothing styles, and beauty routines (Bradley et al., 2021). This effect is not uniform across retailers in different sectors and countries. Most of the increase in market cap is captured by American and Chinese companies, especially by major companies such as Amazon, Pinuoduo, Home Depot, and Walmart, due to the shift in demand and having strong digital shopping and analytics platforms (Bradley et al., 2021). In a broad classification, the majority of market capital gains during the pandemic were obtained by home-economy retailers, value retailers, and online retailers. In the 14 months from February 2020 to April 2021, 25 retail companies accounted for 91% of market cap gains of over $1450 billion (Bradley et al., 2021).

Grocery retailers such as Walmart, Target, Kroger, and Albertsons enjoyed the sales driven by an increase in household and grocery demand mainly due to the work-from-home conditions and stay-at-home orders. Albertsons reported a sales growth of 13.8% in early 2021, and Walmart reported a 7.7% increase in its total revenue in 2021 (Kang, 2021; Walmart, 2021). Kroger's digital sales also doubled during the pandemic as consumers were cautious of in-store shopping (Kang, 2020). On the other hand, several retailers filed for bankruptcy during the pandemic. Brooks Brothers filed for bankruptcy in July 2020 due to the reduction in demand for executive dress clothes. The shift in demand led to a bankruptcy filing by retailers such as J.C. Penney, J. Crew, Neiman Marcus, GNC, Century 21, and others (Markowitz, 2021).

In early 2022, when the spread of COVID-19 eased to some extent, retailers faced a significant amount of inventory arriving at ports and in their warehouses. This high level of inventory was because of consumers' lower spending power due to the high inflation rate, as well as due to a large number of orders by retailers submitted to their suppliers during the pandemic to ensure sufficient inventory in their fulfillment centers and stores amid continued supply chain uncertainties (Young, 2022). Major retailers such as Target changed their strategy and canceled several orders from their suppliers to avoid excess inventory. Prologis, the largest owner of warehouses, reported that it needs an additional 800 million square feet of warehouse space to handle excess inventories. Many retailers also turned into flexible and shared warehouses to handle excess inventory temporarily (Young, 2022). This piled-up inventory provided a great opportunity for liquidators to dispose of the oversupply (Kapner, 2022).

Due to the lockdown, work-from-home, and shifts in demand, several companies gained the most market capital during the pandemic, including home-economy retailers, value retailers, and online retailers (Bradley et al., 2021). Due to working from home, people had the time and motivation to renovate and improve their homes and furnishings. Stress and uncertainties also led people toward money-saving strategies, particularly purchasing from value retailers such as TJ Maxx and Dollar General. Online retailers, retailers with strong online platforms, and online selling and buying platforms were able to gain considerable benefits as people stayed home and shopped online during the pandemic. Interestingly, the market valuation of Amazon increased by 62% from February 2020 to April 2021, while Alibaba only added 6%; this is because Amazon performs beyond a traditional online retailer by entering entertainment, video streaming, and web services markets (Bradley et al., 2021).

Figure 3 shows the retail industry summary. Albertsons shows increased ROA due to sales of certain categories of products and services enabled by the new distribution channel for pickup and deliveries. Big retailers such as Amazon, Walmart, and Target experienced huge inventory build-up at the end of 2021 and beginning of 2022 due to huge orders placed to suppliers during the pandemic (Kapner, 2022). This led Target to warn investors about revenue loss due to huge inventory costs. Similar to other industries, the shortage of labor is a major problem in this industry. However, despite the fact that many companies laid off labor during the pandemic—showing up as an increase in sales per employee—Amazon hired more than 800,000 people, primarily for operations at its current and several newly opened warehouses (Mattioli, 2022), reflected in the drop in sales per employee.

Adjustments Made

One major change in retailers' operations in response to COVID-19 is their approach to how products are delivered to customers, that is, the shift in the distribution channel. Many retailers and department stores such as Macy's, Kohl's, Target, and Best Buy adjusted and revised their distribution channels (Thomas, 2020). Due to the surge in online orders, retailers and grocery stores invested in new distribution channels such as in-store and curbside pickup (Corral, 2020). Some distribution channels, specifically omnichannel services, Buy Online Pickup in Store (BOPIS), and curbside pickup, became exceptionally popular (Berthiaume, 2021). Curbside pickup, for example, increased by 208% during the pandemic, driven by department stores and grocery stores (Thomas, 2020). Starbucks also diverted inventory to improve the retention of customers by delivering coffee to the customer's doorstep and adding window delivery (Starbucks, 2022).

While brick-and-mortar retailers added/expanded their online shopping platforms, online retailers added/expanded their network of physical distribution centers and stores. Due to delivery delays during the pandemic, Amazon aims to expand its fulfillment centers by adding 1000 centers, particularly in suburban areas. Amazon also added several brick-and-mortar locations such as Amazon Go, Amazon Fresh, and Amazon Style stores (Soper, 2020). Retailers also focused their hiring primarily on the workforce for online sales. Other companies such as Nike expanded and accelerated online sales by allowing orders to be fulfilled from the stores. This enabled Nike to sell 35% of its Nike-branded goods online (Silver, 2021).

According to a survey by McKinsey & Co., more than 30% of supply-chain executives decided to bring some production near the point of use from 2020. Several retailers and health and beauty companies also followed the same pattern.

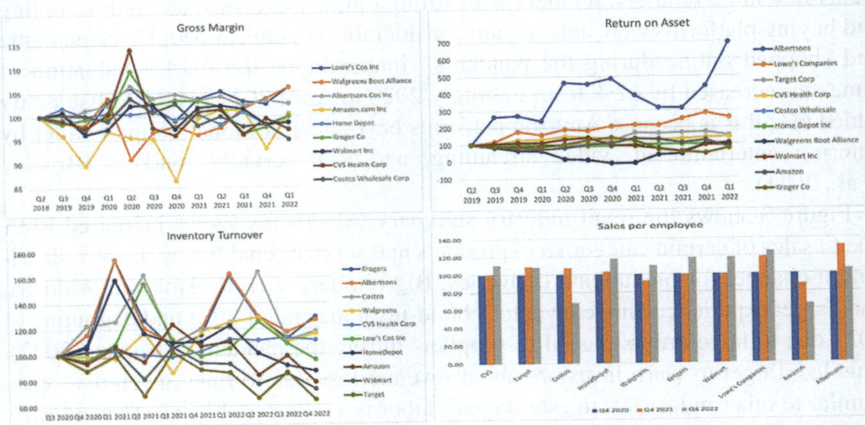

Fig. 3 Summary of the performance of the major companies in the retail industry. Note: Data is collected from Bloomberg. Return on asset = (net income + (1 – tax rate) × interest expenses)/(total assets), gross margin = (net income + (1 – tax rate) × interest expenses)/(total revenue), sales per employee = (revenue)/(number of employees), and inventory turnover = (cost of goods sold)/inventory. The tax rate is assumed to be 35%

For example, the perfume and cologne industry shifted operations to the U.S. although the cost of production is considerably higher than in Asia, showing that companies prioritize reliable production, transportation, and delivery rather than minimizing the total landed costs (Terlep, 2022).

Because many people worked from home during the pandemic, creating a major change in demand patterns, retailers such as Albertsons offered products such as meal kits, fresh seafood, meat, and floral products. Albertsons also provided order pickup services as a new delivery channel for customers due to stay-at-home orders and work-from-home (Kang, 2021). Similarly, Kroger added several new items to its stores due to the higher appetite for shopping when working remotely during the pandemic. To prevent stockpiling by customers during the pandemic, grocery stores and big retailers considered price hikes and enforced a limit on purchases on some items such as sanitizer, flour, and toilet paper (Kang, 2020).

Lessons Learned

- During COVID-19, companies that were able to quickly revise their operations and supply chain to serve customers' demand shifts were more successful. Offering efficient distribution channels, expanding distribution networks, increasing production and distribution capacity, managing inventory of popular and in-demand products, and preventing SKU proliferation toward rationalization are among the most effective strategies for retailers. The collective wisdom did not predict the slowdown after the pandemic eased. The slowdown was caused as much due to a shift in consumption patterns as to inflation. For some companies, it led to excess inventories, whereas for others it led to shortages. The key factor in the success of retailers is to respond to the changes/shifts in demand in an agile way.
- The role of analytics is undeniable for the success of retailers as it makes the collection and analysis of data more accessible and possible. The data can be used to optimize the set of goods for production and offerings, the level of inventory to keep at each location, and optimize the production and distribution network in the supply chain. In addition, digitalization enables several opportunities such as online shopping, as well as delivery of products using the sharing economy. However, companies should consider the potential failure in IT and information management systems and, therefore, the essential role of brick-and-mortar services in their supply chain.

2.4 *The Pharmaceutical Industry*

Impacts of COVID-19

COVID-19 led to the financial growth of several pharmaceutical companies. Abbott's worldwide sales, for example, grew more than 39% in the second quarter of 2021, primarily due to COVID-19 testing-related sales (Abbott, 2021b). Abbott beat expectations in 2022 with a 17.5% increase in sales mainly because of an increase in demand for rapid COVID-19 tests (Slabodkin, 2022). Similarly, AstraZeneca reported a 41% growth in vaccine revenues in 2021 compared to 2020 (Wells, 2022). Bristol Myers Squibb reported 9% full-year 2021 revenue growth and a surge in product sales from $41.3 billion to $45.1 billion (Pharmaceutical Technology, 2022). Gilead Sciences reported an 11% increase in revenue from $24.6 billion to $27.3 billion, and Merck reported a 17.3% increase in revenue in 2021 (U.S. Securities and Exchange Commission, 2022). Pfizer's earnings rose 133% in 2021-Q4 with 60% of it coming from vaccine sales (Isidore, 2021a).

While many pharma companies focused on finding treatments related to COVID-19 and coping with the impacts of COVID, the total pharma patent applications considerably reduced during and after COVID. Particularly, application counts reduced from approximately 55,000 in 2019 to 15,000 in 2021. This could also be because of budget control and workforce limitations and future uncertainties. However, the number of available job postings in pharma industries increased from approximately 47,000 in 2020-Q1 to more than 100,000 in 2021-Q4 (PharmaTech, 2022).

Figure 4 shows the industry summary. Most of the companies related to manufacturing vaccines and test equipment and products for COVID reported a significant growth in gross margin. The rise in revenue for Bristol Myers Squibb was mainly because of Eliquis, immune-oncology, novel product portfolios, commercial execution, and substantial development in its projects (Pharmaceutical Technology, 2022).

Adjustments Made

The essential roles of information, innovative technologies, and analytics tools are inevitable, especially during the pandemic's uncertain situations. Johnson & Johnson (J&J) closely monitors the supply and demand levels of its products to ensure the proper inventory level and efficient distribution of its products and services. Most importantly, they have a strong business continuity and risk management plan in their global supply chain to prepare for unpredictable events and meet the needs of patients, customers, and consumers. J&J invests in leading IoT technology to provide real-time diagnosis and treatment, and it has established the 3D Printing Center of Excellence at the University of Miami for R&D and integration of 3D printing in their operations to ensure flexibility in production and delivery lead time to customers (University of Miami, 2020). J&J also uses data science to detect unusual high-volume orders during the pandemic, mostly ordered by medical centers and governments, for further investigation and fulfillment (Brody, 2020). By analyzing thousands of orders from large customers such as hospitals and governments, the algorithm notifies supply chain professionals about any strange patterns. To manage staff and ensure reliable production of products, J&J uses highly automated scenario risk simulation technology, tracking staffing levels and production rates through worst-case and best-case scenarios. This technology also enables J&J to investigate shifting production to a different location, change shipping methods, and track the need for raw materials and inventory (Brody, 2020). Finally, J&J used smart glass technology such as Google Glass to continue production and train staff

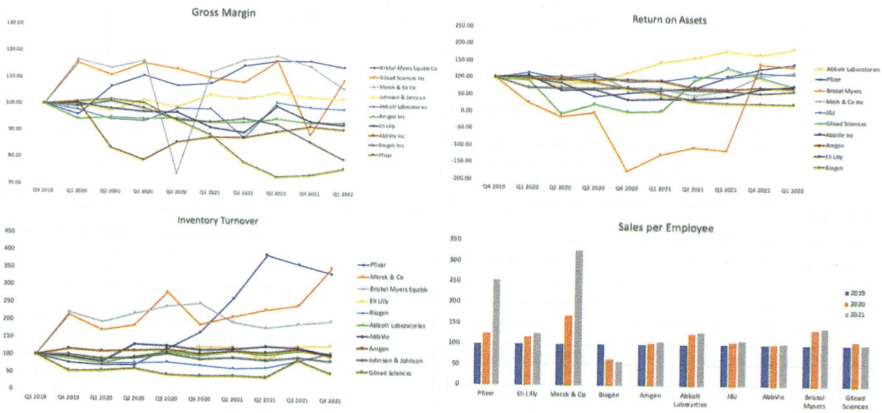

Fig. 4 Summary of the performance of the major companies in the pharmaceutical industry. Note: Data is collected from Bloomberg. Return on asset = (net income + (1 − tax rate) × interest expenses)/(total assets), gross margin = (net income + (1 − tax rate) × interest expenses)/(total revenue), sales per employee = (revenue)/(number of employees), and inventory turnover = (cost of goods sold)/inventory. The tax rate is assumed to be 35%

remotely during the pandemic while lockdown and stay-at-home orders interrupted other companies' manufacturing processes (Brody, 2020).

Due to the shortage of supplies such as sanitizers and masks, some apparel producers and perfume factories adjusted their operations within weeks to produce these healthcare products and essential items (Schatteman et al., 2020). J&J, for example, managed capacity by reducing the production of more complex formulations to be able to produce the medicines in high demand (Brody, 2020). To ensure workforce availability and health risks associated with jobs in pharmaceutical companies, maintaining a healthy workforce was among the highest priorities. Bristol Myers Squibb (BMS), for example, prioritizes keeping employees safe and ensuring compliant supply continuity in its operations (Bristol Myers Squibb, 2021c; Schmukler, 2020).

To effectively respond to the sudden surge in demand, Pfizer completely overhauled its supply chain. Investing $700 million, Pfizer increased its production capacity by building a new production facility, producing vaccines in several facilities in Missouri, Massachusetts, and Michigan (Garland, 2021b). Pfizer also added a parallel distribution system to its current supply chain to be able to reliably distribute vaccines to demand locations. Working with DHL, FedEx, and UPS, vaccines were delivered to the point of use within 2 days using the road or air modes of transportation (Leonard, 2020). Collaborating with Operation Warp Speed, Pfizer used a direct shipment strategy to minimize transportation time from facilities to the point of use. It also utilizes an inventory management system to ensure the availability of second doses and vaccine ancillary supplementary kits (Pfizer, 2022). Pfizer designed a new box that is temperature-controlled and GPS-tracked for reliable storage and distribution of vaccines during the pandemic (Leonard, 2020).

Many pharmaceutical companies added more capacity, including production sites as well as workforce, to respond to the increased demand for testing supplies and vaccines.

Strategic sourcing and supplier diversity are at the core of Bristol Myers Squibb's supply chain, enabling this company to effectively mitigate the disruption caused by the pandemic. BMS developed a Third-Party Risk Management (TPRM) process to manage and monitor risk with its suppliers and to identify, assess, manage, and monitor risks from its third parties (Bristol Myers Squibb, 2021a, 2021b). Merck has a global network of manufacturers and suppliers in nine different countries, which helped it to cope with the pandemic more effectively via regionalization (Merck, 2022a). Similarly, the broad network of suppliers for Abbott, consisting of 70,000 suppliers in 145 countries, enabled Abbott to supply its materials with minimum disruption during the pandemic. Abbott also increased its capacity by adding three new facilities to develop COVID-19 tests (Abbott, 2021a).

Collaborations among pharmaceutical companies increased during the pandemic. Gilead signed several licensing agreements with generic drug makers in India, Egypt, and Pakistan (Gilead, 2021). Biogen signed an agreement with Vir Biotechnology for cell line development, process development, and handling clinical manufacturing (Sagonowsky, 2020). In addition to product development collaborations, some companies collaborated on the manufacturing and production of health and medicine products, primarily by sharing their resources. Merck lent its expertise and capacity to J&J to support the manufacturing and supply of the COVID-19 vaccine (Merck, 2022b). Pfizer also collaborated with Gilead in a multi-year agreement to manufacture and supply the investigational antiviral remdesivir (Pfizer, 2020).

Lessons Learned

- Pharmaceutical companies focused on redesigning their supply and distribution networks to make them more resilient in addition to minimizing costs. Changing the structure of the supply chain network, adding extra production and inventory capacity, local production closer to the consumer market, and geographical dispersion with a focus on low-risk locations are among some of the recent actions made by companies. Further, companies with flexible and agile processes could enhance their resiliency and benefit from the pandemic situation by switching to more popular products with high demand. Having flexible production processes and modularized products facilitated approval and validation processes. An extensive network of geographically dispersed suppliers, as well as accelerated audits, could improve agility, helping enhanced resiliency during the pandemic (Kelleher et al., 2020).
- Similar to the food and beverage industry, the role of digitalization and analytics tools to improve agility and transparency in the pharmaceutical supply chain is undeniable. Companies can collect data about patients and focus on designing a patient-centric supply chain for faster and more reliable healthcare deliveries. In production facilities, automation can also help the collection of data and automate analytics processes and transparency, as well as accelerate auditing tasks

(Kelleher et al., 2020). The importance of digitalization, integration, and building trust and data sharing is critical, especially in the pharma industry (Dunleavy, 2022).
- Major disruptions such as the COVID-19 pandemic encourage collaboration among pharmaceutical companies. Such collaboration could be in the area of drug development, testing and vaccine developments, capacity sharing, outsourcing, digitalization, and more. Such types of collaboration help to improve the profitability of companies, human immunity, and public health.

2.5 *The Semiconductor Industry*

Impacts of COVID-19

COVID-19 has significantly affected the semiconductor industry. This is the first of two industries that supply many others. In industries such as these, disruptions not only create stoppages but also shifts to the highest bidder. The Santa Clara-based company AMD reported a 49% growth in revenues in 2021 compared to 2020 (AMD, 2022). This huge increase was because of a 33% increase in sales of PCs and an 88% increase in game console markets (Markman, 2022). Auto manufacturers had the opposite experience, as discussed in Sect. 2.1. TSMC also reported a 19% growth in revenue in 2021 (Zafar, 2022).

There are two major semiconductor manufacturers, TSMC and Samsung, accounting for more than 91% of chip making for global customers across different industries such as automakers, communication systems, and electronics manufacturers, as well as other companies such as Qualcomm, Broadcom, Nvidia, and AMD. When demand surged, in addition to TSMC becoming a bottleneck in the semiconductor industry supply chain, another bottleneck in this supply chain is the Netherlands-based ASM Holding NV, which has a monopoly providing photolithography equipment required for printing chips onto the wafer. Other common resources in this industry are automation software, which is provided by Cadence Design Systems Inc. and Synopsys Inc. in the U.S. (King et al., 2021).

Figure 5 illustrates the summary of the performances of the major semiconductor companies. Further concentrated manufacturing capacity seems to have exacerbated the effect of the pandemic. It can be seen how bottlenecks, demand surges, and anticipation allowed some fabless firms to make enormous profits. Now that the demand is shifting back to other goods, we see a build-up of inventories in the very same firms. Fabless firms saw an increase in sales per employee, reflecting labor shortages.

Adjustments Made

To increase supply chain resiliency, several chip manufacturers plan to bring production close to the point of use. This probably indicates unraveling bundled capacity to reduce future risk. Intel plans to invest in a $20 billion facility in Ohio for chip making (Bobrowsky, 2022) and new $23.5 billion facilities in Arizona and New

Mexico. Intel also plans to increase its European expansion in France, the Netherlands, and Italy with a total investment of $100 billion in 10 years (Fitch & Davis, 2021). TSMC plans to invest in a $12 billion chip factory in Arizona (Fitch & Davis, 2021) and invest another $100 billion over 3 years to increase manufacturing capacity (Leonard, 2021c). Similarly, Samsung plans to invest $17 billion to build an advanced chip plant in the Austin vicinity of Texas close to its current manufacturing plant (Leonard & Kim, 2021). Due to the supply chain crunch in the automotive industry, several automakers also decided to design their chips, reducing their reliance on semiconductor industries (Sorkin et al., 2021).

Samsung continued to hold strong relationships with its suppliers and customers during the pandemic and support them significantly. Samsung provided $30 million in business operating funds as a part of a co-prosperity program (ProcureCon Events, 2021). These funds are paid in advance with nearly zero interest rates. Samsung also helped its suppliers with freight costs and simplified the parts approval process from its suppliers (ProcureCon Events, 2021). Samsung donated thousands of cell phones and tablets during the pandemic to provide access and remote learning for people in quarantine and people working and studying remotely (Samsung, 2021). AMD donated several additional petaflops of supercomputer processing power to research institutes during the pandemic to increase computing power for research on COVID-19 (Black, 2020). Applied Materials also closely worked with its customers to reduce the processing time of installation to high volume production (Yu, 2022). Finally, Qualcomm switched to different supplier alternatives and used multi-sourcing strategies during the pandemic due to the shortage of raw materials such as resins and epoxies (Cunnane, 2022).

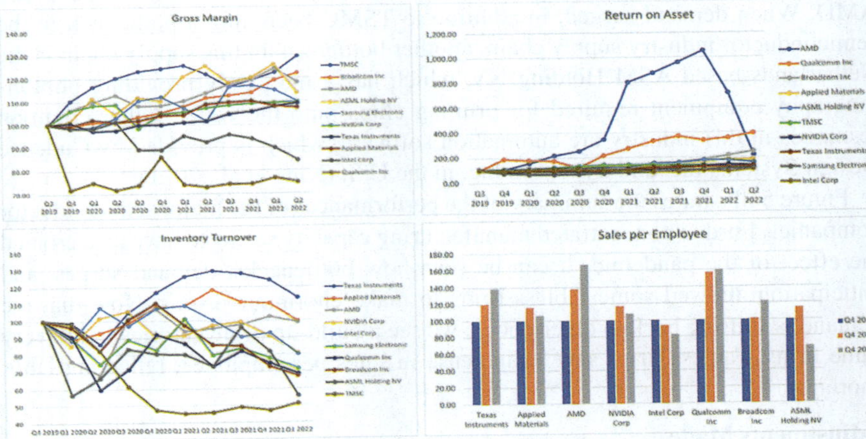

Fig. 5 Summary of the performance of the major companies in the semiconductor industry. Note: Data is collected from Bloomberg. Return on asset = (net income + (1 − tax rate) × interest expenses)/(total assets), gross margin = (net income + (1 − tax rate) × interest expenses)/(total revenue), sales per employee = (revenue)/(number of employees), and inventory turnover = (cost of goods sold)/inventory. The tax rate is assumed to be 35%

Some companies adjusted their focus during the pandemic to reduce complexity and disruptions and increase profitability. AMD optimized its focus during the pandemic on premium gaming, computing, and the graphic portion of the market such as PCs. This focus on premium segments of the market was helpful to make its supply chain more resilient since it reduces the variety and complexity of the supply chain and, therefore, it is less affected by the chip shortage disruption (Hachman, 2022; Hruska, 2021). Similarly, due to limited capacity, Qualcomm focused on high-end products during the pandemic (Cunnane, 2022). Interestingly, while many industries were affected by labor shortages during the pandemic, some semiconductor companies such as Qualcomm were affected comparatively less because of highly automated manufacturing facilities (Cunnane, 2022). Other companies such as Texas Instruments focused mainly on stockpiling inventories to make sure they can satisfy demand (Bloomberg Wire, 2020).

Lessons Learned

- The shortage of semiconductor chips considerably affected manufacturing operations worldwide across different industries such as electronics and auto industries. Semiconductor companies prioritize the mitigation and prevention of risks in the long-term rather than reducing landed costs in the short-term. To enhance capacity, reduce potential future risks and, therefore, increase the resiliency of supply chains, semiconductor manufacturers learned to restructure their supply and production network by adding new facilities closer to the points of use and reducing uncertainties in their supply chains. This decision was supported by governments in the U.S., Italy, France, and the Netherlands.
- Having a common single supplier can add huge risk to the supply chain. This primarily happens because during special situations such as a pandemic, changes in consumer preferences and shifts in types and volume of demands will put significant pressure on the common supplier, leading to a huge bottleneck for some or all of its customers.

2.6 *The Transportation Industry*

Along with semiconductors, this is another industry that serves as a feeder to many other industries. When such industries are hit by surging demand or disruptions, smaller, less profitable firms are affected much more. A similar impact can be seen in the labor market or fuel supply that is related to common supply factors. While this may be obvious, this pandemic has highlighted potential choke points from the supply side and led to conversations about mitigating such effects in the future.

Impacts of COVID-19

When the pandemic happened, its effect on the logistics industry could easily be observed at the ports in China, where containers were logjammed due to the lockdowns and travel restrictions in China and other countries of destination (Miller, 2022b; Saraiva & Murray, 2021). A shortage of truck drivers due to travel restrictions and lockdowns also intensified inventory shortage at manufacturers and, thus, many dependent industries globally.

United States business logistics costs increased by 22.4% in 2021 compared to 2020 (Kearney, 2022). This includes an increase in all logistics costs, including transportation and inventory, and storage. While the increase in transportation costs is due to expedited shipping, the inventory cost increase is because of storing, handling, and financing inventory (Kearney, 2022).

Different carriers in transportation industries underwent rises and falls during the pandemic. For example, during the early stages of the pandemic, trucking volume increased by approximately 30% because of panic-buying, railroad volume declined by 20%, ocean shipping reduced by 25%, and last-mile delivery increased by 1000%. However, by July 2020, road transportation was considerably reduced due to a halt in manufacturing, lockdowns, and a reduction in requests for transportation (Bhattacharjee et al., 2020). The pandemic led to more than 3000 small carrier companies filing for bankruptcy in 2020 (Ronan, 2021). In 2021, air freight costs increased by 19.2% due to the continued increase in demand, delays at ports, and insufficient capacity of shipping lines during the pandemic. Ocean shipping costs also increased by 23.6% in 2021 due to the increased demand. Similarly, motor carriers increased their profits by more than 50% in 2021 while their costs increased by 23.4% (Kearney, 2022). The effect of the pandemic was not only in cargo transportation but also in passenger transportation. The number of airport passenger screenings, for example, plummeted from approximately 2.2 million per day in January 2020 to less than 500,000 for the rest of 2020 (Blunt, 2020).

A shortage of truck drivers and port labor, lockdowns, increased demand for imports, old infrastructure, late-arriving ships, and safety regulations led to thousands of containers piling up at container ports worldwide (Saraiva & Murray, 2021; Sirimanne, 2021). After slight relief from the pandemic in late 2020, the volume of global transportation increased, leading to huge congestion at ports around the world. Hundreds of ships were waiting to unload containers at several ports in the U.S. due to limited unloading capacity at ports and a shortage of truck drivers (Miller, 2021). The number of container ships waiting at the ports of Los Angeles and Long Beach reached a record high of 109 in January 2022, with each ship waiting on average 18 weeks to start unloading the containers (Berger, 2022b; Wills, 2022). This includes more than 815,958 TEUs waiting to be unloaded at ports (Pino, 2022). The total number of containers at these two ports dwelling for 9 days or more increased to 48,905 in November 2021, among which 60% of them are planned for transportation by rail (Miller, 2022a). Figure 6 shows the container traffic at the port of Long Beach. This led to a huge increase in spot prices, container rates, and even rail transportation rates due to the limited capacity of road carriers. The container rate from China to the U.S. west coast increased from approximately $3000 in early 2020 to more than five times pre-pandemic levels in early 2021 (Luman & Soroka, 2022; Tan, 2021). However, since July 2022, the rates have started reducing by more than 15% compared to several months ago, signaling a slow move away from the peak demand (Berger, 2022a).

Adjustments Made

Companies had to tackle several transportation challenges during the pandemic, particularly a shortage of truck drivers and congestion at ports (Isidore, 2021b). These inefficiencies and backlogs in transportation led to the shortage of essential supplies such as healthcare supplies and semiconductor chips for some industries. Many companies such as Tesla had to spend a significant amount of money to transport essential supplies from East Asia to the U.S. by airplanes, paying the premium shipping cost (Isidore, 2021b). These changes in modes of transportation, although costly, enabled Tesla to run factories at full capacity, leading to record high sales during the pandemic (Isidore, 2021b).

Some companies repurposed their resources to increase capacity. Airlines, for example, chartered airplanes to transport cargo during the pandemic (DHL, 2020). Also, due to the huge reduction in passengers, companies removed seats to load cargo in passenger airplanes in addition to the airplane's belly (Horton, 2020). Due to a huge burden on road carriers, some companies leaned toward air carriers, resulting in a slight increase in air transportation rates (IFC, 2020). Observing the surging demand for transportation by motor carriers, truck companies increased the hiring of drivers and bought new trucks to expand capacity (Kearney, 2022).

To overcome congestion issues, ports focused on increasing throughput and capacity. The Georgia Ports Authority (GPA) in Savannah invested $205 million to increase the port's capacity by 20% in 2021 (Ashe, 2021). Due to the lack of space at the ports in Georgia, they also added pop-up container yards around the port to increase space for keeping containers. To this end, they turned five existing inland

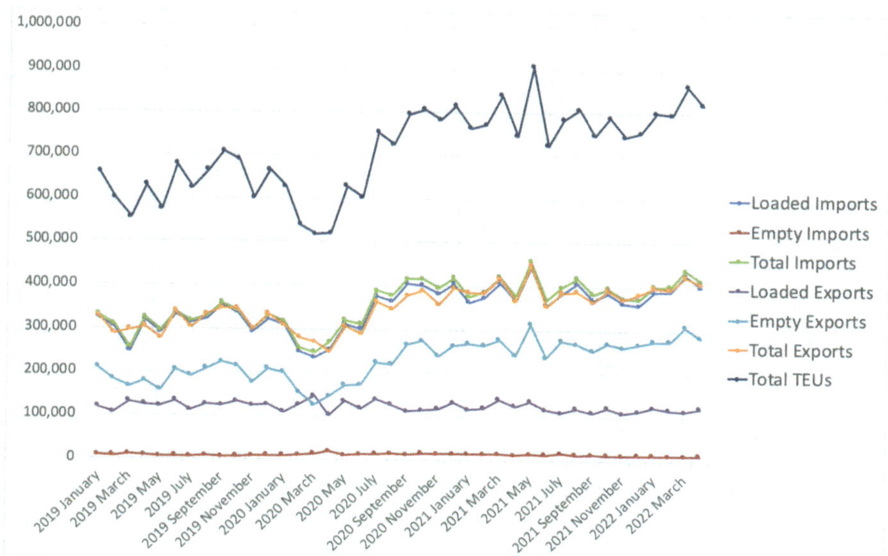

Fig. 6 Container traffic at the port of Long Beach. Data is retrieved from the Port of Long Beach website (POLB, 2022)

facilities in Georgia and North Carolina into container yards (Lopez, 2021). The port of Los Angeles decided to pay a $7.5 million incentive to San Pedro Bay container terminals if they increased the throughput of containers at terminals. The port particularly aimed to reduce the time that it takes to process trucks dropping off and/or picking up cargo at terminals and encouraged trucks to perform delivery and pickup in the same trip (Wills, 2021). This incentive was given to the terminals that can reduce the average turn times to 35 minutes or less (Wills, 2021). Some railroad carriers such as Union Pacific and BNSF also gave incentives of $60 per container to ocean carrier customers if they move their containers out of the ports on the weekends (Marsh, 2021).

Due to the shortage of containers, shipping companies increased prices to more than five times the pre-pandemic prices. Empty shipping containers were also returned to China after leaving the U.S. ports to load quickly with more profitable cargo to send back to the United States. This tremendously slowed down the exports of agricultural goods during the fourth season primarily because the profit obtained by exporting agricultural goods is five to six times less than importing profitable products such as electronics from China to the United States (Clayton, 2021). This is a violation of the Shipping Act of 1984 and resulted in several complaints from U.S. agricultural exporters to the Federal Maritime Commission (Clayton, 2021). The top three destinations for U.S. agricultural goods are Canada, China, and Mexico. Some companies such as Amazon made their shipping containers to better manage container availability and minimize wait time for containers. By chartering ships and using their containers, Amazon was able to reduce wait time at ports to as little as 2 days during peak demand (Kay, 2021a).

Lessons Learned

- The ability to repurpose resources to increase capacity in response to shifts/changes in demand plays a winning role in the transportation industry. Companies were able to repurpose airplanes, change shipping routes, switch to other modes of transportation, and repurpose facilities into temporary yards and warehouses for containers in response to the shortage of space and containers.
- Containers and vehicles are among the shared resources for a majority of businesses. Due to high demand for such shared resources during disruptions, smaller companies and less profitable makers of products are hard hit due to less financial power competing with large companies for these shared resources. Some companies such as Amazon used in-house containers to reduce their reliance on shipping lines' containers as shared resources.
- Governmental agencies play essential roles by giving potential support to ensure that companies follow the rules and act to provide access to resources to all companies. Governmental support and incentives can also enhance throughput and reduce wait time and congestion at ports.
- The labor shortage is a major problem in the logistics industry. Driver shortage, for example, has been the number one problem in the transportation industry for more than 60 years. Lockdowns and stay-at-home orders, on the one hand, and the surge in customer demands, transportation, and deliveries, on the other hand,

intensified the effect of worker shortage in this industry. The role of labor in the transportation industry is inevitable because remote working for drivers and warehouse workers is not an option. In addition, almost all industries rely on the transportation industry for receiving their ingredients and input materials, as well as delivering their finished goods and services. Therefore, attracting and retaining workers in this industry is a high priority.

3 Classification and Lessons Learned

In this section, we summarize some of the key findings and lessons learned in this research. Table 1 shows the summary of supply chain issues and companies' responses to these issues.

Based on the study of the six industries, the summary of the key lessons learned are:

- *Problems with the lean strategy, and the revised lean supply chain*: Before the pandemic, many companies leaned toward operating a lean supply chain, keeping minimum inventory to keep costs down and forcing continuous improvement. However, due to the lockdown during the pandemic, a halt in production, and a surge in demand and panic-buying, many supplies were scarce. This includes products such as emergency and medical supplies, household supplies and toilet paper, and healthcare supplies and disinfection wipes (Weissman, 2020). Not only were finished goods hard to find, but the raw materials required to produce ventilators, masks, and hand sanitizers were also hard to find. The pandemic illustrated that lean manufacturing focused on minimizing inventory as a type of waste is not a reliable approach, especially in the highly uncertain supply situation. Rather, this approach should be strengthened by enhanced real-time information, transparency, and forward visibility in the supply chain to be able to obtain promising results under inevitable uncertainties (Hyder, 2021). Companies with lean supply chains were impacted by this issue and, therefore, arranged to add inventories to their supply chain at least for the short term to cope with later potential waves of COVID. Some companies such as Ford, however, use a mixed approach to tackle other types of uncertainties, especially customer preferences. Ford stockpiles critical parts required for assembly while it reduces the inventory of assembled cars to account for customer shifts in demand and preferences (Garland, 2021a; Leonard, 2021a). Similar lessons have been learned from similar supply chain disruptions during the past decades (Schatteman et al., 2020).
- *Having a flexible, prepared supply chain*: Companies that were prepared in advance were hit less, and they were able to adjust their operations, redesign their products, and readjust product offerings faster in response to the pandemic. Several companies across all the studied industries adjusted their operations and processes to serve the surges in demand during the pandemic. This includes

Table 1 Summary of major problems and adjustments made to supply chains in different industries

		Major problems				
		Supplier disruption	Halted/slowed manufacturing	Distribution difficulties and delays	Labor shortage	Inventory shortage
Major adjustments made by companies	Labor/wage justification				X	
	Improve demand planning	X		X		X
	Increase manufacturing efficiency		X			
	Specialize, focus, and rationalization		X			X
	Remove silo	X				
	Insourcing/outsourcing	X	X	X	X	
	Vertical integration	X	X	X		X
	Streamline vendor choice	X				X
	Focus on agility and speed	X	X	X		X
	Price hikes					X
	Improve supply chain infrastructure	X	X	X	X	X
	Improve traceability and visibility	X	X	X		X
	Improve sales channels	X		X		X
	Localization and regionalization	X		X		X
	Improve digitalization and IT technologies	X	X	X	X	X

repurposing resources such as machines, vehicles, warehouses, and workforce to adjust the mix, variety, and volume of offered products and services. Therefore, having a flexible set of resources and processes is an essential component of having a responsive company.

- *Agility has never been more important*: Not only is flexibility important, but the ability to quickly apply such adjustments is critical to respond to the changes/increases in consumers' demands and obtain quick recovery. Being able to quickly respond to changes in demand, work conditions, jobs, products, and inventory is one of the most critical factors during the pandemic. Our research indicates that those companies which were able to quickly respond to changes are among the winners of companies coping with the pandemic's challenges. Implementing agility depends on several factors such as a digitized supply chain, flexible resources and products, and authorizing workers and managers to facilitate improvement and changes in processes (Saleki-Gerhardt, 2020).
- *Increase in regionalization (localization) by in-shoring, near-shoring, and re-shoring*: To be able to cope with disruptions, it is essential to reduce the distance between sources, producers, and consumers. For decades, companies outsourced to low-cost countries to reduce the total landed cost. However, this approach cannot cope with global disruptions such as the COVID-19 pandemic. Companies in different industries such as health and beauty, manufacturing, and semiconductor industries tend to bring production closer to the point of use although the total landed cost is higher. A study by Kearney on the Reshoring index shows that re-shoring and near-shoring of operations for manufactured goods have increased significantly since 2020 (Luo et al., 2022).
- *The undeniable role of technologies and digitalization*: The roles of technologies such as information technology and digitalization are undeniable in coping with disruptions. Technologies such as IoT and Blockchain are particularly more important for the food, beverage, and pharmaceutical industries to enhance visibility, tracing, tracking, and management of inventory. In addition, technologies for analytics can considerably help to optimize operations, supply, and inventory during disruption and serve the changing consumers' demands. Companies with strong IT platforms were able to offer remote work for their labor while those with online shopping platforms and analytics could provide online shopping options for their consumers and, thus, survive the pandemic. Finally, technologies and digitalization could enable companies to facilitate the transition by providing new distribution channels for customers during the stay-at-home order.
- *Common resources increase risk*: Common resources such as transportation resources, containers, and suppliers increase the fragility of the supply chain, especially for smaller companies. During disruptions, the battle for resources and suppliers was intense, leading to the bankruptcy of several companies such as small carriers in the transportation industry. Having backup plans like backup suppliers, in-house resources and operations, flexibility in product design, and input materials are among some of the main approaches to avoid reliance on common resources in the supply chain.
- *The underestimated importance of labor*: Almost all industries experienced labor shortages during the pandemic due to the surge in demand and stay-home orders. The role of labor is especially critical in some industries in which remote working is not possible, such as in the logistics industry. Hence, companies and governments must consider practical strategies to hire and retain labor.

- *Financial pressures during COVID and optimizing everyday operations*: Similar to consumers who were under financial pressure during the pandemic and tried to optimize their spending, companies also attempted to improve everyday operations to minimize costs. This includes decisions related to, for example, the choice of materials and suppliers, as well as the (re)design of products.

4 Factors That Affect the Performance of the Supply Chains

During the pandemic, several supply chain characteristics, as well as external factors affected companies' performances.

4.1 Internal Factors: Supply Chain Characteristics

- *Resiliency*: Owning a resilient supply chain plays a critical role in coping with disruptions. This can be achieved through different ways such as regionalization, geographically dispersed networks of facilities, increased safety stock, product modularization, postponement of production/assembly operations, and securing multiple suppliers. Some companies such as automakers manage several factories around the world, which can help to satisfy demand in each region. Knowing that the timing and intensity of COVID waves and lockdowns are different in different regions around the world, the factories may be used for production to not only satisfy the demand in the allocated region but in other regions suffering from the lockdown. Companies that invest in supply chain resilience reduce product development cycles by 40–60% as production teams respond faster to changes in the market, leading to higher revenue growth (Schatteman et al., 2020).
- *Flexibility*: Having a flexible supply chain played a key role for several companies. This flexibility may have several dimensions. In the early stages of the pandemic, toilet paper companies, for instance, could adapt their processes to reduce the production of business toilet paper to increase the production volume of residential toilet paper. They also utilized their buffer capacity to increase production volume and serve the unprecedented surged demand. Similarly, designing a flexible supply and production network can be used to effectively adjust production concerning changes in consumer demand and adjust the volume of production at each location and received supplies from each supplier. This directly helps move toward a more resilient supply chain. Flexibility may also depend on flexible resources, processes, product designs, reliable digital platforms, and analytics infrastructure (Mazumdar-Shaw, 2022). A flexible supply chain shows a 10–40% increase in inventory turnover rate (Schatteman et al., 2020).
- *Product offering range and mix*: The types and variety of products offered by companies could considerably affect the resiliency of companies during the

pandemic. Tesla, for example, focuses on a limited number of vehicle types. This reduces the variety of supplies and suppliers needed, enabling them to strengthen their supply network by easily managing multiple suppliers or vertically integrating the suppliers. In addition, providing different products and services for customers could bring a competitive advantage and significant growth for the company. For instance, Alibaba only achieved 6% growth, while Amazon gained more than 60% valuation in 1 year because Amazon also provides several services beyond traditional retailers such as online streaming and web services. Similarly, Chewy provides pet foods with additional types of services such as CarePlus and pet parent services, giving a sense of loyalty and care to its customers (Chewy, n.d.; DealPost, 2021).

- *Product (re)design*: The ability and agility to offer new products and/or revise the types of offered products played a considerable role during the pandemic. For example, as demand for apparel reduced during the pandemic, apparel companies started producing essential supplies such as masks. Other examples of a (temporary) shift in the product offering include Ford teaming up with GE to produce ventilators, and fragrance companies producing sanitizers and disinfecting wipes.
- *Dedicated, talented teams*: Due to several supply shortages, companies leaned toward developing in-house capabilities to mitigate the risks of future supply shortages. For instance, GM plans to develop in-house chips to cope with chip supply shortages. The approach could not only help to tackle chip shortages, especially in the long term, but also helps companies design customized chips, aiming to reduce the number of unique chips used in vehicles and, therefore, enhance supply chain resiliency. It is expected that the leaders be familiar with traditional functions like manufacturing sourcing and logistics as well as with adjacencies such as risk management, customer service, and production introduction (Gartner, 2022). To facilitate the ability to react rapidly to changes during the pandemic, an increase in managers' autonomy is an essential factor (Dunleavy, 2022).
- *Digitalization and information technologies*: Management information systems, IoT, Blockchain, and digitalization could considerably enhance companies' abilities to cope with supply chain disruptions. IoT and MIS enhance visibility in the supply chain, providing the grounds for real-time analysis and decision-making. Digitalization and advanced technologies such as additive manufacturing can also enhance the agility of the supply chain. Many companies used additive manufacturing technologies to design and produce mask shields, and rapidly shared the codes worldwide, accelerating the speed of design and production of essential items during the pandemic. The role of analytics and online platforms can also accelerate switching gears in response to the change in consumer demand. Companies, however, need to consider the risk of IT failures and consider contingency plans for potential disruptions.

4.2 External Factors

While the aforementioned levers are used by companies to cope with the impacts of supply chain disruption, external factors are outside the control of companies:

- *Unequal shifts in demand across industries*: The shift in demand is not equal across industries. While companies in a specific industry need to react quickly to respond to these changes, the shift in demand also provides an opportunity for other companies to benefit from the situation. For instance, automotive companies such as GM and Ford started the production of ventilators, which are healthcare equipment.
- *The ability to work remotely*: Working remotely is not an option for all industries, especially the transportation industry and hospitals. Therefore, adjustments made to processes in these industries are limited compared to other industries with remote working possibilities.
- *The ability of consumers to wait*: In some industries such as pharma, patients prefer to receive medication as soon as it is available, while consumers' patience to wait is comparatively higher for electronics and fashion products. This indicates different levels of urgency for providing goods and services for consumers in different industries and, therefore, the differences in flexibility, processes, technologies, and resources required to produce the requested goods.
- *Supply chain disruptions affect industries differently*: When disruptions happen, the scope and intensity of impacts across different industries are not equal. For instance, congestion and logjam at ports did not affect BigTech companies, while it considerably affected retailers. This variability considerably affects the design of the supply chain, resources, and processes.
- *Role and impact of government*: Although the government can considerably impact the equality of service and resources for companies during the disruption, the role and power of government are not equal across industries and countries. For example, after the deregulation in the 1990s, the role of the government in regulating the transportation industry was considerably reduced.

5 Trends to Be Seen in the Future

Based on the learned lessons from the COVID-19 pandemic and adjustments made by companies, firms continue to adjust their supply chains to cope with future potential disasters. Some of these trends are explained below:

- *Add capacity*: After an intense shortage of supplies, several companies plan to expand their long-term capacities by adding new facilities in different geographical regions and expanding their production and distribution networks. This primarily happened in the semiconductor industry, Intel, Samsung, and TSMC. Other industries also plan to expand short-term capacities, including the pharma and transportation industries.

- *Add multiple suppliers*: Companies may add suppliers to improve supply chain resiliency to cope with future potential disruptions. Some of the suppliers, located in different geographical locations, may be used as backup suppliers in case of disruptions.
- *Production-inventory strategies*: Many companies intend to increase the safety stock of input materials, especially for critical items, and reduce the inventory of finished goods due to uncertainties in customer demands (Alicke et al., 2021). To be able to serve customer demands, they also employ novel postponement strategies and product modularization.
- *Optimize product portfolio*: Companies will tend to reduce SKUs by rationalization and optimizing the mix and volume of products to offer to the market to reduce supply chain complexities, manage shortages of supplies, and tackle shifts in consumers' demands. Retail and automotive industries are among the industries that may follow this trend.
- *Localization and regionalization*: Companies will move toward adding local suppliers and production facilities to avoid the complexities of global sourcing and transportation. Semiconductor, pharmaceutical, and production companies are seen to follow this trend to enhance the resiliency of their supply chain, although the total landed cost could be higher.
- *Digitalization*: Analytics tools, information management systems, IoT, Blockchain, artificial intelligence, and additive manufacturing are among the major technologies which help to cope with disruptions effectively. Many companies adopt and implement such technologies to be prepared for future disruptions. Knowing that the labor shortage is a major issue in various industries, artificial intelligence and advanced automated analytics can potentially alleviate the need for labor. Online shopping platforms, multi-channel, and omnichannel systems were also among the major winning factors during the COVID-19 pandemic.
- *Invest in same-day delivery services*: Due to the increase in customer expectations, companies, particularly retailers and transportation companies, aim to enhance same-day delivery services by adding resources such as vehicles and expanding their distribution networks by adding fulfillment centers and warehouses. The question remains whether customers will continue to require such services in the future to the same degree.

6 Concluding Remarks and Future Research

The COVID-19 pandemic showed that many companies, local or global, do not pay sufficient attention to the resiliency of their supply chains. The pandemic has fueled many companies to rethink their supply chain and revise their resources, technologies, and processes. For future research, the following directions are recommended:

- Flexibility and repurposeability are effective factors in coping with disruptions. Some critical questions for companies in different industries are: How much flexibility should be considered? What are the different ways that flexibility can be enhanced in each industry?
- The extent and duration of the supply chain disruptions are still unknown. Although significant positive observations in the economy and industry operations can be seen in June-August 2022, the question "When will supply chains return to normal?" is not answered as various uncertainties continue to exist. Moreover, conventional methods of extrapolating the past have proved to be disastrous for many firms as they struggle with excess inventories or capacity as much as they struggled with shortages during the pandemic. Do we need different methods of assessing risk?
- As many companies are moving to localization, a critical question is: How much localization should be done? Similarly, how much outsourcing and insourcing should be done to not only keep the costs down but also enhance the resiliency and responsiveness of the supply chains?
- Companies added safety inventory in their supply chains. However, how much inventory should be added, and should the inventory be kept for the short-term or long-term need analysis? Where should inventory be kept in the supply chain?
- The mismatch between demands and supplies led to significant price hikes. To keep customers happy while providing supply availability to customers and ensuring companies' profit, how much can sellers raise prices? On what products should price hikes be done, and in which geographical regions should they be applied?
- The extent of disruption could be mitigated considerably if the demand could be forecasted accurately and early. Better forecasting methods are necessary for pandemics to be able to predict supply chain disruptions and the cascading effect on the demands for various essential products.
- Visibility in the supply chain can be an effective tool. Which organizations in the supply chain are responsible to enhance visibility, and how and how much should this be done effectively? Why did firms keep missing early warnings of shifts?
- Although IT and digitalization can be effective ways to accelerate risk mitigation and battle disruption, they also bring risks to the supply chains. What are some of the risks and what are some of the precautionary measures to consider when considering such technologies? How can we minimize the risks of such technologies to benefit from their advantages in the long term? What are some of the key technologies and innovations that are critical to invest in to be able to cope with future supply chain disruptions?

Acknowledgments We would like to thank the Margolis Lab at the Gies College of Business at the University of Illinois at Urbana-Champaign for providing us with the opportunity to collect industry data from Bloomberg. We thank Mr. Mayank Tripathi for his support in doing this research. We also thank the student of the supply chain management course at the Gies College of

Business for initial data collection. We acknowledge the generous support from the Collaboratory Initiative in the Information, Operations, Supply Chain, and Analytics (IOSA) Area in the Department of Business Administration at the Gies College of Business.

References

Abbott. (2021a). 2020 global sustainability report. https://dam.abbott.com/en-us/documents/pdfs/abbott-citizenship/Abbott-2020-Global-Sustainability-Report.pdf.

Abbott. (2021b). Abbott Q2 earnings: Exceptional performance & momentum. https://www.abbott.com/corpnewsroom/strategy-and-strength/Abbott-Q2-earnings-exceptional-performance-and-momemtum.html.

Accenture. (2021). Supply chain disruption. https://www.accenture.com/us-en/insights/consulting/coronavirus-supply-chain-disruption.

Alicke, K., Barriball, E., & Trautwein, V. (2021). How COVID-19 is reshaping supply chains. https://www.mckinsey.com/business-functions/operations/our-insights/how-covid-19-is-reshaping-supply-chains.

AMD. (2022). AMD reports fourth quarter and full year 2021 financial results. https://ir.amd.com/news-events/press-releases/detail/1044/amd-reports-fourth-quarter-and-full-year-2021-financial.

Ashe, A. (2021). Savannah Port adding capacity to address congestion. https://www.joc.com/port-news/us-ports/georgia-ports-authority/savannah-port-adding-capacity-address-congestion_20210329.html.

Beggin, R. (2020). Michigan manufacturing resumes Monday, stay-at-home order extended to May 28. https://www.bridgemi.com/michigan-government/michigan-manufacturing-resumes-monday-stay-home-order-extended-may-28.

Bellwood, O. (2022, July 11). Mercedes sales drop as supply chain issues take hold. *Jalopnik*. https://jalopnik.com/mercedes-sales-drop-as-supply-chain-issues-take-hold-1849163828.

Beredo III, C. S., Denniston, K., Giaimo, C., & Rathke, S. (2020). Impacts to automotive supply chains from COVID-19. *Global Supply Chain Law Blog*. https://www.globalsupplychainlawblog.com/automotive/impacts-to-automotive-supply-chains-from-covid-19/.

Berger, P. (2022a, July 10). Freight rates are starting to fall as shipping demand wavers. *The Wall Street Journal*. https://www.wsj.com/articles/freight-rates-are-starting-to-fall-as-shipping-demand-wavers-11657454400?

Berger, P. (2022b, February 10). Ship backup at Southern California Ports is receding. *The Wall Street Journal*. https://www.wsj.com/articles/container-ship-backup-at-southern-california-ports-is-receding-11644523945.

Bernstein, J., & Tedeschi, E. (2021). Pandemic prices: Assessing inflation in the months and years ahead. The White House. https://www.whitehouse.gov/cea/written-materials/2021/04/12/pandemic-prices-assessing-inflation-in-the-months-and-years-ahead/.

Berthiaume, D. (2021). The most popular new fulfillment channel during COVID-19. https://chainstoreage.com/survey-most-popular-new-fulfillment-channel-during-covid-19.

Best, D. (2020). Kraft Heinz to reduce SKUs by 20% with sharper focus on innovation. https://www.just-food.com/news/kraft-heinz-to-reduce-skus-by-20-with-sharper-focus-on-innovation/.

Bhattacharjee, D., Gould, R., Greenberg, E., & Kandel, M. (2020). US freight after COVID-19: What's next? https://www.mckinsey.com/industries/travel-logistics-and-infrastructure/our-insights/us-freight-after-covid-19-whats-next.

Black, D. (2020). AMD COVID-19 HPC fund adds 18 institutions and 5 petaflops of supercomputer processing power to assist researchers fighting COVID-19 pandemic. https://insidehpc.com/2020/09/amd-covid-19-hpc-fund-adds-18-institutions-and-5-petaflops-of-supercomputer-processing-power-to-assist-researchers-fighting-covid-19-pandemic/.

Bloomberg Wire. (2020, July 21). Texas instruments' COVID effect: Chip orders rise as customers stock up to avoid supply disruptions. *The Dallas Morning News*. https://www.dallasnews.com/business/local-companies/2020/07/21/texas-instruments-covid-effect-chip-orders-rise-as-customers-stock-up-to-avoid-supply-disruptions/.

Blunt, R. (2020). How COVID-19 is affecting transportation. https://www.rpc.senate.gov/policy-papers/how-covid-19-is-affecting-transportation.

Bobrowsky, M. (2022, January 21). Intel to invest at least $20 billion in Ohio Chip-Making Facility. *The Wall Street Journal*. https://www.wsj.com/articles/intel-to-invest-at-least-20-billion-in-ohio-chip-making-facility-11642750760.

Boudette, N. E. (2021, January 27). Tesla has first profitable year, but competition is growing. *The New York Times*. https://www.nytimes.com/2021/01/27/business/tesla-earnings.html.

Bradley, C., Kohli, S., Kuijpers, D., & Smith, T. R. (2021). Why retail outperformers are pulling ahead. https://www.mckinsey.com/industries/retail/our-insights/why-retail-outperformers-are-pulling-ahead.

Bristol Myers Squibb. (2021a). Supplier diversity. https://www.corporatereport.com/bms/2020/esg/our-people/supplier-diversity.php.

Bristol Myers Squibb. (2021b). Supply chain—Approach. https://www.corporatereport.com/bms/2020/esg/our-people/supply-chain.php.

Bristol Myers Squibb. (2021c). Updated statement: Bristol Myers Squibb on Coronavirus (COVID-19). https://news.bms.com/news/details/2021/Updated-Statement-Bristol-Myers-Squibb-on-Coronavirus-COVID-19/default.aspx.

Brody, B. (2020). 4 high-tech tools Johnson & Johnson is using to get products to you during the pandemic. https://www.jnj.com/innovation/johnson-johnson-supply-chain-technology-during-coronavirus.

Bureau of Labor Statistics. (2021). Consumer prices up 6.8 percent for year ended November 2021. https://www.bls.gov/opub/ted/2021/consumer-prices-up-6-8-percent-for-year-ended-november-2021.htm.

Bureau of Labor Statistics. (2022). United States inflation rate. https://tradingeconomics.com/united-states/inflation-cpi.

Chewy. (n.d.). Chewy launches CarePlus, making wellness and insurance plans available to millions of pet parents. Retrieved August 16, 2022, from https://investor.chewy.com/news-and-events/news/news-details/2022/Chewy-Launches-CarePlus-Making-Wellness-and-Insurance-Plans-Available-to-Millions-of-Pet-Parents/default.aspx.

Clayton, C. (2021). US Ag exporters come up empty. https://www.dtnpf.com/agriculture/web/ag/news/article/2021/01/26/shippers-sending-empty-containers-us.

Colias, M., & Foldy, B. (2021, November 18). Ford, GM step into chip business. *The Wall Street Journal*. https://www.wsj.com/articles/ford-enters-semiconductor-business-amid-chip-shortage-impact-11637242202.

Corral, C. (2020). Macy's adjusting brick & mortar strategy. https://www.hometextilestoday.com/omnichannel/macys-adjusting-brick-mortar-strategy/.

Cosgrove, E. (2020). Kraft Heinz to unite supply chain in 'ops center' to save $2B in 5 years. https://www.supplychaindive.com/news/Kraft-Heinz-supply-chain-SKU-ops-center-Patricio/585325/.

CSCMP. (2021). Coca-Cola bottler takes holistic approach to supply chain resiliency. *Supply Chain Quarterly*. https://www.supplychainquarterly.com/articles/5508-coca-cola-bottler-takes-holistic-approach-to-supply-chain-resiliency.

Cuevas, N. (2022). Strained battery material supply chains threaten EV transition. https://www.automotiveworld.com/articles/strained-battery-material-supply-chains-threaten-ev-transition/.

Cunnane, C. (2022). Qualcomm's answer to the chip shortage and digital transformation strategy. https://logisticsviewpoints.com/2022/08/24/qualcomm-chip-shortage/.

Dawson, S. (2020). Nestle shrugs off Covid-19 impact thanks to pet food and health nutrition. https://www.cnbc.com/2020/10/21/nestle-shrugs-off-covid-19-impact-due-to-pet-food-and-health-nutrition.html.

DealPost. (2021). Chewy has revolutionized pet care customer service. https://www.computerworld.com/article/3619883/chewy-has-revolutionized-pet-care-customer-service.html.

Denton, J. (2021). Tesla price increases caused by major issues sourcing critical parts, Elon Musk says. https://www.msn.com/en-us/money/companies/tesla-price-increases-caused-by-major-issues-sourcing-critical-parts-elon-musk-says/ar-AAKBsvu.

DHL. (2020). DHL global forwarding combats COVID-19 with charter flights and trains. https://www.dhl.com/global-en/home/press/press-archive/2020/dhl-global-forwarding-combats-covid-19-with-charter-flights-and-trains.html.

Dunleavy, K. (2022). Fierce JPM week: 5 Industry execs discuss pandemic supply chain issues, solutions. https://www.fiercepharma.com/manufacturing/fierce-jpm-week-5-industry-execs-discuss-pandemic-supply-chain-issues-solutions.

Eisenstein, P. (2020). Coronavirus starts to take a major toll on automakers, with thousands of jobs at risk. https://www.nbcnews.com/business/autos/coronavirus-starts-take-major-toll-automakers-thousands-jobs-risk-n1162251.

Elliott, R., & Bobrowsky, M. (2022, July 2). Tesla vehicle deliveries tumble after China factory shutdown. *The Wall Street Journal*. https://www.wsj.com/articles/tesla-vehicle-deliveries-tumble-after-china-factory-shutdown-11656779597.

Fitch, A., & Davis, B. (2021, August 14). Intel CEO pitches pricey chip plants to officials at home and abroad. *The Wall Street Journal*. https://www.wsj.com/articles/intel-ceo-pitches-pricey-chip-plants-to-officials-at-home-and-abroad-11628933400.

Garland, M. (2021a). Ford shifts focus to built-to-order to mitigate semiconductor shortage's effects. *SupplyChainDive*. https://www.supplychaindive.com/news/ford-semiconductor-shortage-chip-sales-bank/604270/.

Garland, M. (2021b). How Pfizer transformed its supply chain to deliver vaccines at lightspeed. *SupplyChainDive*. https://www.supplychaindive.com/news/pfizer-jim-cafone-covid-vaccine-manufacturing-distribution-cscmp/606867/.

Garland, M. (2021c). Tesla works with suppliers to source alternative chips amid semiconductor shortage. *SupplyChainDive*. https://www.supplychaindive.com/news/tesla-earnings-elon-musk-semiconductor-chips-shortage/604011/.

Gartner. (2022). Supply chain top 25 for 2022. https://www.gartner.com/en/supply-chain/research/supply-chain-top-25.

Gilead. (2021). Our COVID-19 response. https://www.gilead.com/news-and-press/annual-report/year-in-review-2020/our-covid-19-response.

Giusti, M. (2022). Supply-chain issues drive inflation in the auto industry. *PropertyCasualty360 Digital Reader*. https://www.propertycasualty360.com/2022/07/05/supply-chain-issues-drive-inflation-in-the-auto-industry/.

Grzelewski, J. (2021, March 22). Semiconductor shortage, other supply chain issues cause more auto production disruptions. *The Detroit News*. https://www.detroitnews.com/story/business/autos/2021/03/22/ford-cuts-production-stellantis-holds-back-vehicles-latest-signs-supply-chain-woes/4803411001/.

Guilford, G. (2022a, May 11). Inflation slipped in April, but upward pressures remain. *The Wall Street Journal*. https://www.wsj.com/articles/us-inflation-consumer-price-index-april-2022-11652218520.

Guilford, G. (2022b, May 24). Where is inflation headed? Nine signs to watch. *The Wall Street Journal*. https://www.wsj.com/articles/where-is-inflation-headed-nine-signs-to-watch-11653384601?

Guilford, G., & Cambon, S. C. (2022, April 24). Workers are changing jobs, raking in big raises—And keeping inflation high. *The Wall Street Journal*. https://www.wsj.com/articles/workers-are-changing-jobs-raking-in-big-raisesand-keeping-inflation-high-11650792602.

Hachman, M. (2022). AMD shrugs off COVID chip shortage fears by focusing on premium PCs. https://www.arnnet.com.au/article/697869/amd-shrugs-off-covid-chip-shortage-fears-by-focusing-premium-pcs/.

Harris, M. (2022). These 5 charts help demystify the global chip shortage. https://spectrum.ieee.org/global-chip-shortage-charts.

Hays, K., & Banerjee, H. (2021). Coca-Cola's Q4 sales volumes drop on global COVID-19 shutdowns. https://www.spglobal.com/commodityinsights/en/market-insights/latest-news/petrochemicals/021021-coca-colas-q4-sales-volumes-drop-on-global-covid-19-shutdowns.

Heilweil, R. (2020, May 12). Why Elon Musk disobeyed government orders and reopened a Tesla Factory. *Vox*. https://www.vox.com/recode/2020/5/12/21255812/elon-musk-tesla-factory-coronavirus-reopening.

Horton, W. (2020, June 7). Airlines are removing seats to carry cargo on more planes with capacity shortage likely to persist. *Forbes*. https://www.forbes.com/sites/willhorton1/2020/06/07/airlines-still-removing-seats-to-create-cargo-space-despite-covid-19-easing/?sh=4fc95b816980.

Hruska, J. (2021). AMD's reliance on TSMC isn't harming the company's growth prospects. https://www.extremetech.com/computing/319929-amds-reliance-on-tsmc-isnt-harming-the-companys-growth-prospects.

Hu, K., & Dastin, J. (2020, March 17). Amazon warehouses receive only vital supplies in U.S., Europe amid coronavirus. *Reuters*. https://www.reuters.com/article/us-health-coronavirus-amazon-com-idUSKBN2142IM.

Hyder, S. (2021, February 22). How Covid-19 has changed lean manufacturing practices: A case study with IBASEt. *Forbes*. https://www.forbes.com/sites/shamahyder/2021/02/22/how-covid-19-has-changed-lean-manufacturing-practices-a-case-study-with-ibaset.

IFC. (2020). The impact of COVID-19 on logistics. https://www.ifc.org/wps/wcm/connect/2d6ec419-41df-46c9-8b7b-96384cd36ab3/IFC-Covid19-Logistics-final_web.pdf?MOD=AJPERES&CVID=naqOED5.

Isidore, C. (2021a). Pfizer revenue and profits soar on its Covid vaccine business. https://www.cnn.com/2021/11/02/business/pfizer-earnings/index.html.

Isidore, C. (2021b). Tesla shakes off supply chain issues to post record profit, again. https://www.cnn.com/2021/10/20/business/tesla-earnings/index.html.

Jackson, J. K., Weiss, M. A., Schwarzenberg, A. B., Nelson, R. M., Sutter, K. M., & Sutherland, M. D. (2021). Global economic effects of COVID-19. Congressional Research Service. https://www.wita.org/atp-research/global-economic-effects-of-covid-19/.

Jagt, R., Knipscheer, L., & van Houten, S. -P. (2020). Rethinking food supply chains in times of COVID-19. https://www2.deloitte.com/nl/nl/pages/consumer/articles/food-covid-19-priorities-to-future-proof-supply-chains.html.

Kang, J. (2020, December 3). Kroger reports strong, but slowing, sales growth. *The Wall Street Journal*. https://www.wsj.com/articles/kroger-reports-strong-but-slowing-sales-growth-11607004330.

Kang, J. (2021, January 12). Albertsons' sales growth outpaces rivals amid Covid-19 pandemic. *The Wall Street Journal*. https://www.wsj.com/articles/albertsons-reports-strong-grocery-sales-growth-amid-pandemic-11610462657.

Kapner, S. (2022, July 4). Glut of goods at target, Walmart is a boon for liquidators. *The Wall Street Journal*. https://www.wsj.com/articles/glut-of-goods-at-target-walmart-is-a-boon-for-liquidators-11656927184.

Kay, G. (2021a). Amazon is making its own shipping containers—And waiting as little as 2 days outside ports. https://www.businessinsider.com/amazon-making-own-shipping-containers-bypassing-port-delays-2021-12.

Kay, G. (2021b). Elon Musk says pandemic supply-chain issues and a global microchip shortage resulted in 'insane difficulties' for Tesla. https://www.businessinsider.com/elon-musk-tesla-supply-chain-issues-chip-shortage-insane-difficulties-2021-4.

Kearney. (2022). CSCMP's state of logistics report.

Kelleher, K., Kumar, K., Patel, P., & Schrader, U. (2020). Pharma operations: The path to recovery and the next normal. https://www.mckinsey.com/industries/life-sciences/our-insights/pharma-operations-the-path-to-recovery-and-the-next-normal.

Keller, A. -Q. (2021). From COVID to Coca-Cola: Analyzing distribution models. https://www.supplychain247.com/article/from_covid_to_coca_cola_analyzing_distribution_models/alteryx.

King, I., Wu, D., & Pogkas, D. (2021, March 29). How a chip shortage snarled everything from phones to cars. *Bloomberg*. https://www.bloomberg.com/graphics/2021-semiconductors-chips-shortage/.

Koenig, D., & Miller, Z. (2020, April 3). 3M fires back at trump over order to produce more face masks, stop exports. *PBS News Hour*. https://www.pbs.org/newshour/nation/3m-fires-back-at-trump-over-order-to-produce-more-face-masks-stop-exports.

Kolodny, L. (2020). Tesla's sale of environmental credits help drive to profitability. https://www.cnbc.com/2020/07/23/teslas-sale-of-environmental-credits-help-drive-to-profitability.html.

Lambert, L. (2020, May 7). Real unemployment rate soars past 24.9%—and the U.S. has now lost 33.5 million jobs. *Fortune*. https://fortune.com/2020/05/07/unemployment-33-million-coronavirus/.

Leonard, J., & Kim, S. (2021, November 23). Samsung will build an advanced chip plant in Texas in a win for Biden's drive to increase U.S. production. *Fortune*. https://fortune.com/2021/11/23/samsung-new-chip-plant-texas-biden-us-production-semiconductor/.

Leonard, M. (2020). What we know about Pfizer's coronavirus vaccine distribution plan. *SupplyChainDive*. https://www.supplychaindive.com/news/pfizer-vaccine-supply-chain-BioNTech-fedex-ups-dhl/588784/.

Leonard, M. (2021a). Ford doubles down on lean in the face of semiconductor shortage. https://www.supplychaindive.com/news/ford-lean-inventory-semiconductor-chip-shortage-manufacturing-production-renesas/599422/.

Leonard, M. (2021b). Ford limits production at multiple factories through July due to semiconductor shortages. https://www.supplychaindive.com/news/ford-semiconductor-shortage-manufacturing-supplier-factory/602855/.

Leonard, M. (2021c). TSMC plans $100B investment to battle semiconductor shortages. https://www.supplychaindive.com/news/tsmc-plans-investment-semiconductor-shortage/598535/.

Lepcha, M. (2022). Semiconductor shortage guide: Winners and losers of crisis. https://capital.com/semiconductor-shortage-guide.

Lopez, E. (2021). Georgia Ports Authority to convert 5 facilities into pop-up container yards. https://www.supplychaindive.com/news/pop-up-container-yards-Georgia-Savannah-North-Carolina-STOR/609788/.

Luman, R., & Soroka, O. (2022). Container shipping: Volume growth calms, tariff s remain strong. https://think.ing.com/articles/container-shipping-volume-growth-calms-tariffs-remain-strong.

Luo, S., van den Bossche, P., Ehrig, B., & Troncoso, O. (2022). Kearney finds a bright future for a new style of reshoring that incorporates what used to be thought of as nearshoring. https://www.kearney.com/operations-performance-transformation/us-reshoring-index.

Markman, J. (2022, May 5). AMD crushes earnings as new chip leadership emerges—Leaving Intel in the dust. *Forbes*. https://www.forbes.com/sites/jonmarkman/2022/05/05/amd-crushes-earnings-as-new-chip-leadership-emergesleaving-intel-in-the-dust/.

Markowitz, A. (2021). 14 iconic retailers that fell into pandemic bankruptcy. https://www.aarp.org/money/credit-loans-debt/info-2020/bankrupt-retail-chain-store-list-is-growing.html.

Marsh, J. (2021). UP, BNSF offer incentives to move containers away from LA, Long Beach. https://www.freightwaves.com/news/up-bnsf-offer-incentives-to-move-containers-away-from-la-long-beach.

Mattioli, D. (2022, June 16). Amazon went big during the pandemic. Now it's feeling the hangover. *The Wall Street Journal*. https://www.wsj.com/podcasts/the-journal/amazon-went-big-during-the-pandemic-now-its-feeling-the-hangover/91905217-767d-4446-9c65-24d899040882.

Mazumdar-Shaw, K. (2022). Reinventing supply chains of tomorrow. https://kiranshaw.blog/2022/07/19/reinventing-supply-chains-of-tomorrow/.

McNeil, T. (2020). Kellogg's value soars during COVID-19 crisis. https://www.bakeryandsnacks.com/Article/2020/03/18/Kellogg-s-value-soars-during-COVID-19-crisis.
Merck. (2022a). How we're prioritizing supply. https://www.merck.com/stories/how-were-prioritizing-supply/.
Merck. (2022b). Our COVID-19 response. https://www.merck.com/our-covid-19-response/.
Mikhail, N. (2020). Elementum to #leadboldly by supporting global supply chain organizations with free virtual 'war room' to manage disruptions caused by COVID-19. https://www.elementum.com/chain-reaction/elementum-to-leadboldly-by-supporting-global-supply-chain-organizations-with-free-virtual-war-room-to-manage-disruptions-caused-by-covid-19/.
Miller, G. (2021). New video shows massive scope of California box-ship traffic jam. https://www.freightwaves.com/news/new-video-shows-massive-scope-of-california-box-ship-traffic-jam.
Miller, G. (2022a). California Ports piling up again: Too many containers sitting too long. https://www.freightwaves.com/news/california-ports-piling-up-again-with-long-dwelling-import-containers.
Miller, G. (2022b). East Coast Ports about to get slammed by a lot more ships. https://www.freightwaves.com/news/east-coast-ports-about-to-get-slammed-by-a-lot-more-ships.
Mutikani, L. (2020, March 2). U.S. manufacturing sector stalls as coronavirus hits supply chains. *Reuters*. https://www.reuters.com/article/us-usa-economy-manufacturing-idUSKBN20P29T.
Nadelle, D. (2022). Global chip shortage leaves new BMWs without access to Apple CarPlay and Android Auto. https://www.gobankingrates.com/money/economy/global-chip-shortage-new-bmw-without-apple-carplay-android-auto/.
Nellis, S. (2021, September 25). Intel breaks ground on $20 bln Arizona Plants as U.S. Chip Factory race heats up. *Reuters*. https://www.reuters.com/technology/intel-breaks-ground-20-bln-arizona-plants-us-chip-factory-race-heats-up-2021-09-24/.
Nunes, K. (2020). Kraft Heinz playing catch up in supply chain efficiencies. https://www.foodbusinessnews.net/articles/16878-kraft-heinz-playing-catch-up-in-supply-chain-efficiencies.
O'Brien, S. (2022). With limited inventory due to a computer chip shortage, 82% of consumers are paying above sticker price for a new car. https://www.cnbc.com/2022/02/17/more-than-80percent-of-consumers-are-paying-above-sticker-price-for-new-car.html.
Pfizer. (2020). Pfizer announces agreement with gilead to manufacture remdesivir for treatment of COVID-19. https://www.pfizer.com/news/press-release/press-release-detail/pfizer-announces-agreement-gilead-manufacture-remdesivir.
Pfizer. (2022). Manufacturing and distributing the COVID-19 vaccine. https://www.pfizer.com/science/coronavirus/vaccine/manufacturing-and-distribution.
Pharmaceutical Technology. (2022). Bristol Myers Squibb reports 9% full-year 2021 revenue growth. https://www.pharmaceutical-technology.com/news/bms-full-year-2021-revenue/.
PharmaTech. (2022). COVID-19 impact on pharma. *Pharmaceutical Technology*. https://www.pharmaceutical-technology.com/covid-19-in-pharma/.
Pino, D. (2022, January 10). Line of ships waiting at LA/Long Beach at all-time high. *National Review*. https://www.nationalreview.com/corner/line-of-ships-waiting-at-la-long-beach-at-all-time-high/.
Plume, K. (2020, May 14). Truckers hit by Coronavirus pandemic face rocky road to recovery. *Reuters*. https://www.reuters.com/article/us-health-coronavirus-trucking-idUSKBN22Q1J5.
POLB. (2022). TEUS archive: 1987 to present by month. https://polb.com/business/port-statistics/#teus-archive-1995-to-present.
ProcureCon Events. (2021). How Samsung has supported its suppliers during the COVID-19 pandemic. https://procureconeu.wbresearch.com/blog/samsung-supported-its-suppliers-during-the-pandemic.
Ronan, D. (2021). Trucking bankruptcies surged in 2020 as pandemic hit small carriers. https://www.ttnews.com/articles/trucking-bankruptcies-surged-2020-pandemic-hits-small-carriers.
Sagonowsky, E. (2020). Biogen signs on to manufacture clinical supplies for Vir's COVID-19 antibodies. https://www.fiercepharma.com/manufacturing/biogen-signs-to-develop-manufacture-vir-antibodies-for-covid-19.

Saleki-Gerhardt, A. (2020). Ensuring patients around the world get medicines during COVID-19. https://stories.abbvie.com/stories/ensuring-patients-around-world-get-medicines-during-covid-19.htm.

Samsung. (2021). Our response to COVID-19. https://www.samsung.com/us/aboutsamsung/samsung-pandemic-response/.

Saraiva, A., & Murray, B. (2021, November 23). Every step of the global supply chain is going wrong—All at once. *Bloomberg*. https://www.bloomberg.com/graphics/2021-congestion-at-americas-busiest-port-strains-global-supply-chain/#xj4y7vzkg.

Schatteman, O., Woodhouse, D., & Terino, J. (2020). Supply chain lessons from Covid-19: Time to refocus on resilience. https://www.bain.com/insights/supply-chain-lessons-from-covid-19/.

Schmukler, L. (2020). Global supply chain management during the COVID-19 pandemic and beyond. https://www.bms.com/life-and-science/news-and-perspectives/managing-a-global-supply-chain-during-the-covid-19-pandemic.html.

Silver, S. (2021). How Kellogg's, Nike, and HP handled 2020 supply chain disruptions. https://www.fm-magazine.com/news/2021/jan/coronavirus-supply-chain-disruptions-kelloggs-nike-hp.html.

Sirimanne, S. N. (2021). Container shipping in times of COVID-19: Why freight rates have surged, and implications for policymakers. https://unctad.org/system/files/official-document/presspb2021d2_en.pdf.

Slabodkin, G. (2022). Abbott reports $900M Q1 revenue beat on COVID-19 test demand. https://www.medtechdive.com/news/abbott-q1-2022-revenue-covid-19-test/622367/.

Soper, S. (2020, September 16). Amazon plans to put 1,000 warehouses in suburban neighborhoods. *Bloomberg*. https://www.bloomberg.com/news/articles/2020-09-16/amazon-plans-to-put-1-000-warehouses-in-neighborhoods.

Sorkin, A. R., Karaian, J., Kessler, S., Gandel, S., de la Merced, M. J., Hirsch, L., & Livni, E. (2021, November 19). Ford has a D.I.Y. plan for computer chips. *The New York Times*. https://www.nytimes.com/2021/11/19/business/dealbook/ford-computer-chips.html.

Starbucks. (2022). At-a-glance: Our response to COVID-19. https://stories.starbucks.com/stories/response-to-covid/.

Stinson, J. (2021). A dip in chips slows truck production. https://www.transportdive.com/news/semiconductor-chip-shortage-class-8-truck-OEM/597712/.

Tan, W. (2021). An 'aggressive' fight over containers is causing shipping costs to rocket by 300%. https://www.cnbc.com/2021/01/22/shipping-container-shortage-is-causing-shipping-costs-to-rise.html.

Terlep, S. (2022, July 10). Fed up with China, one boss tries removing it from the supply Chain. *The Wall Street Journal*. https://www.wsj.com/articles/fed-up-with-china-one-boss-tries-removing-it-from-the-supply-chain-11657445401?

Thomas, L. (2020). Curbside pickup at retail stores surges 208% during Coronavirus pandemic. https://www.cnbc.com/2020/04/27/coronavirus-curbside-pickup-at-retail-stores-surges-208percent.html.

Ting-Fang, C., & Li, L. (2021). COVID slows Apple and Google production shift away from China. https://asia.nikkei.com/Business/China-tech/COVID-slows-Apple-and-Google-production-shift-away-from-China.

UKEssays. (2020). Evaluation of Tesla's supply chain management. *UKEssays*. https://www.ukessays.com/assignments/evaluation-of-teslas-supply-chain-management-2021.php.

University of Miami. (2020). J & J Collaboratory. https://www.coe.miami.edu/research/shared-facilities/engineering-johnson-and-johnson-shared-facility/j%2D%2Dj-collaboratory/index.html.

U.S. Department of Statistics. (2022). Consumer Price Index—Bureau of Labor Statistics. https://www.bls.gov/news.release/pdf/cpi.pdf.

U.S. Securities and Exchange Commission. (2022). 10K—Merck & Co, Inc. https://www.sec.gov/ix?doc=/Archives/edgar/data/310158/000031015822000003/mrk-20211231.htm.

Walmart. (2021). Walmart annual report 2021. https://corporate.walmart.com/media-library/document/q4-fy21-earnings-release/_proxyDocument?id=00000177-b235-d73b-a9f7-b2f591660001.

Wayland, M. (2020). GE, Ford sign $336 million Federal Contract to make ventilators for Coronavirus outbreak. https://www.cnbc.com/2020/04/16/ge-ford-sign-336-million-federal-contract-for-ventilator-production.html.

Weissman, R. (2020). Today's supply chains are too lean. https://www.supplychaindive.com/news/lean-supply-chain-jit-inventory-covid-19/574693/.

Wells, D. (2022). AstraZeneca reports 41% growth in FY 2021 total revenue. https://www.pharmaceutical-technology.com/news/astrazeneca-fy-2021-revenue/.

Wiener-Bronner, D. (2020). Coke is canceling 200 drink brands. https://www.cnn.com/2020/10/22/business/coke-zico-tab/index.html.

Wills, K. L. (2021). Port of LA will pay container terminals for efficiency gains. https://www.freightwaves.com/news/port-of-la-will-pay-container-terminals-for-efficiency-gains.

Wills, K. L. (2022). Ports of LA, Long Beach clear containers, set January records. *American Shipper*. https://www.freightwaves.com/news/ports-of-la-long-beach-clear-containers-set-january-records.

World Health Organization. (2020). Novel Coronavirus (2019-NCoV): Strategic preparedness and response plan. https://www.who.int/publications/i/item/strategic-preparedness-and-response-plan-for-the-new-coronavirus.

Young, L. (2022, August 2). Surging retail inventories are swamping U.S. warehouses. *The Wall Street Journal*. https://www.wsj.com/articles/retailers-seeking-more-warehouse-space-to-stow-excess-inventory-11659460929?

Yu, J. (2022). Applied materials stock a supply chain regain play. https://www.entrepreneur.com/article/429462.

Zafar, R. (2022). TSMC more than doubles revenue growth to end 2021 on strong note. https://wccftech.com/tsmc-more-than-doubles-revenue-growth-to-end-2021-on-strong-note/.

Post-pandemic Online Grocery Delivery Services: Trends, Challenges, and Empirical Evidence from Germany

Jakob Schmidt and Konstantinos Nikolopoulos

1 Introduction

The Coronavirus disease 2019 (COVID-19) pandemic changed the world as we know it: mobility was severely constrained, health services became of paramount importance, and demand collapsed in most markets (Lodni et al., 2021; McKinsey, 2021a; Veselovská, 2020). Ultimately, the consumption shock in the leading industrial nations was many times higher than that in the global economic crisis between 2007 and 2009 (McKinsey, 2021a). In Germany, consumption plummeted by 13% at the pandemic's beginning (McKinsey, 2021a).

Nevertheless, there were markets and sectors, albeit few, which experienced a substantial increase in demand at the beginning and during the COVID-19 pandemic (Chowdhury et al., 2021; McKinsey, 2021b; Veselovská, 2020). These included, for example, demand for personal health protection and demand for groceries (Chowdhury et al., 2021; McKinsey, 2021a). This increase in demand for groceries during the pandemic was due to the fact that during the lockdowns in Germany, restaurants and cafés were closed for an extended time, which meant that there were very few—if any, options for eating out (Dannenberg et al., 2020; Deutschland.de, n.d.). In addition to the general increase in grocery demand, the online grocery business model has benefited in particular (Dannenberg et al., 2020; McKinsey, 2021b). This business model has experienced a tailwind in two ways: On the one hand, from the increased demand for groceries and, on the other hand, from the general increase in e-commerce business in connection with the COVID-19 pandemic (Lodni et al., 2021).

Firstly, Germany's demand for groceries increased by 12.3% between 2019 and 2020 (McKinsey, 2021b). This number represents an almost two percentage point

J. Schmidt · K. Nikolopoulos (✉)
Business School, Durham University, Durham, UK
e-mail: kostas.nikolopoulos@durham.ac.uk

M. Moshref-Javadi, S. Seshadri (eds.), *Impacts of COVID-19 on Supply Chains*, Springer Business Cases, https://doi.org/10.1007/978-3-031-47734-8_2

higher increase in Germany compared to the European average. Secondly, total e-commerce sales increased by 14.7% in 2020 and another 19% in 2021 and are now close to 100 billion € (Bundesverband E-Commerce und Versandhandel Deutschland e.V. (BEVH), 2022). This rise symbolises a significant increase, considering that in the pre-COVID-19 year, sales in e-commerce amounted to just 72.6 billion € (BEVH, 2022). Furthermore, and even more important, experts expect this trend to be sustainable (Gruntkowski & Martinez, 2022; Lodni et al., 2021; McKinsey, 2021b; Shen et al., 2022).

Undoubtedly, online grocery has received an external boost from COVID-19 and its aftermath (McKinsey, 2021b). Nonetheless, customers have adopted and appreciate its convenience, making it likely to remain, at least partially (McKinsey, 2021a, 2021b; Shen et al., 2022). According to Spryker and Appinio (2022) research, time savings, crowd avoidance and comfort are the main reasons consumers shop for groceries online. Moreover, 33% of German consumers buy at least some of their groceries online in 2022. According to McKinsey (2021b), online grocery growth was 39.2% in Germany between 2019 and 2020, while the weighted European average was 53.9%. The different growth figures from BEVH (2021) and McKinsey (2021b) are due to different definitions of the grocery category. The reasons for Germany's slower adoption are, on the one hand, problems in the implementation and execution, especially challenges in the last mile delivery of orders (Dannenberg et al., 2020). On the other hand, it also concerns the Germans' general cultural characteristics and behaviour patterns. These behaviours will be discussed in more detail in the next section, and the companies' operational challenges will be considered from several angles throughout the thesis.

Looking at the online grocery delivery market in Germany, there are essentially three business models, which differ from each other and will be explained in more detail in the course of this chapter: Standard grocery delivery with a pre-selected time window for delivery, delivery of meal kit boxes for pre-determined meals and on-demand, so-called quick-commerce, ordering of groceries with an immediate delivery (Heard et al., 2019).

2 Working Definitions

First, the phrase 'post' COVID-19 pandemic should be explained and defined. The COVID-19 virus has so far infected millions of people in Germany, and thousands have died in connection with the virus (Robert Koch Institute, 2022). Even in the summer of 2022, thousands of people are infected with the virus daily (Robert Koch Institute, 2022). Therefore, the fight against the virus is certainly not over yet. However, on the other hand, the 'epidemic situation of national scope' (Deutschland.de, n.d., 28.10.2021) has been lifted in Germany since November 25th 2021, most of the population has been vaccinated, and all drastic restrictions are currently abolished (Deutschland.de, n.d.). Thus, the end of the pandemic situation does not have to go hand in hand with the end of the virus (Telenti et al., 2021). Moreover, other authors, such as Shen et al. (2022) and East (2022), also classify the situation and examine the grocery market 'after' the COVID-19 pandemic. Therefore, this chapter does not address the possible return of restrictions and associated effects on the industry.

Secondly, online or electronic grocery (e-grocery) purchasing or delivery should be defined and distinguished from other ordering and delivery options. 'Groceries' are broadly defined as 'food and household items as well as other fast-moving consumer goods' (Leyerer et al., 2020, p. 587). This definition does not include ready-cooked meals from restaurants, which are delivered by delivery services (Leyerer et al., 2020).

E-grocery is defined as the electronic purchase of groceries regardless of physical location during the ordering process and subsequent delivery to the place of residence (Seidel, 2021). This variant is examined in the chapter as it is the preferred delivery option of Germans when ordering groceries online (Ehrler et al., 2021; Lodni et al., 2021; Seidel, 2021). A similar variant is the click-and-collect model, where the customer picks up the pre-ordered groceries at the supermarket, which this will not examine.

Before examining the different models, comparing them and highlighting the operational challenges, it is important to briefly describe the overarching cultural characteristics of the Germans concerning shopping. Besides the operational challenges, these specifics partly explain why e-grocery is not yet as widespread in Germany as in comparable countries (McKinsey, 2021b).

On the one hand, digitalisation in Germany is not yet as advanced as in other similar countries of the European Union. The reasons for this are complex, and it would go beyond the scope of this report to go into all of them. However, new providers of innovative and digital business models find a digital environment in Germany that is only average in Europe (European Commission, 2022). In addition, there is a general scepticism towards innovation in German society (Lodni et al., 2021; Seitz, 2013). Furthermore, this is often accompanied by increased customer complaint density and lower customer satisfaction (Lodni et al., 2021). Finally, Germans also have a trust deficit towards credit card payments on the internet and are advocates of cash, especially the older generations. With just under 63% cash payments in transactions, Germany stands out compared to the economically strong European nations, where the average is just under 40%.

The fact that there is still hope for online grocery delivery providers and that it is interesting to examine the market in Germany is also due to two statistics. On the one hand, the share of cash payments has fallen from 83 to 58.7% between 2007 and 2020. On the other hand, Germans' general online spending per capita has been increasing for years.

3 Literature Review

Before examining the differences and specifics of each business model in the following sub-sections, there are also challenges and circumstances that all three models have in common. These are partly due to the grocery market's operation in general, implications of e-commerce or overarching delivery issues (Lodni et al., 2021). Looking at the German grocery market in general, it is noticeable that it is a highly competitive market with strong participating companies (Frank & Peschel, 2020; McKinsey, 2021b). These persistent conditions have led to a high concentration and essentially four dominating companies in Germany (Wortmann, 2021). The Edeka Group, REWE Group, Schwarz Group and Aldi Group held 75.5% of the market share in 2020 and have been duelling for decades with price wars and innovations (Wortmann, 2021). As a result, margins in the grocery industry are small, and cost pressure is high, even without the additional aspect of home delivery and related costs (McKinsey, 2021b; Piroth et al., 2020). Furthermore, the entry of pure online players into the market, the general increase in the online and delivery business, and the rising expectations of customers are leading to further pressure on margins (Lagorio & Pinto, 2021; McKinsey, 2021b). Consequently, companies must pay extreme attention to costs at every step of their commercial chain.

Another common challenge is the grocery industry's highly complex and demanding supply chain (Alftan et al., 2015; Lagorio & Pinto, 2021). As will be shown later, this supply chain is modified for the three business models, but basic regulations and requirements remain. Firstly, there is a need for an uninterrupted refrigerated supply chain (Dannenberg et al., 2020; Fikar, 2018; Lagorio & Pinto, 2021). This persistent cooling chain is necessary to bring the various fresh groceries to the customer in perfect quality and to comply with the legal requirements (Centobelli et al., 2020). Such a cooling supply chain requires detailed planning, reliable partners and is much more cost-intensive than an ordinary supply chain (Ali et al., 2018; Lagorio & Pinto, 2021; Lodni et al., 2021). Moreover, strict sanitary regulations must also be observed throughout the supply chain (Lagorio & Pinto, 2021).

Secondly, a decisive factor in the supply chain, which several authors identified for all grocery home delivery services, is the last mile distribution (Capgemini, 2019; Dannenberg et al., 2020; Ehrler et al., 2021; Seidel, 2021). The last mile refers to the last step in the supply chain, where the shipment is delivered to the consumer. It is often a significant cost driver; therefore, numerous authors have looked at optimising this step in the supply chain (Lagorio & Pinto, 2021; Lodni et al., 2021; McKinsey, 2021b). Leyerer et al. (2020) have investigated the last mile's structural shortening by commissioning refrigerated lockers as an alternative to the consumers' door. Seidel (2021) also supported this idea and additionally brought up the idea of a 'milk-man principle' (Seidel, 2021, p. 1928), where the routes are fixed. Consequently, costs could be reduced, and capacity utilisation increased (Seidel, 2021). However, overall, there is a need for action on this topic regardless of the business model since, in addition to the already costly delivery, cost drivers such as unsuccessful delivery attempts and ever-smaller delivery windows drive up costs and devour profits (Fikar, 2018; Fikar et al., 2021). Frank and Peschel (2020) and Lim et al. (2017) also see last mile distribution as central and one of the few options in grocery retailing to differentiate from competitors. Vakulenko et al. (2019) support this view and attribute a crucial link between the ordering experience and customer satisfaction to the last mile distribution. However, the existing literature deals more generally with the problem of the last mile distribution, which exists not only in Germany and the sector of groceries.

Another specific issue for the grocery industry is the rapid perishability of the products (Fikar et al., 2021; Lagorio & Pinto, 2021). Even if the cooling chain and sanitary standards are maintained, vulnerable and fresh grocery products have a short shelf life (Fikar et al., 2021). In the worst case, failed delivery attempts or increased traffic can lead to food being disposed of. This food waste problem is ubiquitous in the grocery industry in general (Teller et al., 2018). However, the extent to which German grocery delivery services are affected by this problem can only be rudimentarily deduced from the existing literature.

High demand uncertainty is a further general difficulty associated with online retailing (Jing & Lewis, 2011). Online business is much more volatile, trends come and go faster, and there is information asymmetry between suppliers and buyers (McMaster et al., 2020; Yang et al., 2021). In addition, since the outbreak of the COVID-19 pandemic, there has been uncertainty throughout the grocery industry about further developments (McKinsey, 2021b). This uncertainty results in purchasing and inventory forecasting being much more difficult for companies and can, among other things, lead to stockouts (Jing & Lewis, 2011). This problem is even more severe for pure online players, as they cannot sell goods via brick-and-mortar stores. Ulrich et al. (2021) have also recognised this problem and developed a distributional regression model, which should provide more precise forecasting and has also outperformed models from practice in a test scenario. However, the extent of the problem of stockouts for the individual models will be explained in the sub-sections.

A further criticism of some potential customers is that the goods cannot be physically inspected for quality and freshness (Dannenberg et al., 2020; Olsson et al., 2021). However, this is an insurmountable disadvantage of online retail and can only be minimised through good supplier selection, quality controls and a lean supply chain.

Moreover, Gruntkowski and Martinez (2022) identified that customers perceive risk when they order groceries online. In addition to the mentioned scepticism regarding online payment, including data protection and quality of the products, this risk relates to potential delivery problems and return difficulties (Gruntkowski & Martinez, 2022). Lastly, some customers do not accept paying a premium for the home delivery service (Lodni et al., 2021). Of course, this does not apply to all customer groups, but some are price-sensitive when shopping for groceries (Fikar et al., 2021; Lodni et al., 2021). All in all, German customers, in particular, are considered to be very price-oriented and are often referred to as the 'most complicated customers in the world' (Expansion, n.d.; Spryker & Appinio, 2022). In summary, the significant challenges for the e-grocery business are more operational and fewer strategic issues (Mkansi et al., 2018; Piroth et al., 2020). Bain and Company (2022) also concludes in its report that the fulfilment of operational processes will be a decisive factor in determining who prevails in the market.

3.1 Standard Delivery

The standard or traditional grocery delivery method is the most prolonged of the three delivery methods in Germany (Dannenberg et al., 2020; Seidel et al., 2016). After several failed attempts of companies to enter the e-grocery market, the pioneer was today's market leader REWE in 2011, the first full-range grocery retailer to enter the online market (Dannenberg et al., 2020; Lodni et al., 2021). From the customer's point of view, the business model works that the customer first enters his postal code to see if his place is supplied (Inside Germany, 2021). If this is the case, customers can choose their products and place them in the shopping basket (Inside Germany, 2021). After reaching the respective minimum order value, a delivery window can be selected and confirmed (Inside Germany, 2021). Depending on the provider and capacity utilisation, this may be on the same day or from the following day onwards (Amazon, n.d.; Inside Germany, 2021). The last step is payment, which is possible with most providers using all common online payment methods (Amazon, n.d.; Inside Germany, 2021).

The current market shares of the dynamic grocery delivery market are difficult to find, as the participants do not want to show their cards too precisely. However, it can be stated that REWE is the market leader from the economic data and the people's awareness (Dannenberg et al., 2020; Kolf, 2022; Lodni et al., 2021; Spryker & Appinio, 2022). They are followed by companies like Amazon Fresh / Pantry and smaller players like Bringmeister, Picnic and Knuspr (European Supermarket Magazine, 2019; Lodni et al., 2021; Spryker & Appinio, 2022; Startbase, 2022). The providers also prefer to keep the turnover a secret, leaving only room for speculation. What is public is that the REWE Group achieved a total turnover of 76.5 billion € in the financial year 2021, of which 18.52 billion € was generated by the independent retail segment, to which the grocery delivery business belongs (REWE Group, 2022). Amazon Germany achieved net sales of $37.3 billion in 2021 (Amazon, 2022a). According to forecasts made by the German trade journal 'Lebensmittelzeitung' in 2017, Amazon Fresh was expected to have a turnover of approximately 120 million € in 2021. For REWE, Kolf (2022), writing in the German newspaper 'Handelsblatt', estimated the pick-up and delivery business turnover at around 700 million € for the year 2021.

The smaller market players publish more information: the supplier Knuspr reports its turnover for the first business year in Germany at 23 million € (Knuspr, 2022b). Bringmeister, which started as an offshoot of the Edeka Group and now belongs to a venture capital investor, generated around 58 million € in sales in 2020 while projected an increase to over 100 million € in 2021 (Kapalschinski & Kolf,

2021a). Picnic, which the Edeka Group now supports, reported total sales of 455 million € for 2020, of which 78 million € was generated in Germany (Kapalschinski & Kolf, 2021a; Krisch, 2022).

There are also differences in the delivery areas: While REWE is leading here as well, and delivery is possible in all large and small cities, the other providers tend to concentrate on fewer or smaller cities (Amazon, 2022b; Bringmeister, n.d.; Knuspr, 2022a; Picnic, n.d.; REWE, n.d.). Amazon Fresh and Bringmeister are available in four cities each, and the Knuspr and Picnic services in several, but mainly smaller cities (Amazon, 2022b; Bringmeister, n.d.; Knuspr, 2022a; Picnic, n.d.). What all models have in common, however, is that orders are limited to urban or suburban areas (Seidel, 2021).

Another distinction made by Bain and Company (2022) and Dannenberg et al. (2020) is between omnichannel retailers and pure online retailers. Only REWE can be considered a true omnichannel retailer of the five mentioned companies. Although the Edeka Group is a 35% shareholder of Picnic and provides some of the products their own brand, it is still more of a strategic partner and not an operational partner that allows Picnic to engage in stationary retail (Ecommerce News, 2019). On the other hand, Amazon Fresh, Bringmeister and Knuspr are pure online players and have no stationary shops. Omnichannel companies like REWE often have an advantage over pure online companies because they purchase larger quantities and can thus achieve better prices through economies of scale (Bain & Company, 2022; Eriksson et al., 2022). These more complex sales opportunities online and offline also enable multi-channel providers to offer a broader range of products, which appears to be an essential criterion for many customers (Altay et al., 2022; Bain & Company, 2022). In addition, it is easier for them to build reliable partnerships with their suppliers, and they already have a customer base that they can activate more easily online (Bain & Company, 2022; Eriksson et al., 2022). The assortment size of the providers mentioned above varies significantly in some cases: REWE states its assortment as 15,000–20,000 products depending on the location, Knuspr offers 12,000 products, and Amazon Fresh itself only speaks of 'thousands of products' (Amazon, 2022b; REWE Group, n.d.). Bringmeister states over 17,000 products and no information are available about Picnic (Bringmeister, n.d.). Of course, more products potentially attract more customers but also entail increased operational effort and challenges (Lim et al., 2018).

Before presenting the challenges of this ordering method, Table 1 summarises all the essential aspects of the leading providers.

In addition to the general challenges of the German online grocery market described in Sect. 3, some particularly stand out for delivery with a fixed delivery window.

Firstly, the adherence to the previously agreed delivery windows, which is essential for the customers on the one hand, and extremely challenging for the last mile distribution of the companies on the other hand (Fikar, 2018; Seidel, 2021). Moreover, the smaller the delivery window, the less flexibility of routes is possible, and the more effective the delivery must be, which is consequently more expensive (Fikar et al., 2021; Seidel, 2021). One delayed delivery or high traffic volume can delay the entire tour and lead to annoyance of the customers. This challenge leads

Table 1 Information about standard grocery delivery companies

	Category					
Company	Launch year in Germany	Delivery areas	Revenue in 2021	Assortment (SKUs)	Delivery window	Costs
REWE	2011	75 cities	~ 700 million €	~ 15,000–20,000	2 or 4 h[a]	0–5.90 €[b]
Amazon Fresh	2017	Berlin, Potsdam, Hamburg, Munich	~ 120 million €	Several thousands	2 h	0–1.99 €[d]
Bringmeister	1997[d]	Berlin, Potsdam, Munich, Augsburg	~ 100 million €	~ 17,000	1, 2 or 4 h	0–6.99 €[e]
Knuspr	2021	Munich, Frankfurt, Mainz, Wiesbaden, Darmstadt, and smaller cities nearby	23 million €	~ 12,000	3 h	0–4.99 €[f]
Picnic	2018	25 small cities	78 million €[g]	Unknown	1 day[h]	0 €[i]

Sources: Amazon (2022b); Bringmeister (n.d.); Knuspr (2022a, 2022b); Kolf (2022); Krisch (2022); Picnic (n.d.); REWE Group (n.d.)
[a]Customer choice
[b]Depends on selected delivery window, order value and postal code
[c]0 € for orders >80 €
[d]Relevant operational start was in 2017 after acquisition from Edeka Group (Kapalschinski & Kolf, 2021b)
[e]Depends on selected delivery window
[f]0 € for orders >79 €
[g]In 2020
[h]On the morning of the selected delivery day, the delivery window is concretised
[i]Minimum order value is 35 €

directly to the second issue of whether companies prefer to rely on their own fleet for delivery or leave it in the hands of logistics companies (Leyerer et al., 2020). With their own delivery fleet, companies have more control over factors such as cooling chain, handling of the goods and delivery window (Leyerer et al., 2020). At the same time, it is capital and resource-intensive, especially if companies want to operate in various locations (Leyerer et al., 2020). However, the existing literature does not clarify how serious this problem for the companies is and what relevance this punctuality factor has for the customers.

Another problem is a well-known one from the supply chain sector: location planning (Silva et al., 2020). Suppliers must decide how many warehouses they want to implement and where to place them to deliver in the most efficient possible way (Silva et al., 2020). This decision is an even more significant challenge for omnichannel providers, as they must decide whether to combine the warehouses for brick-and-mortar retail and online delivery or to set up new ones for this purpose (Eriksson et al., 2022; Seidel, 2021). Seidel (2021) proposed so-called micro hubs in the cities between the warehouse and the customer to shorten the last mile and deliver more efficiently. In addition, she suggests thinking about a fixed route, where the customer does not choose the delivery window but is informed of one (Seidel, 2021). The extent to which this would meet customer acceptance remains to be seen. Leyerer et al. (2020) also proposed refrigerated lockers, which would then be delivered to. It should be noted, however, that these lockers would have to be complex with different temperature zones and would no longer be home delivery, as customers would then have to pick up their orders at the lockers (Leyerer et al., 2020).

Lastly, order picking is another resource-intensive process in the operations chain (Seidel, 2021). The share of automated warehouses has increased considerably in recent years due to various factors, and REWE just opened fully automatic warehouses in Cologne and Berlin (Seidel, 2021). However, this is not yet the standard, and consequently, orders are mainly picked manually by warehouse staff (McKinsey, 2021b; Seidel, 2021; Spryker & Appinio, 2022). Thereby, the larger the warehouses, the longer the distances and the longer the picking and packing process is (Eriksson et al., 2019; Seidel, 2021). In addition, the criterion of the best-before date should also be considered when selecting goods (Fikar, 2018). On the one hand, it is desirable to deliver goods with a short shelf life first, but on the other hand, customers show lower satisfaction when they receive goods with a short shelf life (Fikar, 2018).

In summary, Germany's traditional grocery delivery market with a fixed delivery window is on the move. Although REWE is the clear industry leader in terms of turnover, awareness, and spread in the country, it is followed by powerful companies, some of which have well-known and capital-rich investors behind them. The central challenges are the same for all competitors: Effective distribution to meet delivery windows, location planning of warehouses and logistics sites, efficient order picking and integration of increasing automation.

What remains open by the existing literature is, on the one hand, which currently the most urgent operational challenges for the companies are. On the other hand, there is also a lack of detailed insights into customers' preferences and decision criteria.

3.2 *Meal Kit Delivery*

Another option to order groceries online to the customer's home is meal kit delivery. The concept of meal kits differs from traditional grocery delivery in that all the ingredients are already pre-portioned for the chosen dishes (Heard et al., 2019). The ingredients for several dishes usually will be delivered to the customer in a box with cooling packs and the respective recipes. While ordering, the customer enters his postal code and depending on this and the provider, customers can add a specific day or even time window in the week for delivery (Dinnerly, n.d.; HelloFresh, n.d.; Marley Spoon, n.d.). The boxes can also be delivered in the absence of the customers and be parked in the stairwell if the customers permit.

Looking at the market for meal kit deliveries in Germany, the Berlin-based company HelloFresh is the clear leader (Dannenberg et al., 2020). Founded in 2011, the company is active in 17 countries, generated a turnover of 5.9 billion € in 2021 and employs almost 15,000 people worldwide (HelloFresh, 2022a). The revenue share of HelloFresh's German business is unfortunately not public. Nevertheless, the two main competitors in Germany, Marley Spoon and Dinnerly, cannot compete with the size

(HelloFresh, 2022a; Marley Spoon, 2022). Marley Spoon achieved a turnover of 322.4 million € in eight countries worldwide in 2021, of which 23 million € was generated in Germany (Marley Spoon, 2022). The low-cost variant Dinnerly, which belongs to Marley Spoon, has been active in Germany since 2020 but does not disclose any turnover data (Marley Spoon, 2022). However, with HelloFresh as the dominant player, Germany's market for cooking boxes can be seen as somewhat monopolistic (Beckmann, 2021). The Berliners promptly announced a turnover target of 10 billion € for the latest 2025 (HelloFresh, 2021). Of course, the figures should be taken with caution, as the share of the German business is unknown. However, of the almost 15,000 employees, 2973 were employed in Germany in 2021, which should reveal at least an approximate size of the German turnover (HelloFresh, 2022a).

Another development illustrates the volatility of the online grocery market again: the HelloFresh share price first skyrocketed with the onset of the COVID-19 pandemic from around 18 € per share in December 2019 to an interim 95 € per share in November 2021, registering an increase of over 500% (Yahoo Finance, n.d.). However, the virtual end of all COVID-19 restrictions, the associated return to restaurants, and rising inflation put HelloFresh heavily under pressure and have caused the share price to fall to 30 € at the beginning of July 2022 (Felsted & Kim, 2022; Yahoo Finance, n.d.). Besides the macroeconomic headwinds, HelloFresh and other market participants face operational challenges (Gee et al., 2019; Heard et al., 2019). Before analysing them, we will look at the advantages. In addition to streamlining the supply chain through fewer stations, the difference between a push and pull concept is crucial. HelloFresh has much higher planning reliability for the supply chain due to the orders, which are often placed weeks in advance compared to conventional supermarkets, where the customer decides in the shop which product to select (HelloFresh, 2022c). HelloFresh can then carry this advantage of early customer demand data through the supply chain and efficiently source its ingredients (HelloFresh, 2022c).

However, both Gee et al. (2019) and Heard et al. (2019) conclude that only in terms of transportation and the specific last mile distribution, meal kit boxes cause fewer emissions than physical shopping at the supermarket. The meal kit method is often harshly criticised from an environmental perspective due to the high packaging consumption (Gee et al., 2019; Heard et al., 2019; Lewis, 2021). While convenient for the customer, the pre-portioned ingredients for the exact dishes are individually packaged in small quantities, creating a lot of packaging waste (Gee et al., 2019; Heard et al., 2019). In this assessment, Gee et al. (2019) and Heard et al. (2019) agree that the conventional supply chain takes up less packaging than meal kit deliveries. However, pre-portioning provides an environmental advantage, resulting in less food loss, as the consumer typically uses everything delivered (HelloFresh, n.d.). Heard et al. (2019) concluded that the conventional supply chain produces overall 33% more emissions on average than the meal kit supply chain. On the contrary, Gee et al. (2019) came to the opposite conclusion and saw meal kit boxes as more environmentally harmful overall. This evaluation is mainly due to the high packaging consumption (Gee et al., 2019). The market leader HelloFresh is aware of this issue and states in its current sustainability report a reduction of the packaging weight per meal by 11% from 2020 to 2021 (HelloFresh, 2022b). Plastic and mixed packaging weight has even fallen by 21% in the same period (HelloFresh, 2022b). However, the company is reticent about concrete targets for the future, stating, for example, only 'our aim in Australia and New Zealand is to achieve 100% reusable, recyclable or compostable packaging by 2025' (HelloFresh, 2022b, p. 24).

Overall, the meal kit model has recently enjoyed high popularity in Germany and could attract more customers. The model is profitable, and the market leader HelloFresh is expanding rapidly (HelloFresh, 2021). With the currently still quite environmentally harmful and high packaging waste, the industry still has a big task ahead of it. The existing literature leaves a few gaps open: How vital sustainability or sustainable packaging is to customers when purchasing groceries and how companies respond to recurring issues like stockouts of products.

3.3 On-Demand Delivery

The last method, also the last to enter the delivery market, is on-demand or instant delivery of groceries (McKinsey, 2021b; Spryker & Appinio, 2022). The business model, which gained importance in Germany with the onset of the COVID-19 pandemic and the associated lockdowns, works as follows from the customer's point of view: The customer downloads the app of the respective provider onto his smartphone and enters the desired delivery address (Altay et al., 2022). If delivery is available for this address, the customer selects preferred items for his shopping basket from the various product categories (Altay et al., 2022). As soon as he has finished, he chooses one of the standard payment methods he would like to use and places the order (Altay et al., 2022). Depending on the provider and customer address, the delivery time is only a few minutes, in most cases by electric bike (Altay et al., 2022). The companies initially started with a delivery time promise of 10 min. Meanwhile, major suppliers in the market only promise delivery in 'a few minutes' (Flink, n.d.; Gorillas, n.d.) or delivery in 'about 10 min' (Getir, n.d.). However, the existing literature has not clarified where this time could settle in the medium term and what priority the shortest possible delivery time has for the companies.

The German market has three strong players in the on-demand grocery delivery sector: Gorillas, Flink and Getir (Klauth & Gassmann, 2021; Rest, 2022). Gorillas and Flink are both German companies, which were also both founded in 2020 (Flink, n.d.; Gorillas, n.d.). The Turkish provider Getir has been around since 2015 but has only been operating in Germany since 2021 (Getir, n.d.). The companies prefer not to disclose their exact turnover figures, orders and customer numbers. However, at least the numbers of downloaded apps are known for 2021, shown in Fig. 1, and should provide a rough ballpark for their respective market shares.

Moreover, it is known that the companies are focusing on rapid expansion and debt capital (Rest, 2022). All essential information about their operational areas and most important numbers are listed in Table 2.

The rate of expansion of the companies is impressive. Within the short time of 2 years, many cities in Germany were opened up and supplied. After selecting a suitable city, the companies open several small warehouses, so-called dark stores, in central locations and determine a delivery radius from there (Ladd, 2022). Besides meaningful marketing budgets, this strong presence seems to affect the Germans: While in a survey in 2021, less than 10% knew Gorillas and Flink, in 2022, it was around 40% (Spryker & Appinio, 2022). For Spryker and Appinio (2022), there is, therefore, no doubt that 'Gorillas, Flink and other on-demand providers are the talk of the town' (Spryker & Appinio, p.28). The assortments of around 2000 stock keeping units (SKUs) are typical for this business model but, of course, well below the approx. 15,000 SKUs of a regular supermarket (Bain & Company, 2022; REWE Group, n.d.).

With all the attention around on-demand suppliers, the main problem is that they are still far from being profitable (Bain & Company, 2022; Ladd, 2022; Luu et al., n.d.). There are several reasons for this: On the one hand, there is tough competition between the three companies, which is currently being fought out mainly through significant discounts and promotions (Altay et al., 2022; Klauth & Gassmann, 2021). The race for market share at any price seems to be the strategy of choice, also for investors (Klauth & Gassmann, 2021). On the other hand, the operational costs, such as order picking or delivery, are currently far too high (Bain & Company, 2022; McKinsey, 2021b). In addition, the average order value (AOV) is currently less than 20 €, which is too low to cover the costs (Bain & Company, 2022, Luu et al., n.d.). In a nutshell, suppliers are currently making a loss with every single order (Bain &

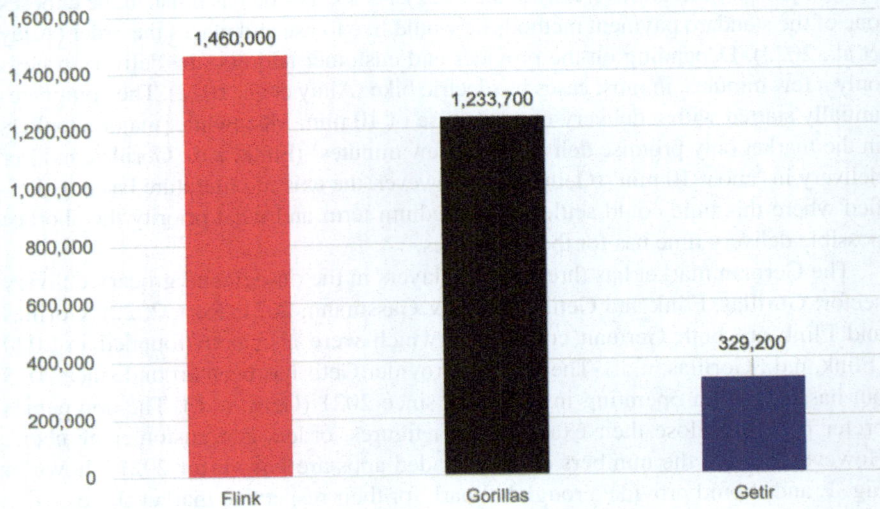

Fig. 1 Number of downloads of leading on-demand apps in Germany in 2021

Table 2 Key information about on-demand delivery companies

	Category					
Company	Founded	Last valuation	Active countries[a]	Active cities in Germany[f]	Assortment	Costs
Gorillas	2020	$2.1 billion[b]	7	25	>2000 SKUs	1.80 €
Flink	2020	$2.85 billion[c]	4	33	>2200 SKUs	1.99 €
Getir	2015[d]	$11.8 billion[e]	9	7	>1500 SKUs	1.80 €

Sources: Flink (n.d.); Getir (n.d.); Gorillas (n.d.)
[a]As of 4 July 2022
[b]Valuation October 2021
[c]Valuation December 2021
[d]Operating in Germany since 2021
[e]Valuation in March 2022

Company, 2022; Luu et al., n.d.). And not by a small margin: Luu et al. (n.d.) estimate that those companies make a loss of about 11–40 € per order in Germany, and Rest (2022) calculates that Gorillas, for example, currently burns 50 million € per month. As a result, half of the staff in Berlin was fired recently, and an intense search for new partners and investors is underway (Rest, 2022).

Consequently, parameters have to change to ensure that the instant delivery model is not over before it takes off. Firstly, the AOV must increase to at least 30 € (Bain & Company, 2022; Luu et al., n.d.). This increase could be achieved, for example, through a broader assortment, a minimum order value or a better understanding of customer needs (Luu et al., n.d.). Secondly, costs must be reduced (Bain & Company, 2022; Luu et al., n.d.). To cut costs, the picking process must be optimised further and preferably automated wherever possible (Bain & Company, 2022). Furthermore, delivery routes and rider utilisation must be improved or the promised time increased (Luu et al., n.d.). Lastly, partnerships should reduce purchasing prices (Bain & Company, 2022; Luu et al., n.d.). Flink has already started on this matter and has been cooperating with REWE since mid-2021 (REWE Group, 2021). In addition, companies should continue to use their agility and identify opportunities. Gorillas, for example, has been selling its private label of essential products since June 2022 to offer customers a cheaper product alternative (Gorillas., 2022).

4 Empirical Findings

To gain further insights into the comparatively new and dynamic market, first semi-structured interviews were conducted with industry experts. The three interviews were conducted in English via video calls and lasted on average 21 min and 34 s. The audio track was recorded and transcribed promptly afterwards for use (McGrath et al., 2019). The partners were informed about the recording of the interviews before the start of the interview. Moreover, all interview partners received all the required information on the research project and their data privacy and agreed to participate in writing. In addition, the researcher took care not to interview any vulnerable groups. When analysing the interviews, the interviewees are anonymised, and no conclusions can be drawn about which person they are or at which company they work.

Furthermore, a survey was conducted as a quantitative method to obtain current customer preferences and information on the market penetration of grocery delivery services. This survey results should also complement the existing literature with more explicit information on preferences, habits and patterns, as these are often superficial or generalised (Fikar et al., 2021).

The exploratory survey was created using *Qualtrics* survey software and published to respondents in July 2022. A pre-test ($n = 8$) was conducted before the final version to avoid typos, grammatical errors or ambiguities. The use of *Qualtrics* allowed high usability on smartphones, tablets or laptops, which may influence the quality of the answers (Malhotra, 2019). The survey was completely anonymous, and the results do not allow any conclusions to be drawn about individual persons. Respondents were informed about the research objective and the privacy policy before the survey started. In addition, the respondents could stop answering the questionnaire without giving reasons and were informed about this before the survey began.

In total, the survey contained 33–39 questions, depending on the answers and the associated display logic, and took about seven minutes to complete. Four to ten questions were asked about previous experience with online grocery delivery, 18 about participants' grocery shopping preferences and 11 questions related to respondents' characteristics. When formulating the questions, care was taken to ensure neutrality to avoid tendencies or bias (Malhotra, 2019). For the questions on participants' preferences, a 5-point Likert scale was primarily used. This is widely used in science and provides survey participants with an intuitive way to agree or disagree with the statements presented (Malhotra, 2019). Moreover, simple vocabulary was used, and no expertise was assumed so as not to exclude people from answering (Malhotra, 2019). The survey was shared through the researcher's *LinkedIn*, *Instagram*, *Facebook* and *WhatsApp* networks.

4.1 Interviews

Thematic analysis was chosen for the analysis of the qualitative data. This approach supports the search for patterns and is particularly suitable for the chosen inductive approach to analyse the grocery delivery market in Germany (Braun & Clarke, 2006). Moreover, the thematic analysis offers enough flexibility to identify and analyse thematic foci after the interviews have been conducted and transcribed (Braun & Clarke, 2006). In addition, this method better allows highlighting different or similar views of the interviewees on specific topics while making them understandable to all readers (Braun & Clarke, 2006).

The approach was to familiarise oneself with the three interview transcripts through repeated reading (Braun & Clarke, 2006). Then, potentially interesting and valuable passages of the transcripts were marked (Braun & Clarke, 2006). The gaps in the current literature identified in the literature review were particularly present and an important criterion for the selection. Subsequently, the relevant statements were compiled and sorted according to superordinate themes (Braun & Clarke, 2006; Tracey et al., 2011). After all statements were assigned to the broad themes, the themes were further subdivided, and the statements were classified accordingly (Braun & Clarke, 2006). Finally, the themes were named as briefly and concisely as possible (Braun & Clarke, 2006). For clarity and comprehensibility, a tabular form of presentation was chosen, based on Tracey et al. (2011), and further developed. The results in a table can be found in Table 3. Person A works in the on-demand delivery sector for company AA, Person B in company BB from the meal kit industry and Person C in company CC, which belongs to the standard delivery industry.

Looking at the results of the interviews, it is striking that there are common themes and assessments across all three models and different emphases.

For company AA and BB, the balance between supply and demand as and the handling of peak demand are current bottlenecks. For company CC, which has a large stationary supermarket chain as a partner, it is less the products but more the onboarding of new staff that limits growth.

When asked about the current challenges in operations, Person A and Person B mentioned the stockout of popular products, which is always a challenge. Person C denied having these challenges to any significant extent and referred to its reliable partner, who reliably supplies it with products. Questioned about the biggest challenge in operations, Company CC referred to scaling the business without losing quality in operations. This also represents a central building block for the company's success and is therefore classified accordingly. For company AA, the specific rider utilisation, and for company BB, sickness and corresponding quarantines in the labour-intensive warehouse were added as challenges.

All three companies estimate the delivery window differently. It is important for company AA to keep the delivery window as small as possible and stick to it. In case of doubt, they would also prefer to reduce the delivery radius rather than increase the promised time. Company BB only points out that having their own delivery fleet is resource-intensive and that they, therefore, have to rely on third-party providers to

Table 3 Interview results

Superordinate theme	Subordinate topic	Respondent	Quote
Current bottlenecks in company development	Reaching a broader market	Person A	– "(…) we obviously have a bit more struggles in terms of reaching the rest of the market (…)."
		Person B	– "(…) you still have the traditional supermarkets, where you have more room to market and to communicate some promotions (…)."
	Matching supply and demand	Person A	– "(…) this constant matching of supply and demand is going to be super-difficult for us, as we obviously need to plan really accurately." – "Exactly, the demand planning is, I think, probably [challenge] number one."
		Person B	– "And we had to modify the ingredients in order to be able to cater to the big demands, (…) and the lower supplies that we had."
	Onboarding	Person C	– "(…) onboard new pickers very, very fast. (…). And that was, again, before COVID, within COVID, and let's say we are now after COVID, maybe the biggest problem (…)."
Operational challenges	Rider utilisation	Person A	– "And then from the operations side, we have on the rider side, the utilisation per rider, which we call UPR or OPH, orders per hour." – "And we keep the top performers and cut out the negative performers or the bad performers to drive this UPR. (…) on a monthly basis (…) have to cut the bottom 20%"
	Out-of-stock-rate	Person A	– "(…) it's obviously super-important for us to keep a low out-of-stock rate, which is a bit difficult for us. Because we have the super-small MFCs, like micro fulfilment centres, where we just cannot act like super-high safety stocks."
		Person B	– "(…) we try to communicate as much as possible that the reason why you don't have this ingredient in your bag is because we are a farm-to-warehouse-to-door service, and if we can't provide you with fresh ingredients from the farm, then we would rather provide you with a different fresh ingredient from the farm (…)."
		Person C	– "Stockout of certain products are not a big problem." – "First sector's everything we get from wholesalers. This is more or less secured."
	Sickness	Person B	– "I would say the biggest challenge that we would face right now (…) is people getting sick at the warehouse. Because if that's the case, (…) most of the warehouse has to quarantine."

Table 3 (continued)

Superordinate theme	Subordinate topic	Respondent	Quote
Delivery	Delivery window	Person A	– "But overall, say we are aiming to achieve 15 minutes on average, and would also rather (...) go down to the 10 minutes again than to say, okay, we want to increase our radius to now, let's say 4km, to reach more people, and take into account that we deliver in 20 minutes." – "So keeping it below 20 minutes is super-important, and that's also what we aim for, to have basically 90% of the orders below 20 minutes."
		Person B	– "Now, obviously, it's very difficult for us to have our own delivery fleet all over the markets where we operate in, just because it's not exactly very profitable in the long run."
		Person C	– "We have three options. A one-hour, two-hour, and four-hour delivery window. And so I don't think that we want to change that kind of stuff." – "Like delivery windows are, for us, products as well."
	Delivery condition	Person B	– "(...) when it comes to third-party suppliers, we try to make sure to just have as much quality control as possible. Yet, of course, as we know, and in all cases, there might be some damages at some points."
Product assortment	Product range	Person A	– "At the moment, we are fully fine with the 2,000 and do not want to extend it, at least not super-much." – "We actually recently also launched our own private label, so we're a strong believer that this will in the future also be a strong margin driver for us."
		Person B	– "Though, also, when we are expanding into ready-to-heat, that's when we're also tapping into not only house routines, but also work routines."
		Person C	– "Our assortment is about 15,000 SKUs (...)." – "I would not go for an assortment lower than 10,000. Because then I don't get that real value of that online stuff." – "I would say something between the that 15,000 and maybe 20,000 SKUs."

(continued)

Table 3 (continued)

Superordinate theme	Subordinate topic	Respondent	Quote
Competitors	Biggest competitors	Person A	– "Personally, I think it will be the other q-commerce players, because I just think that we are working in a different field than the classic retailer or HelloFresh or Picnic."
		Person B	– "I would say currently it's definitely in the meal kit industry, because we do have a lot of (…) local competitors, rather than us being a global brand."
		Person C	– "I would say, let's say, the biggest competitors are the, let's say, traditional online delivery window players." – "And when it comes to quick-commerce, I don't think they are our competitors. Because they're just serving a different customer group."
Company success	Focus on core customers	Person A	– "So to really focus on our core customers is, I think, the one thing. (…). So they will even be prioritised on the delivery, to have a better experience (…)."
		Person C	– "(…) the most important thing about that is to keep the customers active."
	Increase AOV	Person A	– "And then the other huge thing is to drive our AOV, because this obviously has a huge, huge impact."
	Efficiency	Person A	– "(…) and then it's obviously the efficiency, and then it's mainly the rider." – "(…) so the rider cost is basically our biggest chunk of the order that goes away."
		Person C	– "I think making next steps in terms of automation in warehouses is always an important topic, (…) to increase capacity from existing warehouses."
	Expanding business	Person B	– "But when we're expanding towards ready-to-heat products, for example, we're tapping into people at work, we're tapping into people who need to eat on the go."
		Person C	– "I would say scaling a business with high efficiency, and pretty much no mistakes in the picking operations."
	Funding	Person C	– "(…) without having funding, it will be pretty hard to survive against these other big competitors over a longer time."

Table 3 (continued)

Superordinate theme	Subordinate topic	Respondent	Quote
Outlook	Market assessment	Person A	– "(...) I think that brick-and-mortar will still be dominant, but in the city centres and high-density areas, you will definitely see a decrease (...) in their presence (...)."
		Person B	– "I think definitely the world is drifting more towards online delivery. And I think that growth is going to probably take over, but it's going to take a very long time."
		Person C	– "(...) I think at least for the next, well nearly all the time, they [stationary retail] will have the majority of the market." – "(...) I can imagine that online gets a, let's say, total share of, on long-term, something between 10% or maybe even 20% or 25% of the game."

stick to the delivery window and the condition of the goods. Company CC sees the delivery window as a kind of additional product and lets the customer choose freely between three options and pay a surcharge accordingly.

There are also different views on the future of the product range. While company AA sees itself well positioned and does not plan to increase the product range significantly, companies BB and CC see potential to distinguish in a gradual expansion of the product range.

However, there is again agreement regarding the assessment of the largest competitors. All three companies see the greatest threat from their industry and not from companies that operate one of the other business models. Person A and C explicitly pointed out that they address different customer groups and can co-exist with the other grocery delivery models.

Concerning the factors that determine future success or failure, the companies named both common and different factors. For company AA, these are primarily the increase of AOV, the increase in efficiency, which refers above all to the better utilisation of the riders, and the focus on the core customer. These could also be given preferential treatment, e.g. through prioritised delivery. Person C agrees with the focus on active customers and sees this as one of its main tasks. In addition, it is important for company CC to gain access to further funding to, first of all, survive in the capital-intensive market and, secondly, be able to pursue the vital goal of further expansion. Efficiency is also a focus for this company, and Person C mentioned the automation of the warehouses in particular. Company BB is convinced of its model and sees the key to further success in expansion, which is also to be achieved through new product groups that attract a different target group.

There is also fundamental consensus regarding the outlook for the online grocery delivery business in Germany. All interview partners see the online business on a strong upward trend but, at the same time, see the stationary trade as dominant for the foreseeable future due to its historical predominance.

4.2 *Survey*

This section will provide detailed data analysis, mainly including descriptive analysis, which analyses the traits and patterns of the samples and fits with the exploratory approach. Moreover, some inferential tests about correlation and difference tests were carried out. All analyses were conducted with the support of *SPSS (Statistical Product and Service Solutions), Version 28* and *Microsoft Excel, Version 16.63.1*.

4.2.1 Participants' Demo.graphics

Of the 164 participants who opened the survey, 49 (29.9%) data sets were removed because they did not fill out the survey sufficiently and failed to complete it. Out of the remaining 115 participants, 75 (65.2%) were male, and 40 (34.8%) were female. A detailed overview of the participant's characterisation can be found in Table 4.

The characteristic of age is worth looking at even more closely with the help of the central statistics.

As can be seen in the table, the mean age of the sample is just over 30 years, with a minimum expression of 18 years and a maximum expression of 63 years. However, the centre of the distribution is clearly in the mid-20s, as the calculation of the median, the 16th and 84th percentiles, and a look at Table 5 make clear. Some outliers in the older age range thus clearly lift the average, making the median more sensible to use as an average measure since this is more robust against outliers.

The key characteristics of the monthly disposable income and the weekly expenditure on groceries were examined next. The monthly income distribution across the different levels is almost equally distributed within the sample. Also, the weekly expenditure on groceries looks equally distributed, with a tendency towards the middle group (71–100 €). The distribution of both characteristics is slightly skewed to the right and thus towards a higher disposable income and higher weekly expenditure on groceries. Detailed results can be found in Table 6.

Another characteristic that was investigated is the distance from the place of residence to the nearest supermarket. For this purpose, the required walking minutes between the residence and the nearest supermarket were asked. The result can be seen in the following histogram with normal distribution in Fig. 2.

It can be seen that the majority of the data is in the range of less than or equal to 10 min, and a higher proportion of people living further than average from the nearest supermarket gives the frequency distribution a rightward skew. It is also striking that many participants live within five minutes of the nearest supermarket.

4.2.2 Descriptive Statistics

Most, 93 (80.9%), of the participants have already used online grocery delivery services in Germany, while 22 (19.1%) have not used it so far. Of the 93 participants who have already ordered groceries online for delivery, 89 stated which model they had used predominantly.

Table 4 Participants' characteristics

Characteristic	Description	*n*	%
Gender	Male	75	65.2
	Female	40	34.8
	Prefer not to say	0	0.0
Age	18–22 years	14	12.2
	23–30 years	60	52.2
	31–40 years	22	19.1
	40–63 years	15	13.0
	Prefer not to say	4	3.5
Current status	Employed	57	49.6
	Student	40	34.8
	Self-employed	13	11.3
	Unemployed	4	3.5
	Apprentice	1	0.9
Have you ever used online grocery delivery services in Germany?	Yes	93	80.9
	No	22	19.1
Do you have car available?	Yes	79	68.7
	No	36	31.3
Do you have a lift in your house to get to your floor?	Yes	24	20.9
	No	91	79.1

Table 5 Analysis of the age variable

	n	Mean	SD	Min.	16th PCTL	Median	84th PCTL	Max.
Age (years)	111	30.34	10.50	18.00	23.00	26.00	35.08	63.00

Table 6 Participants income and grocery expenditure

Characteristics	Description	*n*	%
Disposable income per month	Below 500 €	14	12.2
	500–1000 €	17	14.8
	1001–1500 €	12	10.4
	1501–2500 €	18	15.7
	2501–3500 €	18	15.7
	3501–4500 €	14	12.2
	Over 4500 €	20	17.4
Groceries spending per week (household)	Below 30 €	3	2.6
	30–70 €	26	22.8
	71–100 €	44	38.6
	101–150 €	26	22.8
	Over 150 €	15	13.2

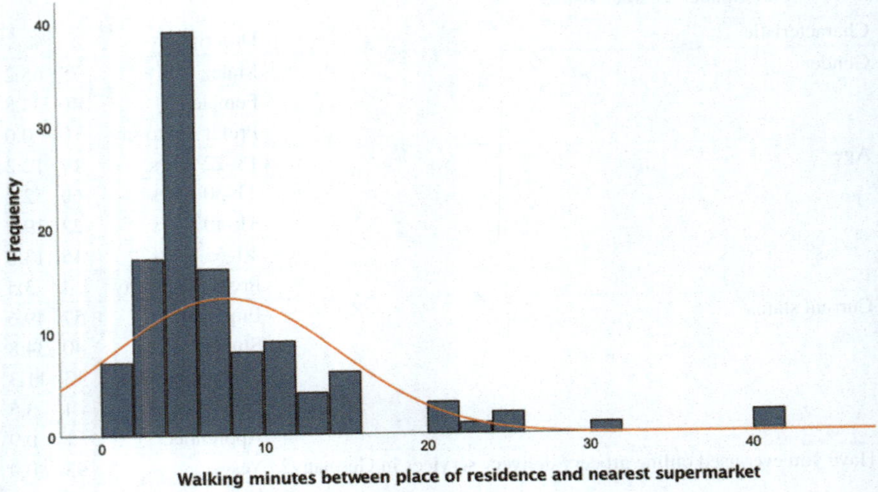

Fig. 2 Histogram of walking minutes to next supermarket

It is striking that the on-demand delivery method was tried out and predominantly used by most participants. Out of the group, 81 participants have already used on-demand delivery at all, and 68 (76.4%) have mainly used this method. This is followed by the standard delivery method, which has been used at least once by 41 participants and is primarily used by 15 (16.9%). In last place is the meal kit delivery which has been used by 24 participants and is preferred by 6 (6.7%). It should be noted that multiple selections were possible for the question of which method the participants have used at all, and therefore the values cannot be added up to 100%.

When asked about the reasons for ordering groceries online, the 93 participants overwhelmingly stated 'comfort' (n = 75) and 'time saving' (n = 74). This reason was followed by 'impulse buying' (n = 23), 'dislike of physical shopping' (n = 11), 'personal safety' (n = 8) and 'other reason' (n = 7). Here, too, multiple selections were possible.

It is prominent how satisfied most users were with their experience: Cumulatively, 80 respondents (86%) of previous users were happy or very happy with the experience. Only seven users (7.5%) were unhappy or very unhappy with the experience they had, and six users (6.5%) were neither happy nor unhappy with it. Nevertheless, 22 participants somewhat agree (n = 19) or strongly agree (n = 3) that they have been upset at least once in the past after placing an order. Reasons for that could be the following: 75 persons had at least once one of the following issues when they placed an order: 'delayed delivery' (n = 45), 'missing items' (n = 38), 'poor condition of the groceries' (n = 17), 'entire order cancelled' (n = 4), 'other' (n = 7).

On the other hand, for the 22 respondents who have not yet ordered groceries online, 'no need for it' (n = 18) was the main reason that prevented them from ordering. Less critical factors were 'too expensive' (n = 6) and 'too much waste' (n = 6).

Almost no or no obstacles were 'other reasons' ($n = 2$), 'not reliable enough' ($n = 1$), as well as 'risk of online payment' and 'problems with the order process' (both $n = 0$).

It was also essential to learn about the sample's grocery shopping preferences. For this purpose, the participants could indicate their agreement or disagreement with certain statements with the help of a Likert scale. The percentage distribution in Fig. 3 shows how strongly each statement was agreed with.

Suppose the two agreeing categories of the Likert scale are taken together, a wide product selection (84.8%), the freshness of the products (86%) as well as a previously determined (82.6%) and adhered to the delivery window (88.7%) seem to be particularly important for consumers. On the other hand, the lowest price of the groceries (73.1%) and the possibility of live tracking (45.3%) of the order do not seem to be quite as important. Moreover, the agreement to pay a premium is significantly higher if this is linked to higher product quality (88.7% vs. 50.5%). Accordingly, asked about what premium they would pay for a delivery worth 30 €, only four respondents stated that they would pay no premium. The total sample had a mean of 2.52 € and a median of 2 € as a premium of a delivery worth 30 €.

A total of 93 (80.9%) participants would like a delivery window limited to less than one hour. This is divided into 40 participants (34.8%) who see a delivery window of up to 30 minutes as appropriate and 53 participants (46.1%) who can arrange for 60 min. The remaining participants see a delivery window of up to 90 min (9.6%), 120 min (5.2%) or over 120 min (4.3%) as suitable.

In addition to the stated preferences, the participants could sort eleven different product groups from important (1) to unimportant (11) by drag & drop. For the calculation, the rankings (1–11) were multiplied by the respective number of participants and added up for each product group. The lower the total for a product group, the higher and thus more popular the ranking of this group was. For the category 'fruit & vegetables', for example, the distribution was as follows (Table 7):

These complete selections resulted in the following ranking as a weighted frequency table (Table 8):

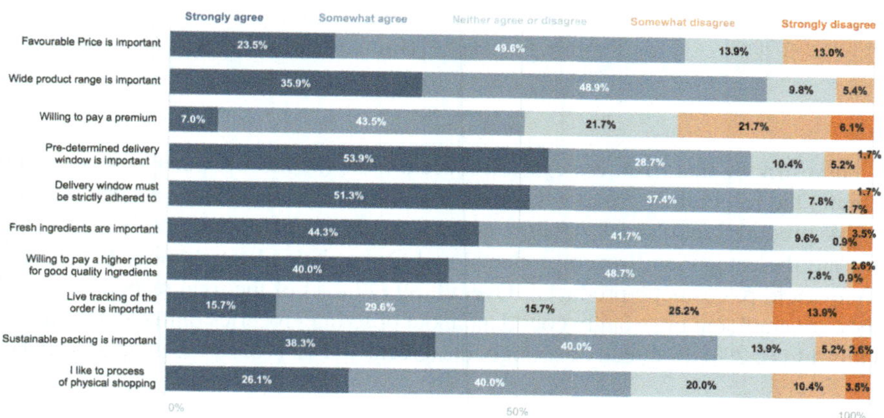

Fig. 3 Key preferences of participants

Table 7 Example calculation for fruit & vegetable category

Rank	Participants (*n*)	Product (*Rank × n*)
1	35	35
2	21	42
3	10	30
4	13	52
5	8	40
6	6	36
7	3	21
8	11	88
9	4	36
10	1	10
11	3	33
Sum	*115*	*423*

Table 8 Weighted product group ranking

Rank	Product group	Product sum
1	Fruit & vegetables	423
2	Shelf-stable products (pasta, rice, sauces etc.)	555
3	Snacks (sweets, crisps, nuts etc.)	571
4	Alcoholic drinks	627
=	Cheese & cold cuts	627
6	Non-alcoholic drinks	679
7	Bakery products	724
8	Ready-made dishes (salads, bowls, sushi etc.)	805
9	Frozen products	816
10	Fresh meat & fish	859
11	Household & cosmetic products	904

It is striking that 'fruit & vegetables' seem to be the most popular product group among the respondent group when ordering groceries online. The categories 'shelf-stable products' and 'snacks' follow with a considerable gap. At the lower end of the list are the categories 'frozen products' and further behind 'fresh meat & fish' and 'household & cosmetic products'. Overall, 89 (77.4%) of the total respondents said they are confident or strongly confident about ordering groceries online in the future. Only 14 (12.2%) disagreed or strongly disagreed, and 12 (10.4%) seemed undecided.

5 Discussion of Findings

The first thing is that the online grocery market in Germany is growing strongly in some areas but is still lacking penetrating power, also in European comparison. This assessment was confirmed by the interviewees when the on-demand company talked about having 'a bit more struggles in terms of reaching the rest of the market', and the meal kit company as well sees the need to reach more people and expand the target group with the new ready-to-heat product group.

However, it should give the suppliers confidence when over 80% of the survey respondents have already ordered groceries online, many of them tried different models, and almost 80% are convinced that they will order groceries online in the future. These stats also have the potential to significantly increase the 33% of consumers who order at least some of their groceries online, which was found by Spryker and Appinio (2022). Furthermore, this increase recognised in the survey confirms how dynamic the development of this business field in Germany continues to be and is on the rise.

In addition to this indication of further dynamic growth in the industry, another finding from the survey can deliver further ambitions for the existing companies. Bain and Company (2022) and Luu et al. (n.d.) highlighted the importance of a higher AOV and calculated that, especially for on-demand companies, it must increase to around 30 € to become profitable. This importance was confirmed by interviewee A, who described that the AOV 'has a huge, huge impact'. Moreover, the findings from the survey suggest that the potential is not yet reached: 72.8% of the participants spend over 70 € a week on groceries. So, with a target AOV of 30 €, the potential of at least two weekly orders per household is given (Bain & Company, 2022). Customers will not do all their grocery shopping online, but the general willingness to pay is there, with over 35% of the sample spending even over 100 € a week. However, the figures must be put into perspective, considering the income level of the sample. Overall, 45.3% of the participants have a disposable income of over 2500 € per month, which is higher than the average German net wage in 2021 of 2170 € per month. Due to this slight overrepresentation of high earners, the results cannot be applied one-to-one to the whole population. Moreover, no statistically significant correlation between a higher disposable income and a higher conviction to order groceries online in the future was found.

However, more steps are needed to achieve further penetration of the market and to realise the potential. For this, it is essential that companies understand their customers' motives and preferences and derive the correct conclusions and actions from this.

The motives of the interviewed participants essentially coincide with those that emerge from the existing literature. Spryker and Appinio (2022) identified time saving, crowd avoidance and convenience as the main motives for consumers to order groceries online. In the survey, the most frequently mentioned motives were comfort, time saving and impulse buying. Only crowd avoidance has almost disappeared as a motive, as only eight participants mentioned 'personal safety' as a motive, probably due to the waning of the COVID-19 pandemic. Companies should therefore continue to emphasise the motives of time saving and comfort and communicate them to customers.

Customers' preferences and critical decision criteria have only been treated superficially in the existing literature and have received little attention (Fikar et al., 2021). With the help of the survey, this gap could be at least partially closed.

It looks vital to the customers that the pre-determined delivery window is adhered to. Over 88% agreed with this criterion to some extent or very much, and late delivery was also the most frequently cited reason for participant complaints. Of 93 participants who have already ordered groceries online, almost half ($n = 45$) have already had the issue of late delivery. Moreover, it could be shown that late delivery negatively impacts the overall experience of ordering groceries online and the likelihood of ordering groceries online in the future.

The companies, however, are only partly aware of this fact. Person A discusses to 'keep 90% of the orders below 20 min'. In case of doubt, however, he claimed it is better to reduce the delivery radius than to increase the delivery time promise. This could be the wrong approach looking at the survey results. Only just over a third of the customers surveyed see a delivery window of less than 30 min as necessary, and a large proportion (46.1%) can accept terms with a delivery window of up to one hour or even more (19.1%). Therefore, the delivery window's length does not seem to be the decisive criterion, but adherence to this window is even more.

Company BB also sees the decisive point with adherence to the promised delivery window but cannot imagine nationwide delivery with its own fleet for profitability reasons. However, the execution and the customer experience are one of the few ways to (positively) differentiate from competitors in the online grocery business (Lim et al., 2017).

The approach of Company CC, which introduced its delivery windows of different lengths as a kind of additional product and takes a premium from the customer, who is willing to pay extra for a shorter window, is interesting. This idea could also be worth looking at for the other models, especially as Company AA is also considering focusing on core customers. Shorter premium delivery windows could be an option to provide them preferential treatment and thus try to increase the order frequency.

Surprising and contradictory to the literature, which has classified German customers as particular price-sensitive, the lowest price is not one of the essential criteria in the survey. While currently, delivery fees of on-demand companies are just under 2 €, the average willingness to pay delivery costs for a delivery worth 30 € was 2.52 €. That suggests there is still room for additional premium options for the customers. However, it should be noted that AOV is not yet at 30 € and that the delivery fee for standard delivery companies varies greatly depending on the delivery location and size of the shopping basket.

More important criteria for customers are product variety and assortment. For almost 85% of the participants, a wide range of products is an important criterion when buying groceries. More concrete, the three product categories 'fruit & vegetables', 'shelf-stable products' and 'snacks' are on top of the wish list. In this case, the standard delivery companies have an advantage over the on-demand companies with a significantly wider product range. They want, like company CC, to expand this further and not reduce their range. On-demand companies, on the other hand, naturally have the disadvantage of smaller warehouses, but at the same time do not see the need to expand them, if person A says, 'we are fully fine with the 2,000 and do not want to extend it, at least not super-much'. Meal kit companies are naturally somewhat limited in product expansion due to their business model or can only indirectly increase their product variety by expanding the recipe portfolio. Nevertheless, CC wants to address a new target group with the ready-to-heat dishes and thus increase its sales.

For the other two models, it is also decisive which products they offer and what effort they involve. For example, the three categories 'ready-made dishes', 'fresh meat & fish' and 'frozen products' tend to rank at the bottom of the survey, the question arises whether the offer of these refrigeration- and cost-intensive categories should be discontinued or limited. However, one argument against this is that cooling chains are also required for more popular categories such as 'cheese & cold cuts' or 'fruit & vegetables', albeit probably to a lesser extent. Moreover, for the companies surveyed, partly also in response to explicit requests, maintaining the cooling chain was not a significant and cost-intensive challenge. This finding is somewhat contrary to Lagorio and Pinto (2021) or Lodni et al. (2021).

Another challenge that emerged from the literature and was again at least largely confirmed is stockouts. In particular, Jing and Lewis (2011) have drawn attention to this problem. Companies AA and BB experience this problem in practice and are working on an improvement. While company AA again has the disadvantage of small warehouses and would like to improve primarily through learning effects, company BB would like to communicate as much as possible and transparently with the customer. For person C, 'stockouts of certain products are not a big problem', probably due to their reliable partner. For customers, however, missing products are the second most mentioned problem after late delivery ($n = 38$). Of course, this can also be caused by faulty order picking in the warehouse. Furthermore, no statistically significant correlation between a missing product and a worse overall experience could be proven.

These stockouts are also due, among other things, to the volatile, dynamic and thus difficult-to-predict demand of the online grocery business. This market assessment was already the result of Yang et al. (2021) and could also be confirmed in the interviews of person A and B. Person A even says that 'the demand planning is, I think, probably [challenge] number one'. Additionally, person B says that his company repeatedly has problems 'to be able to cater to the big demands, (...) and the lower supplies that we had'. This volatility and unpredictability go hand in hand with the survey results and statistical calculations in that hardly any trends, patterns, correlations or causalities in consumers' decision-making are apparent. This unpredictability can have several causes, but it makes forecasting and planning capacities and resources incredibly challenging for companies.

The survey and interviews could not support two other challenges from the literature. Firstly, restrained market penetration in Germany was also partly argued with the aversion to online payments and the cultural adherence of Germans to cash transactions. This reason was not given by any of the 22 participants in the survey who had never ordered groceries online. Besides a general increasing openness towards online payment, the low average age (median = 26 years, mean = 30.34 years) could also explain this, as young people are more familiar with the technology. Even the 84th percentile of the sample was just above 35 years, which means that 84% of the sample were 35 years or younger. In contrast, the average age in Germany in 2020 was 44.6 years.

Secondly, the main criticism from the literature of the meal kit model of too much packaging waste could only be confirmed to a limited extent. Just 6 of the 22 non-online customers gave 'too much waste' as a reason for not ordering groceries online. These six people are still a good 27%, but significantly less than the 18 participants who gave 'no need for it' as reason. Additionally, in the preference part of the survey, many participants (78.3%) fully or partially agreed with the statement that sustainable packaging is essential. At the same time, however, there were also various statements for which the agreement was even more remarkable. Person B from the meal kit industry was aware of the problem but only said that the team was working hard to reduce packaging weight and waste.

Put it all together, the qualitative and quantitative results provided interesting insights, some of which are surprising considering the existing literature and some of which go hand in hand with it. Furthermore, it is striking that hardly any statistically significant patterns were discernible in the sample, which comprised 115 valid data sets. This finding indicates that the topic of grocery delivery in Germany is not yet fully developed and that providers and customers can still learn from each other.

The results have to be limited in two respects in particular: Firstly, only one company from each of the three different business models was interviewed for the qualitative analysis. This structure has certainly already clarified commonalities and differences between the three approaches, but the focus of companies can still vary even within the three models. In the early stages, in which many companies are still operating, requirements, expectations, and strategies are still changing, sometimes in leaps and bounds. Using several companies could result in a more comprehensive picture but would have gone beyond the scope of this chapter.

Secondly, the results of the quantitative analysis cannot be directly generalised. This is mainly because high earners and younger people, for example, were overrepresented in the sample and cannot be easily related to the entire German population. On the other hand, a sample of $n = 115$ is not bad for a first impression but not necessarily sufficient for more in-depth statements and correlations. For future analyses, an attempt should be made to obtain a larger sample representing a cross-section of the population and more concretely questions individual preferences and habits regarding grocery purchases.

References

Alftan, A., Kaipia, R., Loikkanen, L., & Spens, K. (2015). Centralised grocery supply chain planning: improved exception management. *International Journal of Physical Distribution & Logistics Management, 45*(3), 237–259.

Ali, I., Nagalingam, S., & Gurd, B. (2018). A resilience model for cold chain logistics of perishable products. *The International Journal of Logistics Management, 29*(3), 922–941.

Altay, B. C., Okumuş, A., & Mercangöz, B. A. (2022). An intelligent approach for analyzing the impacts of the COVID-19 pandemic on marketing mix elements (7Ps) of the on-demand grocery delivery service. *Complex & Intelligent Systems, 8*, 129–140.

Amazon. (2022a). *Annual report 2021*. Retrieved June 27, 2022, from https://s2.q4cdn.com/299287126/files/doc_financials/2022/ar/Amazon-2021-Annual-Report.pdf.

Amazon. (2022b). *Amazon Fresh feiert Geburtstag*. Retrieved June 28, 2022, from https://amazon-presse.de/Amazon-Prime/Presseinformationen/Newsdetail/amazon/de/Prime/220504_Amazon-Fresh_Anniversary/.

Amazon. (n.d.). *Amazon Fresh*. Retrieved June 27, 2022, from https://www.amazon.de/alm/storefront?almBrandId=QW1hem9uIEZyZXNo.

Bain & Company. (2022). *Online grocery strategy: A reality check for disruptors and incumbents*. Retrieved June 24, 2022, from https://www.bain.com/insights/online-grocery-strategy/.

Beckmann, A. (2021). Scenario analysis of online food supply chains. In *31st Proceedings of the Hamburg international conference of logistics (HICL)* (pp. 585–609).

Braun, V., & Clarke, V. (2006). Using thematic analysis in psychology. *Qualitative Research in Psychology, 3*(2), 77–101.

Bringmeister. (n.d.). *Homepage*. Retrieved June 28, 2022, from https://www.bringmeister.de.

Bundesverband E-Commerce und Versandhandel Deutschland e.V. (BEVH). (2021). *Revenue from the sale of groceries in online retail in Germany from 2014 to 2021*. Retrieved July 26, 2022, from https://www-statista-com.ezphost.dur.ac.uk/statistics/989659/revenue-from-groceries-bought-online-germany/.

Bundesverband E-Commerce und Versandhandel Deutschland e.V. (BEVH). (2022). *E-commerce revenue from goods in Germany from 2000 to 2021*. Retrieved July 19, 2022, from https://www-statista-com.ezphost.dur.ac.uk/statistics/434303/consumer-goods-e-commerce-revenue-germany/.

Capgemini. (2019). *The last-mile delivery challenge: Giving retail and consumer product customers a superior delivery experience without impacting profitability*. Retrieved July 12, 2022, from https://www.capgemini.com/wp-content/uploads/2019/01/Report-Digital-—-Last-Mile-Delivery-Challenge1.pdf.

Centobelli, P., Cerchione, R., & Ertz, M. (2020). Food cold chain management: what we know and what we deserve. *Supply Chain Management: An International Journal, 26*(1), 102–135.

Chowdhury, P., Paul, S. K., Kaisar, S., & Moktadir, M. A. (2021). COVID-19 pandemic related supply chain studies: A systematic review. *Transportation Research Part E: Logistics and Transportation Review, 148*, 1–26.

Dannenberg, P., Fuchs, M., Riedler, T., & Wiedemann, C. (2020). Digital transition by COVID-19 pandemic? The German food online retail. *Tijdschrift voor economische en sociale geografie, 111*(3), 543–560.

Deutschland.de. (n.d.). *Latest coronavirus updates*. Retrieved July 6, 2022, from https://www.deutschland.de/en/news/coronavirus-in-germany-information.

Dinnerly. (n.d.). *Frequently asked questions*. Retrieved July 1, 2022, from https://support.dinnerly.com/hc/de/articles/360001355396-Wann-und-wo-liefert-Dinnerly-.

East, R. (2022). Online grocery sales after the pandemic. *International Journal of Market Research, 64*(1), 13–18.

Ecommerce News. (2019, June 27). Edeka increases stake in picnic. Retrieved June 29, 2022, from https://ecommercenews.eu/edeka-increases-stake-in-picnic/.

Ehrler, V. C., Schöder, D., & Seidel, S. (2021). Challenges and perspectives for the use of electric vehicles for last mile logistics of grocery e-commerce—Findings from case studies in Germany. *Research in Transportation Economics, 87*, 1–9.

Eriksson, E., Norrman, A., & Kembro, J. (2019). Contextual adaptation of omni-channel grocery retailers' online fulfilment centres. *International Journal of Retail & Distribution Management, 47*(12), 1232–1250.

Eriksson, E., Norrman, A., & Kembro, J. (2022). Understanding the transformation toward omnichannel logistics in grocery retail: A dynamic capabilities perspective. *International Journal of Retail & Distribution Management* [Peer-reviewed accepted version]. Retrieved June 29, 2022, from https://www.emerald.com/insight/content/doi/10.1108/IJRDM-10-2021-0508/full/pdf?title=understanding-the-transformation-toward-omnichannel-logistics-in-grocery-retail-a-dynamic-capabilities-perspective.

European Commission. (2022). *Digital Economy and Society Index (DESI) 2021*. Retrieved July 7, 2022, from https://ec.europa.eu/newsroom/dae/redirection/document/80481.

European Supermarket Magazine. (2019, May 29). Picnic expands its delivery service in Germany. Retrieved July 13, 2022, from https://www.esmmagazine.com/technology/picnic-expands-delivery-service-germany-75550.

Expansion. (n.d.). *Germans are the most complicated customers in the world*. Retrieved June 23, 2022, from https://expansion.eco/germans-are-the-most-complicated-customers/.

Felsted, A., & Kim, T. (2022, March 23). Food-delivery services will struggle to outrun inflation. *Washington Post*. Retrieved July 1, 2022, from https://www.washingtonpost.com/business/energy/food-delivery-services-will-struggle-to-outrun-inflation/2022/03/23/681dff08-aa9d-11ec-8a8e-9c6e9fc7a0de_story.html.

Fikar, C. (2018). A decision support system to investigate food losses in e-grocery deliveries. *Computers & Industrial Engineering, 117*, 282–290.

Fikar, C., Mild, A., & Waitz, A. (2021). Facilitating consumer preferences and product shelf life data in the design of e-grocery deliveries. *European Journal of Operational Research, 294*, 976–986.

Flink. (n.d.). *Frequently asked questions*. Retrieved July 4, 2022, from https://www.goflink.com/de-DE/faq/.

Frank, D.-A., & Peschel, A. O. (2020). Sweetening the deal: The ingredients that drive consumer adoption of online grocery shopping. *Journal of Food Products Marketing, 26*(8), 535–544.

Gee, I. M., Davidson, F. T., Speetles, B. L., & Webber, M. E. (2019). Deliver Me from food waste: Model framework for comparing the energy use of meal-kit delivery and groceries. *Journal of Cleaner Production, 236*, 1–11.

Getir. (n.d.). *Frequently asked questions*. Retrieved July 4, 2022, from https://getir.com/de/faq.html.

Gorillas. (n.d.). *Frequently asked questions*. Retrieved July 4, 2022, from https://gorillas.io/en/customer-support.

Gorillas. (2022). *Gorillas enters the private label market*. Retrieved July 5, 2022, from https://gorillas.io/en/blog/gorillas-enters-the-private-label-market.

Gruntkowski, L. M., & Martinez, L. F. (2022). Online grocery shopping in Germany: Assessing the impact of COVID-19. *Journal of Theoretical and Applied Electronic Commerce Research, 17*(3), 984–1002.

Heard, B. R., Bandekar, M., Vassar, B., & Miller, S. A. (2019). Comparison of life cycle environmental impacts from meal kits and grocery store meals. *Resources, Conversation & Recycling, 147*, 189–200.

HelloFresh. (2021). *Capital markets day 2021*. Retrieved June 30, 2022, from https://ir.hellofreshgroup.com/download/companies/hellofresh/Capital_Markets_Day/CMD_Final_Presentation.pdf.

HelloFresh. (2022a). *Annual report 2021*. Retrieved June 30, 2022, from https://ir.hellofreshgroup.com/download/companies/hellofresh/Annual%20Reports/DE000A161408-JA-2021-PN-EQ-E-00.pdf.

HelloFresh. (2022b). *Sustainability report 2021*. Retrieved July 1, 2022, from https://ir.hellofreshgroup.com/download/companies/hellofresh/Annual%20Reports/HelloFresh_Sustainability_Report_2021_Non_Financial_Report.pdf.

HelloFresh. (2022c). *Supply chain infographic*. Retrieved July 1, 2022, from https://drive.google.com/drive/folders/1CJ5T2KDThY44Z5Iqcz8C_PwqJxMtW80i.

HelloFresh. (n.d.). *Frequently asked questions*. Retrieved July 1, 2022, from https://www.hellofresh.de/about/faq?categoryId=DEFAQ05-Lieferung&questionId=DEFAQ0502NoDelivery.

Inside Germany. (2021, August 29). *This is how you do your grocery shopping online with home delivery in Germany!* Retrieved June 27, 2022, from https://insidegermany.co/online-grocery-shopping-in-germany/.

Jing, X., & Lewis, M. (2011). Stockouts in online retailing. *Journal of Marketing Research, 48*(2), 342–354.

Kapalschinski, C., & Kolf, F. (2021a, March 9). Edeka verkauft Bringmeister—und heizt dadurch den Wettlauf der Onlinesupermärkte an. *Handelsblatt*. Retrieved July 13, 2022, from https://www.handelsblatt.com/unternehmen/handel-konsumgueter/einzelhandel-edeka-verkauft-bringmeister-und-heizt-dadurch-den-wettlauf-der-onlinesupermaerkte-an/26988896.html.

Kapalschinski, C., & Kolf, F. (2021b, May 29). Dieser tschechische Investor will Rewe, Amazon und Aldi die Kunden abjagen. *Handelsblatt*. Retrieved July 13, 2022, from https://www.handelsblatt.com/unternehmen/handel-konsumgueter/jakub-havrlant-dieser-tschechische-investor-will-rewe-amazon-und-aldi-die-kunden-abjagen/27236238.html.

Klauth, J., & Gassmann, M. (2021, October 1). Gorillas, Getir, Flink—die wilde Schlacht der Lieferdienste. *Welt*. Retrieved July 5, 2022, from https://www.welt.de/wirtschaft/article234125270/Gorillas-Getir-Flink-Die-wilde-Schlacht-der-Lieferdienste.html.

Knuspr. (2022a). *Online-Supermarkt Knuspr ab sofort auch in der Metropolregion Rhein-Main*. Retrieved June 28, 2022, from https://www.knuspr.de/seite/pressemitteilungen.

Knuspr. (2022b). *Knuspr wächst monatlich um fast 30% und liefert in den ersten 9 Monaten über 320.000 Bestellungen*. Retrieved June 27, 2022, from https://www.knuspr.de/seite/pressemitteilungen.

Kolf, F. (2022, May 2). Milliardenmarkt der Lieferdienste: Rewe kontert Gorillas, Picnic und Knuspr. *Handelsblatt*. Retrieved July 13, 2022, from https://www.handelsblatt.com/unternehmen/handel-konsumgueter/e-commerce-milliardenmarkt-der-lieferdienste-rewe-kontert-gorillas-picnic-und-knuspr/28284310.html.

Krisch, J. (2022, January 10). Picnic lag 2020 bei Umsätzen von 455 Mio. €, davon 78 Mio.€ in D. *Exciting Commerce*. Retrieved July 13, 2022, from https://excitingcommerce.de/2022/01/10/picnic-lag-2020-bei-umsaetzen-von-455-mio-e-davon-78-mio-e-in-d/.

Ladd, B. (2022, March 18). Will rapid grocery delivery have to slow down to survive? *Forbes*. Retrieved July 4, 2022, from https://www.forbes.com/sites/forbescommunicationscouncil/2022/03/18/will-rapid-grocery-delivery-have-to-slow-down-to-survive/?sh=7139a9401496.

Lagorio, A., & Pinto, R. (2021). Food and grocery retail logistics issues: A systematic literature review. *Research in Transportation Economics, 87*, 1–14.

Lewis, M. (2021, March 8). The case for meal kits: Environment's friend or foe? *EcoWatch*. Retrieved July 13, 2022, from https://www.ecowatch.com/case-for-meal-delivery-kits-2650927816.html.

Leyerer, M., Sonneberg, M. O., Heumann, M., & Breitner, M. H. (2020). Shortening the last mile in urban areas: optimizing a smart logistics concept for e-grocery operations. *Smart Cities, 3*(3), 585–603.

Lim, S. F. W., Jin, X., & Srai, J. S. (2018). Consumer-driven e-commerce: A literature review, design framework, and research agenda on last-mile logistics models. *International Journal of Physical Distribution & Logistics Management, 48*(3), 308–332.

Lim, S. F. W., Wang, L., & Srai, J. S. (2017). Wal-Mart's omni-channel synergy. *Supply Chain Management Review, 21*(5), 30–37.

Lodni, C., Najmaei, M., & Mansori, S. (2021). The effect of COVID-19 pandemic on the German E-grocery industry with respect to challenges for retailers and customer satisfaction. *Journal of Marketing Management and Consumer Behaviour, 3*(3), 1–31.

Luu, H., Schäfer, R., & Muttenthaler, L. (n.d.). Geld verbrennen in 10 Minuten: Das Geschäftsmodell von Gorillas, Flink & Co. *hy—the Axel Springer Consulting Group*. Retrieved July 5, 2022, from https://hy.co/2021/10/28/geld-verbrennen-in-10-minuten/.

Malhotra, N. (2019). *Marketing research: An applied orientation* (7th ed.). Pearson.

Marley Spoon. (2022). *Annual report 2021*. Retrieved June 30, 2022, from https://ir.marleyspoon.com/DownloadFile.axd?file=/Report/ComNews/20220225/02492132.pdf.

Marley Spoon. (n.d.). *Frequently asked questions*. Retrieved July 1, 2022, from https://support.marleyspoon.com/hc/de/articles/360001926216-Wie-kann-ich-herausfinden-an-welchen-Tagen-ihr-an-meine-Adresse-liefert-.

McGrath, C., Palmgren, P. J., & Liljedahl, M. (2019). Twelve tips for conducting qualitative research interviews. *Medical Teacher, 41*(9), 1002–1006.

McKinsey. (2021a). *The consumer demand recovery and lasting effects of COVID-19*. Retrieved July 19, 2022, from https://www.mckinsey.com/industries/consumer-packaged-goods/our-insights/the-consumer-demand-recovery-and-lasting-effects-of-covid-19.

McKinsey. (2021b). *Disruptions and uncertainty—The state of grocery retail 2021: Europe*. Retrieved July 12, 2022, from https://www.mckinsey.com/~/media/mckinsey/industries/retail/our%20insights/the%20path%20forward%20for%20european%20grocery%20retailers/disruption-and-uncertainty-the-state-of-grocery-retail-2021-europe-final.pdf.

McMaster, M., Nettleton, C., Tom, C., Xu, B., Cao, C., & Qiao, P. (2020). Risk management: Rethinking fashion supply chain management for multinational corporations in light of the COVID-19 outbreak. *Journal of Risk and Financial Management, 13*(8), 173.

Mkansi, M., Eresia-Eke, C., & Emmanuel-Ebikake, O. (2018). E-grocery challenges and remedies: Global market leaders perspective. *Cogent Business & Management, 5*(1), 1–28.

Olsson, J., Osman, M. C., Hellström, D., & Vakulenko, Y. (2021). Customer expectations of unattended grocery delivery services: mapping forms and determinants. *International Journal of Retail & Distribution Management, 50*(13), 1–16.

Picnic. (n.d.). *Wohin liefert Picnic?* Retrieved June 28, 2022, from https://picnic.app/de/alle-orte/.

Piroth, P., Rüger-Muck, E., & Bruwer, J. (2020). Digitalisation in grocery retailing in Germany: an exploratory study. *The International Review of Retail, Distribution and Consumer Research, 30*(5), 479–497.

Rest, J. (2022, 24 May). Radikaler Kahlschlag bei Gorillas. *Manager Magazin*. Retrieved July 5, 2022, from https://www.manager-magazin.de/unternehmen/tech/gorillas-massenentlassung-bei-express-lieferdienst-a-c7a0afaf-f709-44aa-bad3-917912739ca9.

REWE Group. (2021). *REWE setzt auf flink und auf weiteres dynamisches Wachstum von rewe.de*. Retrieved July 5, 2022, from https://www.rewe-group.com/de/presse-und-medien/newsroom/pressemitteilungen/rewe-setzt-auf-flink-und-auf-weiteres-dynamisches-wachstum-von-rewe-de/.

REWE Group. (2022). *Annual report 2021*. Retrieved June 27, 2022, from https://www.rewe-group-geschaeftsbericht.de/documents/Key_Figures_2021.pdf.

REWE Group. (n.d.). *Struktur und Vertriebslinien*. Retrieved June 29, 2022, from https://www.rewe-group.com/de/unternehmen/struktur-und-vertriebslinien/rewe/.

Robert Koch Institute. (2022). *Coronavirus disease 2019—Daily situation report—6 July 2022*. Retrieved July 6, 2022, from https://www.rki.de/DE/Content/InfAZ/N/Neuartiges_Coronavirus/Situationsberichte/Jul_2022/2022-07-06-en.pdf?__blob=publicationFile.

Seidel, S. (2021). One goal, one approach? A comparative analysis of online grocery strategies in France and Germany. *Case Studies on Transport Policy, 9*(4), 1922–1932.

Seidel, S., Mareï, N., & Blanquart, C. (2016). Innovations in e-grocery and logistics solutions for cities. *Transportation Research Procedia, 12*, 825–835.

Seitz, C. (2013, June 19–21). E-grocery as new innovative distribution channel in the German food retailing. In *Proceedings of the management, knowledge and learning international conference, Zadar (Croatia)* (pp. 125–133).

Shen, H., Namdarpour, F., & Lin, J. (2022). Investigation of online grocery shopping and delivery preference before, during, and after COVID-19. *Transportation Research Interdisciplinary Perspectives, 14*, 1–10.

Silva, A., Coelho, L. C., Darvish, M., & Renaud, J. (2020). Integrating storage location and order picking problems in warehouse planning. *Transportation Research Part E: Logistics and Transportation Review, 140*, 1–22.

Spryker and Appinio. (2022). *Ultimate overview of online food retailing in Germany in 2022 and beyond*. Retrieved June 23, 2022, from https://www.efoodinsights.com/de-online-grocery-report/.

Startbase. (2022). *Online-Supermarkt Knuspr liefert erste Zahlen*. Retrieved June 27, 2022, from https://www.startbase.de/news/online-supermarkt-knuspr-liefert-erste-zahlen/.

Telenti, A., Arvin, A., Corey, L., Corti, D., Diamond, M. S., García-Sastre, A., Garry, R. F., Holmes, E. C., Pang, P. S., & Virgin, H. W. (2021). After the pandemic: Perspectives on the future trajectory of COVID-19. *Nature, 596*(7873), 495–504.

Teller, C., Holweg, C., Reiner, G., & Kotzab, H. (2018). Retail store operations and food waste. *Journal of Cleaner Production, 185*, 981–997.

Tracey, P., Phillips, N., & Jarvis, O. (2011). Bridging institutional entrepreneurship and the creation of new organizational forms: A multilevel model. *Organization Science, 22*(1), 60–80.

Ulrich, M., Jahnke, H., Langrock, R., Pesch, R., & Senge, R. (2021). Distributional regression for demand forecasting in e-grocery. *European Journal of Operational Research, 294*(3), 831–842.

Vakulenko, Y., Shams, P., Hellström, D., & Hjort, K. (2019). Online retail experience and customer satisfaction: the mediating role of last mile delivery. *The International Review of Retail, Distribution and Consumer Research, 29*(3), 306–320.

Veselovská, L. (2020). Supply chain disruptions in the context of early stages of the global COVID-19 outbreak. *Problems and Perspectives in Management, 18*(2), 490–500.

Wortmann, M. (2021). The German variety of grocery retailing: A historical institutionalist analysis of a non-core industry. *Competition & Change, 25*(3–4), 453–477.

Yahoo Finance. (n.d.). *HelloFresh SE—Historical data*. Retrieved July 1, 2022, from https://uk.finance.yahoo.com/quote/HFG.DE/history?p=HFG.DE.

Yang, M., Zhang, T., & Wang, C. X. (2021). The optimal e-commerce sales mode selection and information sharing strategy under demand uncertainty. *Computers & Industrial Engineering, 162*, 1–13.

Forecasting and Planning with Auxiliary Data During a Pandemic: Evidence from U.K. Google Trends

Maryam Mojdehi, Konstantinos Nikolopoulos, and Vasileios Bougioukos

1 Introduction

This chapter aims to give some insights into how COVID-19 growth rates and the subsequent government decisions regarding social and retail restrictions affected buyer behavior and supply chain management. The primary hypothesis of this work is that COVID-19 impacted retailers' abilities to maintain their supply chains, leading to demand exceeding supply. More specifically, the secondary hypotheses are that (1) the higher the level of national restrictions that the government imposed, the greater the excess demand for a number of key retail items became; (2) this excess demand was also impacted as COVID-19 cases increased; and (3) as the percentage of people in the United Kingdom who had both vaccinations increased, the impact of increasing cases on these excess demand levels was expected to decline. At the height of the pandemic, various predictions were made regarding different levels of government restrictions, though many of them were based on extrapolations from the small amount of data available at the time. After several different governments "imposed lockdowns," much more information became available; this information is used as the basis for this research. Data from social media were also sought out, highlighting the growth of "panic buying" and hoarding behaviors in the retail sector, and providing additional context to these sources.

Scientists suggest that it is highly likely that at some point such restrictions may need to be imposed again, perhaps due to a similar pandemic in the future. It will

M. Mojdehi
Alliance Manchester Business School, Manchester, UK

K. Nikolopoulos (✉)
Durham University & IHRR Forecasting Laboratory, Durham, UK
e-mail: kostas.nikolopoulos@durham.ac.uk

V. Bougioukos
Notre Dame & Durham University Business School, Durham, UK

M. Moshref-Javadi, S. Seshadri (eds.), *Impacts of COVID-19 on Supply Chains*, Springer Business Cases, https://doi.org/10.1007/978-3-031-47734-8_3

then be vital for the retail sector to be able to predict changes in buyer behavior (and subsequent disruptions to supply chains) based on models that assume different levels of government restrictions. This will allow retailers and suppliers to make adjustments according to the specific health conditions and restrictions imposed. This chapter focuses on the development of forecasting models based on the correlation between the severity of the pandemic and the demand for a number of key items across the retail sector. Through these models and the insights that they provide, retailer planners and government statisticians can predict excess demand and prepare for similar disruptions in future pandemics, based on virus case growth rates, national vaccination levels, and the current level of national restrictions.

Literature Review
This chapter investigates disruptions to supply chains caused by COVID-19. The primary hypothesis is that excess demand (ED) for key retail items increased due to the pandemic. The secondary hypotheses are that (1) ED increased as cases increased, (2) ED increased as greater restrictions were imposed, and (3) increases in vaccinations decreased the effect of increased cases and restrictions on ED. This review therefore evaluates works that (1) model supply chain disruption as a result of COVID-19 and (2) consider consumer behavior during the pandemic, and how social media reflected and drove it.

Forty academic articles, papers, and reports were located covering these areas, and gaps were identified in the existing research to which this work can contribute. Alongside the primary term "COVID-19," keywords used in different search combinations included "supply chain," "disruption, "modeling," "retail," "consumer"/"consumer behavior," "panic buying"/"stockpiling," "social media," and "government." Setting a target of 40 papers, these results were categorized into those concerned primarily with "supply chain disruption" and those addressing "consumer behavior." Although some overlapped, there were significantly more articles published regarding the former than the latter (30 and 10, respectively).

1.1 Consumer Behavior

In preparation for this work, ten articles focusing on consumer behavior during the pandemic, and how it was reflected in and driven by social media, were reviewed. Kirk and Rifkin (2020) consider the phenomenon of consumer overreaction to perceived shortages itself driving these shortages, and techniques retailers adopted to combat this: "retailers often began limiting purchases of in-demand items to one per customer per day, perhaps giving consumers more confidence that product choices would be there when they need them." The paper considers consumer phases of "reacting," "coping," and "adapting," but acknowledges further research is required into how consumers' attitudes toward retailers have been changed by the COVID-19 pandemic. Chen et al. (2020) note that stockpiling "will deepen the immediate and longer-term impact on retail operations," "could instantly empty essential products in stores before restocking," and "will initialize an improper competing shopping environment which impairs the fair opportunities for accessing essential commodities [for] the aged and disabled people, as well as those working in the essential businesses," but also that "the fear of commodity scarcity becomes contagious and spreads expeditiously over media channels including social media."

Leung et al. (2021) examine panic buying/stockpiling of toilet paper during COVID-19 restrictions, as reflected on Twitter, concluding that tweets were 3.5 times more likely to indicate negative sentiments than positive. They suggest that more analysis is required on use of social media during this time to provide sufficient data for predicting hoarding behavior in any future pandemic.

Naeem (2020) also explores the impact of social media through phone interviews with U.K. consumer volunteers, age 18 and older, with longstanding active social media accounts educated at the undergraduate level or beyond. Although the results are illuminating, this sample is not representative of the totality of U.K. social media users who may have driven stockpiling behaviors. Naeem (2021) then revisits this topic, building on the same research to conclude that social media can be both a help and a hinderance: "the unprecedented level of real-time information on COVID-19 at users' fingertips can give them the tools they need to make smart decisions, but also make them more anxious about what is to come" leading to stockpiling behaviors. Although primary interviews were not carried out for this work, general social media sources that take into account a wider range of users will be considered in the present review.

Other works covering consumer habits during the COVID-19 era include that by Martin-Neuninger and Ruby (2020), who state, "Under the new shopping conditions of the COVID-19 pandemic, food choices will depend heavily on product availability and restrictions on how many products consumers can buy." According to Pantano et al. (2020), "Sudden disruption of consumer demand (such as panic buying of staples such as toilet tissue and pasta, as seen in the UK) leads to negative impacts on supply chain performance." Schleper et al. (2021) note, "Although many items were sufficiently stocked in warehouses (e.g., toilet paper), supply disruptions, together with unpredictable demand pattern changes, inevitably led to empty shelves in supermarkets. Panic buying and stockpiling among consumers … exacerbated shortages at the retail stage." Sayyida et al. (2021) explore exclusively online retail consumer behavior, concluding in the U.K. market that "Although online retail has increased, offline retail sales are still quite large. Online retail sales are above 70% of total retail sales." Given the growing importance of online channels during the COVID-19 pandemic and going forward, it is even more important to undertake research (such as the present review) that can help retailers predict excess demand for particular products and categories in any future pandemic.

Investigating a connected topic, Wu et al. (2021) explore how (similar to social media) news can be used to predict oil price and consumption (as a key component of the supply chain for logistics and as a raw material). These authors conclude that "social media information contributes to the forecasting of oil price, production, and consumption," showing how even this raw commodity is affected by consumer behavior.

1.2 Supply Chain Disruption

Ivanov (2020) uses projections to predict which specific aspects of global supply chains (GSCs) could be disrupted by COVID-19 or any other pandemic. In Ivanov (2021a) and Ivanov (2021b), the same author examines solutions based on supply chain (SC) resilience. Ivanov and Dolgui (2021) considers the future research implications of COVID-19's impact on SCs asserting they "point toward numerous opportunities for substantial contributions to develop and test new theories, models, and resilience mechanisms for the control and mitigation of disruption propagation in SC's." The present review, for example, seizes the opportunity to model excess demand prediction in any future pandemic.

Alkahtani et al. (2021) focus on controllable production rates in the early stages of SCs, suggesting that the solution to COVID-19-related disruption is "incorporating a controllable production rate for flexible manufacturing, inventory level control, and best resource utilization to cope with the fluctuating demand due to the emergency levels determined by the government to control the transmission of the virus." They propose extending research to retailers and wholesalers, but do not focus on these parties. Their identification of this gap highlights an area where the present research on which items will increase in demand at specific stages of any future pandemic can add to the existing work on the topic.

Panzone et al. (2021) investigate COVID-19's impact specifically on U.K. food retail operations, for which a basic principle applies: Government restrictions increased sales for these stores, compared to nonfood stores, as nonessential stores closed and fewer workers purchased food from convenience and hospitality stores at lunch and after work. These authors also observe that supermarkets demonstrated flexibility in maintaining market share, evidenced by their operational changes and development of online channels. They employ methodologies generally used to calculate excess deaths, factoring in increased expenditures, rather than basing their analysis on which products faced excess demand.

Sharma, Adhikary, et al. (2020) consider COVID-19's impact on U.S. markets' SCs, using aggregated Twitter data as a source. Hobbs (2020) considers similar issues in Canada, concluding that "Steps to mitigate panic buying and stockpiling behavior by consumers in the event of future crises … deserve consideration." The same author expresses concerns for "the impact of supply chain disruptions on vulnerable populations, including low-income consumers"—a concern that is equally valid for such groups within the U.K. population.

On an associated topic, although Xu et al. (2020) consider GSCs, they note that COVID-19 "adversely affected GSCs throughout all their stages with major turbulences in manufacturing, processing, transport, and logistics, as well as significant shifts in demand," and that "massive disruptions to food supplies caused by COVID-19 are expected to double the number of people suffering from chronic hunger." This draws urgent attention as to *why* it is important to predict which products might see an increase in demand during future pandemics, but does not focus on *which* products might be affected in this way.

As well as covering prediction of the growth of the pandemic itself, Nikolopoulos et al. (2021) formulate least squares/coefficient formulae to predict excess demand, based on Google trend data as a proxy indicator across several countries. Although the present work will follow a similar path, it will focus on the supermarket retail sector—which also includes food and some electronic goods but does not primarily cover fashion (though some low-cost clothes are sold) or automotive products. The work of Nikolopoulos et al. (2021) will be expanded on here using similar proxy-indicator methodologies, but focusing in more detail on products indicative of supermarket consumer trends and sold solely within the U.K. retail sector. Those authors' research also evaluates and predicts increased demand over specific periods of the lockdown, whereas this work will consider changes from March 2020 to July 2021, providing additional modeling data.

Other works reviewed approach the topic from different angles using different sources. For example, Gunessee and Subramanian (2020) compare the impact of the COVID-19 pandemic to that of natural disasters. Kumar (2020) examines how blockchain technology can be used to address shrinkage, misplacement, and "ghost demand" in SCs during the COVID-19 pandemic, though not when demand increases. Garnet et al. (2020), meanwhile, discuss the internationally integrated nature of U.K. food supply chains, concluding that "The business objective of maintaining low stock levels, especially for short shelf-life products … relies on the Dover Strait and Channel Tunnel routes," which were easily disrupted by COVID-19 (and Brexit)—a situation the present research will address by predicting which product categories might see increased demands in any future pandemic.

Bogards and Czudaj (2021) focus on the commodity futures market, highlighting that "Since commodities of all classes … are strongly involved in the supply chain, recent academic studies have also analysed the impact of the Covid-19 pandemic on the commodity market." Sharma, Luthra, et al. (2020) consider how SCs can become sustainable in the post-COVID-19 world. Then, in a later paper, Sharma et al. (2021) survey experts within the industry to evaluate COVID-19's impact, though they acknowledge this sampling choice presents a skewed version of consumer experience. The use of Google Trends data here as a proxy for evaluating consumer demand will add to this research.

Although Choi (2021) focuses on modeling a medical operating room (OR) response to COVID-19, the impact on and planning by business are also discussed, with existing research classified into "before pandemic," "during pandemic," and "after pandemic." As this report was published in March 2021, its analysis of these impacts is based on the most up-to-date statistical data at that time, though data were more limited then than they are now. With several more months of data on COVID-19 growth rates, governmental pandemic management efforts, and associated supply chain trends now available, the present review will add to the area of "after pandemic" research.

Similarly, Kamar et al. (2021) focus on forecasting demand for medical supplies during the pandemic but use formulations for calculating excess demand that will be used here in the context of the retail sector. Finally, the extensive literature review undertaken by Golan et al. (2020) cites other sources considered here, and notes that "the fear of contagion results in unanticipated market trends, such as price spikes and hoarding." Meanwhile, Chowdhury et al. (2021) identify 74 articles published before September 2021 that cover, among other themes, "supply chain sustainability in the light of the pandemic," though they acknowledge it remains unclear which aspects have and have not yet been studied. The remaining nine works reviewed for the present study were Marquez et al. (2021), Punia et al. (2020), Queiroz et al. (2020), Zhu et al. (2020), Ishida (2020), Mitchell et al. (2020), Pichler et al. (2020), del Rio-Chanona et al. (2020), and McMaster et al. (2020), all covering the areas outlined previously, and with many of the same weaknesses.

Overview
As noted in the literature review, there are two gaps in the existing research related to the topic of interest here. First, much of the existing research cited in this literature review was written between March and December 2020, meaning that the authors were unable to access data now available. The existing research is therefore largely predictive and speculatory, whereas the current study uses much more real data in training and testing the models. Data covering a wider range of restriction levels are also available now, as are—crucially—data on the widespread rollout of vaccines across the United Kingdom. Much of the extant research was written before or early on in the vaccine rollout, so it did not evaluate the effects of this development on consumer confidence and other SC issues. As such, the data used to determine COVID-19's impact on SCs (as indicated by increased excess demand) in this study are more accurate, more wide-ranging, and more complete than the datasets employed in the extant literature.

Second, the reviews published to date show a gap in the existing research regarding the evaluation and modeling of the combined impact on SCs of case levels, government restrictions, and national vaccination percentages. This work will map Google Trends proxy SC data against restriction levels, cases, and vaccination rates. The aim is to demonstrate the direct impact of COVID-19 on SCs as reflected in excess demand, and to produce accurate, practical models that retailers and statisticians can use to predict and plan for similar disruptions in any future pandemic, thereby protecting supply chains when the country needs it most.

2 Data Preprocessing and Preliminary Analysis

2.1 Determining Restriction Level

The primary source used for the "restriction level" variable in the main dataset was a "COVID-19 Restrictions Time Series" document for lockdown levels in London, later uploaded to the government COVID-19 site (https://data.london.gov.uk/dataset/covid-19-restrictions-timeseries). The weekly statistics it contained were cross-referenced with other lockdown-timeline sources and minor adjustments made. For each week from March 2020 to July 2021, this document indicates which, if any, of the following government measures were in place in the London area (thereby including national and some local restrictions):

- **Schools closed**
- **Shops closed**
- **Eating places closed**
- **Household mixing indoor banned**
- **"Work from home if you can" rule in force**
- Pubs closed
- "Stay at home" rule in force
- "Rule of six indoors" in force
- Curfew in force

The first five measures (in bold) in this list were used for the purpose of assigning a national restriction level to each week in question, as these generally applied more to the whole of the United Kingdom than the others did. With the five measures noted (and for the purposes of this work, each being assigned the same weighting), it was possible to assign a score of 0–5 based on how many were in force for each week in the considered time period.

- Apart from three specific weeks, the level assigned to the national restriction status was determined by how many of the five restrictions were in place across the United Kingdom at that point, in the range 1–5 (one restriction = Level 1, two restrictions = Level 2, etc.).
- In the weeks beginning 14 December 2020 and 21 December 2020, only the last two restrictions were in place for the whole of England, but with Tier 4 restrictions for much of the southeast, the assessment of national restriction level in the main dataset here was elevated to "3."
- In the week beginning 28 December 2020, only the last two restrictions were in place for the whole of England, but at this point 78% of the United Kingdom was in Tier 4, so the assessment of the national restriction level in the main dataset here was elevated to "4."

2.2 *Data Preprocessing and Preliminary Analysis*

Data for the variables to be used in analysis were created from the raw data gathered, with some normalized as noted here:

- *Toiletries* is the mean of weekly excess demand for bleach, toilet paper, and nappies (diapers) for each week evaluated (using Google Trends data as a proxy measure).
- *Groceries* is the weekly mean of excess demand for flour, pasta, and rice.
- *Electronics* is the weekly mean of excess demand for food processors, televisions, and vacuum cleaners.

- All nine sets of Google Trends data used to create values for these variables were already normalized, with the week with highest demand allocated a value of 100.
- *Weekly_Growth_Rate* was calculated using the following formula (Nikolopoulos et al., 2021):

$$\text{Weekly\_Growth\_Rate\%} = \left(\left(\text{Cases}_{t+1} - \text{Cases}_t\right) / \text{Cases}_t\right)$$

- Normalized values for *Weekly_Cases* and *Weekly_Growth_Rate* values were calculated using the standard formula *(value/max_value) × 100.*
- *Vaccination1* and *Vaccination2* data were gathered and then presented as percentages.
- *Restriction_Level* is a categorical value equal to 0, 1, 2, 3, 4, or 5 (calculated through analysis of restriction timelines, as outlined previously, and directly transposed into the equivalent of the normalized values 0, 20, 40, 60, 80, and 100).

The data analyzed here were split into two time periods—the first when vaccinations were not available, and the second when they were:

- Period 1 is from the week ending 9 February 2020 (first week of available data) to the end of December 2020.
- Period 2 is from the week ending 3 January 2021 (first week when vaccines first became available) to 25 July 2021 (the last week in the time period analyzed).

To allow for training and testing of the models that were to be built, the data in each time period were split into two data sets.

- Period 1
  - Training data: week ending 9 February 2020 to week ending 13 March 2020
  - Test data: week ending 20 September 2020 to week ending 21 December 2020
- Period 2
  - Training data: week ending 3 January 2021 to week ending 16 May 2021
  - Test data: week ending 23 May 2021 to week ending 25 July 2021

3 Variable Selection, Modeling, and Forecasting

3.1 Variable Selection

To investigate the correlation between *Excess_Demand* in all three retail areas and the other variables noted earlier, two variable selection techniques were used: analysis of variance (ANOVA) and correlation analysis. If the *p*-value resulting from these techniques is determined to be less than 0.05, and hence significant, this indicates there is a significant change in *Excess_Demand* as other variables change, whereas a value of 0.5 or greater indicates this is not the case. In addition, to further investigate the relationship between all variables, forward stepwise selection was then used.

ANOVA

One-way ANOVA is a hypothesis-based technique that can be used to determine if a correlation exists between the values of two or more variables. This method was chosen because it works best when the independent variable is categorical and the dependent variable is numerical. In the data under consideration here, *Restriction_Level* is the former and *Excess_Demand* is the latter, and the analysis produced the results shown in Table 1.

The ANOVA results for both periods suggest there *is* a significant change in *Excess_Demand* for electronics and groceries as *Restriction_Level* changes, whereas there *is not* a significant change in *Excess_Demand* for toiletries as *Restriction_Level* changes.

> Based on these results, *Restriction_Level* should be excluded from modeling the value of *Excess_Demand* for toiletries but included in the models for electronics and groceries.

Correlation Analysis

Correlation analysis is another hypothesis-based technique that can be used to determine if a correlation exists between the values of two or more variables. This method was chosen because it works best when both the independent and dependent variables are numerical, as all other variables apart from *Restriction_Level* are here. The analysis produced the results shown in Table 2.

When broken down into two time periods, the results of this analysis show the following:

Table 1 Results of ANOVA for association of Excess_Demand and Restriction_Level

	Restriction_Level (independent variable)			
	Period_1		Period_2	
Dependent variables	p_value	R_Square	p_value	R_square
ED_Electronics	<0.0001	0.62	<0.0001	0.79
ED_Toiletries	0.53	0.12	0.67	0.10
ED_Groceries	<0.0001	0.71	0.003	0.56

Table 2 Results of correlation analysis for association of Excess_Demand and numerical variables

	Independent variables					
	p-Value_Period-1		p-Value_Period-2			
Dependent variables	Weekly growth rate	Weekly cases	Weekly growth rate	Weekly cases	Vaccination1	Vaccination2
ED_ Electronics	0.02	0.003	0.8	0.0003	< 0.0001	< 0.0001
ED_Toiletries	0.23	0.37	0.46	0.17	0.20	0.68
ED_Groceries	0.32	<0.0001	0.29	0.002	<0 .0001	< 0.0001

Period 1

(*Vaccination1* and *Vaccination2* do not apply here, as vaccinations were not yet available.)

- *Excess_Demand* for electronics was more closely correlated with *Weekly_Cases* than with *Weekly_Growth_Rate* (with *p*-values 0.003 and 0.02, respectively).
- *Excess_Demand* for groceries was more closely correlated with *Weekly_Cases* than with *Weekly_Growth_Rate* (with *p*-values <0.0001 and 0.32, respectively).
- *Excess_Demand* for toiletries was not highly correlated with *Weekly_Growth_Rate* or *Weekly_Cases* (with *p*-values 0.23 and 0.37, respectively).

Period 2

- *Excess_Demand* for electronics was more closely correlated with *Weekly_Cases* than with *Weekly_Growth_Rate* (with *p*-values 0.0003 and 0.8, respectively). It was also highly correlated with *Vaccination1* and *Vaccination2* (with *p*-values < 0.0001 for both).
- *Excess_Demand* for groceries was more closely correlated with *Weekly_Cases* than with *Weekly_Growth_Rate* (with *p*-values 0.002 and 0.2,9 respectively). It was also highly correlated with *Vaccination1* and *Vaccination2* (with *p*-values <0.0001 for both).
- *Excess_Demand* for toiletries was again not highly correlated with *Weekly_Growth_Rate* and *Weekly_Cases* (with *p*-values 0.17 and 0.45, respectively). It was not highly correlated with either *Vaccination1* or *Vaccination2*, as both have larger *p*-values (0.2 and 0.68, respectively).

Based on these results, when modeling *Excess_Demand*:

In Period 1 models for electronics, no variables should be excluded, but in period 2 *Weekly_Growth_Rate* should be excluded.
In models for groceries in both periods, *Weekly_Growth_Rate* should be excluded.
In models for toiletries, although none of the *p*-values was significant, the least insignificant variable was *Weekly_Growth_Rate* in Period 1 and *Weekly_Cases* in Period 2, so all other variables should be excluded.
The lack of clarity in these findings led to further analysis with the technique outlined next.

Forward Stepwise Selection

Forward stepwise selection is a technique that can be used to test the statistical significance of each independent variable iteratively. It begins with no variable in the model and selects the variable that gives highest *R*-square value (coefficient of determination). The adjusted *R*-square increases only if the added variable improves the model. This technique was chosen to further investigate the results of the previous analysis method, with the following results produced using the function *ols_step_forward_p()* in R. A different formula was also used to analyze each period:

- In Period 1, vaccinations were not yet available, so *Vaccination1* and *Vaccination2* do not apply. The formula used in R was therefore:

$$\text{Excess Demand} \approx \text{Weekly\_Cases} + \text{Weekly\_Growth\_Rate} + \text{Restriction\_Level}$$

- In Period 2, vaccinations became available, though only the percentage of the U.K. population who had received their first vaccination (*Vaccination1*) was used in the analysis. This is due to pre-analysis indicating that both vaccination variables have a very similar effect on this model across all three retail areas. In addition, a model with only the first vaccination is more flexible for use by statisticians in any future pandemic. The formula used in R was therefore:

$$\text{Excess Demand} \approx \text{Weekly\_Cases} + \text{Weekly\_Growth\_Rate} + \text{Restriction\_Level} + \text{Vaccination1}$$

Using these formulae, the results shown in Tables 3, 4, and 5 were produced for each retail type in each time period.

Electronics

- Period 1
  - The correlations between *Excess_Demand* and both *Restriction_Level* and *Weekly_Growth_Rate* were statistically significant, with close adjusted *R*-square values of 0.38 and 0.40, respectively.

Table 3 Results of forward stepwise regression of Excess_Demand (**electronics**)

Selection summary							
Period	Step	Variable entered	*R*-square	Adj. *R*-square	*c*(*p*)	AIC	RMSE
1	1	Restriction Level	0.38	0.38	3.96	215.88	6.64
	2	Weekly Growth Rate	0.45	0.40	2.98	214.76	6.43
2	1	Vaccination1	0.77	0.75	23.80	105.22	3.05
	2	Restriction Level	0.90	0.90	2.36	89.45	2.01
	3	Weekly Growth Rate	0.91	0.89	3.10	89.84	1.99

Table 4 Results of forward stepwise regression of Excess_Demand (**groceries**)

Selection summary							
Period	Step	Variable entered	*R*-square	Adj. *R*-square	*c*(*p*)	AIC	RMSE
1	1	Weekly Cases	0.66	0.65	13.06	243.55	10.23
	2	Restriction Level	0.76	0.74	3.36	234.82	8.80
	3	Weekly Growth Rate	0.77	0.77	4.00	235.30	8.74
2	1	Vaccination1	0.77	0.76	20.12	109.78	3.41
	2	Weekly Cases	0.89	0.87	4.03	97.89	2.48
	3	Weekly Growth Rate	0.90	0.88	4.07	97.58	2.42

Table 5 Results of forward stepwise regression of excess demand (**toiletries**)

Selection summary							
Period	Step	Variable entered	*R*-Square	Adj. *R*-Square	*c*(*p*)	AIC	RMSE
1	1	Weekly Growth Rate	0.50	0.02	1.89	256.78	12.58
	2	Weekly Cases	0.10	0.04	2.14	256.86	12.41
2	1	Weekly Cases	0.10	0.05	2.06	73.09	1.63
	2	Weekly Growth Rate	0.19	0.10	2.28	73.01	1.33
	3	Restriction Level	0.25	0.11	3.18	73.61	1.33

  - The RMSE values of 6.64 for *Restriction_Level* and 6.43 for *Weekly_Growth_Rate* suggest that keeping both variables in the model may improve the forecasting results.

- Period 2
  - The correlations between *Excess_Demand* and all other variables (*Vaccination1, Restriction_Level*, and *Weekly_Growth_Rate*) were statistically significant, with adjusted *R*-square values of 0.75, 0.89, and 0.89, respectively.
  - The RMSE values of 3.05 for *Vaccination1,* 2.01 for *Restriction_Level*, and 1.99 for *Weekly_Growth_Rate* suggest that keeping the first two variables in the model will greatly improve the forecasting results, but adding *Weekly_Growth_Rate* is less likely to do so.

Groceries

Period 1

- The correlations between *Excess_Demand* and all other variables (*Weekly_Cases*, *Restriction_Level*, and *Weekly_Growth_Rate*) were statistically significant, with adjusted *R*-square values of 0.65, 0.74, and 0.77, respectively.
- The RMSE values of 10.23 for *Weekly_Cases,* 8.80 for *Restriction_Level*, and 8.74 for *Weekly_Growth_Rate* suggest that keeping the first two in the model will greatly improve the forecasting results, but adding the last variable is likely to improve it only slightly.

Period 2

- The correlations between *Excess_Demand* and all other variables (*Vaccination1, Weekly_Cases*, and *Weekly_Growth_Rate*) were most statistically significant, with adjusted *R*-square values of 0.76, 0.87, and 0.88, respectively.
- The RMSE values of 3.42 for *Vaccination1*, 2.48 for *Weekly_Cases*, and 2.42 for *Weekly_Growth_Rate* suggest keeping the first two in the model will greatly improve the forecasting results, but adding the last variable is likely to improve it only slightly.

Toiletries

Period 1

- The correlations between *Excess_Demand* and both *Weekly_Growth_Rate* and *Weekly_Cases* were statistically significant, with adjusted *R*-square values of 0.02 and 0.04, respectively.
- The RMSE values of 12.58 for *Weekly_Growth_Rate* and 12.41 for *Weekly_Growth_Rate* suggest that keeping both variables in the model may improve the forecasting results.

Period 2

- The correlations between *Excess_Demand* and all other variables were statistically significant, with adjusted *R*-square values of 0.05, 0.10, and 0.11, respectively.
- The RMSE values of 1.63 for *Weekly_Cases* and 1.33 for both *Weekly_Growth_Rate and Restriction_Level* suggest keeping the first two in the model will greatly improve the forecasting results, but adding *Restriction_Level* is likely to improve it only slightly.

Based on these results, when modeling *Excess_Demand*:

- In both period models for electronics, *Weekly_Cases* should be excluded.
- In Period 1 models for groceries, no variables should be excluded; in Period 2, *Restriction_Level* should be excluded.
- In Period 1 models for Toiletries, *Restriction_Level* should be excluded; in Period 2, *Vaccination1* should be excluded.

3.2 Modeling

Predictive modeling techniques enable statisticians to use past and present data to predict the future. It is therefore essential to choose useful inputs and to optimize the complexity to achieve a good prediction. The next stage of this work was to use the insights and results from the variable selection analysis carried out in Sect. 4.1 to determine the best models to use for forecasting.

3.2.1 Model Types

Three different models were used to predict the excess demand in the three different retailer areas:

- Regression analysis
- Decision trees
- Neural networks

3.2.2 Applying the Models

Once the models were chosen, the training dataset was randomly partitioned into two segments, train (two-thirds of the dataset) and validation (one-third), using the data partition node in SAS Enterprise Miner Workstation. A sequence of models with increasing complexity was produced, one for each of the three modeling techniques. For each retail type in each of the two periods, the models were then set up with the following values in SAS, depending on modeling type:

- Regression
  - *Regression type*: linear regression with Logit Link function
  - *Model selection*: forward
  - *Selection criteria*: validation error
  - *Optimization technique*: default
  - *Convergence criteria*: default
- Decision tree
  - *Leaf size*: 25 (to prevent creating small leaves)
  - *Split size:* 50
  - *Assessment measure:* average squared error
  - *Interval target splitting rules*: ProbF
- Neural network
  - *Neural type*: multilayer Perceptron architecture
  - *Number of hidden units*: 5
  - *Hidden layer activation function*: default
  - *Target layer combination function:* default
  - *Maximum iterations:* 50
  - *Maximum iterations for preliminary training*: 50
  - *Number of runs*: 5
  - *Assessment measure*: average error

After selecting the modeling techniques to be used and then producing the results and subsequent analyses, the next stage was to determine which of the models was most appropriate for each of the retail types, in the two different time periods. Each model's performance was rated using the validation data in the Model Assessment Node in SAS to select the best model with the highest validation assessment. The Score Node was used to score the best model on the full test dataset created earlier.

3.2.3 Modeling Results

The three different models were applied to each of the retail areas, using the most appropriate variables suggested by the ANOVA and correlation analysis. The results of this are displayed in Tables 6, 7, and 8.

Table 6 Modeling accuracy RASE and RMSE and MAE (maximum absolute error) for both train and validation datasets (**electronics**)

Period	Model	Train			Valid		
		RASE	RMSE	MAE	RASE	RMSE	MAE
1.00	Neural Network	4.60	4.06	13.17	4.07	4.07	10.72
	Regression	5.43	6.23	13.11	4.13	4.13	10.39
	Decision Tree	5.71		11.36	6.22	6.22	11.97
2.00	Neural Network	0.65		1.63	3.54	3.64	8.46
	Regression	1.58	1.90	3.74	3.70	3.71	8.46
	Decision Tree	4.20		6.33	3.54	3.54	5.16

Table 7 Modeling accuracy RASE and RMSE and MAE (maximum absolute error) for both train and validation datasets (**groceries**)

Period	Model	Train			Valid		
		RASE	RMSE	MAE	RASE	RMSE	MAE
1.00	Neural Network	1.89		3.43	9.38	9.38	23.28
	Regression	3.15	3.73	6.90	12.21	12.21	23.69
	Decision Tree	16.98		30.44	17.37		33.11
2.00	Neural Network	0.93		2.25	7.63	7.63	11.53
	Regression	2.44	2.79	4.68	2.18	2.18	3.45
	Decision Tree	6.54		12.13	7.34		10.80

Table 8 Modeling accuracy RASE and RMSE and MAE (maximum absolute error) for both train and validation datasets (**toiletries**)

Period	Model	Train			Valid		
		RASE	RMSE	MAE	RASE	RMSE	MAE
1.00	Neural Network	5.20	9.10	13.29	14.10	14.10	45.77
	Regression	8.90		25.26	17.30	17.30	51.60
	Decision Tree	8.90		25.26	17.30		51.60
2.00	Neural Network	1.37	1.43	1.03	1.38	1.41	2.25
	Regression	1.37	1.43	3.28	1.41	1.41	2.04
	Decision Tree	0.50		3.28	1.41	1.39	2.04

To improve the results, the variables suggested by forward stepwise selection were then used in the models. Validation data results for these improved models are discussed next and shown in Tables 9, 10, and 11, together with the outcomes and—where noted—improvements to the original model, as broken down into two periods for each retail type.

Electronics

Period 1

- RASE values: neural network, 4.07; regression, 4.13; decision tree, 6.22.
- Max-AE values: neural network, 10.72; regression, 10.39; decision tree, 11.97.
- The model was not improved.

Table 9 Modeling accuracy RASE and RMSE and MAE (maximum absolute error) for both train and validation datasets **(electronics)—improved model**

Period	Model	Train			Valid		
		RASE	RMSE	MAE	RASE	RMSE	MAE
1.00	Neural Network	4.60	4.06	13.17	4.07	4.07	10.72
	Regression	5.43	6.23	13.11	4.13	4.13	10.39
	Decision Tree	5.71		11.36	6.22	6.22	11.97
2.00	Neural Network	0.44		1.13	5.13	5.13	9.24
	Regression	1.58	1.90	3.74	3.70	3.71	8.46
	Decision Tree	4.40		7.50	3.54	3.54	5.16

Table 10 Modeling accuracy RASE and RMSE and MAE (maximum absolute error) for both train and validation datasets **(groceries)—improved model**

Period	Model	Train			Valid		
		RASE	RMSE	MAE	RASE	RMSE	MAE
1.00	Neural Network	1.54		3.40	11.86	11.86	21.48
	Regression	3.15	3.73	6.90	12.21	12.21	23.69
	Decision Tree	16.98		30.44	17.37		33.11
2.00	Neural Network	0.21		0.46	2.07	2.07	3.10
	Regression	2.44	2.79	4.68	2.18	2.18	3.45
	Decision Tree	6.54		12.13	7.34		10.80

Table 11 Modeling accuracy RASE and RMSE and MAE (maximum absolute error) for both train and validation datasets **(toiletries)—improved model**

Period	Model	Train			Valid		
		RASE	RMSE	MAE	RASE	RMSE	MAE
1.00	Neural Network	1.83	18.54	3.79	7.65	7.65	20.44
	Regression	8.90		25.26	17.30	17.30	51.60
	Decision Tree	8.90		25.26	17.30		51.60
2.00	Neural Network	0.42	1.43	0.99	0.75	0.75	1.30
	Regression	1.37	1.43	3.28	1.41	1.41	2.04
	Decision Tree	1.37		3.28	1.41	1.39	2.04

Period 2

- RASE values: neural network, 3.54; regression, 3.70; decision tree, 3.54.
- Max-AE values: neural network, 9.24; regression, 8.46; decision tree, 5.16.
- The model was not improved.

Groceries

Period 1

- RASE values: neural network, 11.86; regression, 12.21; decision tree, 17.37.
- Max-AE values: neural network, 21.48; regression, 23.69; decision tree, 33.11.
- RMSE increased by 1.98, though Max-AE was reduced by only 1.8.

- Max-AE is a more appropriate measure of the accuracy of a model where being off by 8 is only twice as bad as being off by 4 (rather than exponentially bad).
- The reduction in Max-AE means these improvements to the model are still desirable.

Period 2
- RASE values: neural network, 2.07; regression, 2.18; decision tree, 7.34.
- Max-AE values: neural network, 3.10; regression, 3.45; decision tree, 10.80.
- Max-AE was reduced by 0.35 and RMSE was reduced by 0.11, with the winning model changing from regression to the neural network. The final result was improved.

Toiletries

Period 1
- RASE values: neural network, 7.65; regression, 17.30; decision tree, 17.30.
- Max-AE values: neural network, 20.44; regression, 51.60; decision tree, 51.60.
- Max-AE was reduced by 25.33, and RMSE was reduced by 6.45. The model was therefore improved.

Period 2
- RASE values: neural network, 0.75; regression, 1.41; decision tree, 1.41.
- Max-AE values: neural network, 1.30; regression, 2.04; decision tree. 2.04.
- Max-AE was reduced by 0.95, and RMSE was reduced by 0.66. The model was therefore improved.

The model with the highest validation assessment result is clearly a neural network for all retail types in both periods except electronics in Period 2, where it is a decision tree.

3.3 *Forecasting Excess Demand*

3.3.1 Results

After selecting the best model for each retail type in each period, the next step was to use these models to forecast the impact of the other variables on excess demand in any future pandemic, with or without the availability of vaccinations. The results produced by this forecasting are discussed next.

Electronics
- **Period 1**

At the beginning of the test period, *Weekly_Growth_Rate* was almost 2%, leading the government to increase *Restriction_Level* (40 in the data here), while *Excess_Demand* also increased from 40 to 50. Later in the period, as *Restriction_Level* increased from 40 to 100, *Excess_Demand* also increased, before dropping to its lowest level as *Restriction_Level* also dropped. *Weekly_Growth_Rate* remained below its trend line as *Restriction_Level* increased.

- **Period 2**

Throughout the test period, as *Vaccination1* increased, *Excess_Demand* remained stable, despite *Weekly_Growth_Rate* fluctuating and *Restriction_Level* remaining at 20.

Groceries

- **Period 1**

In the middle of the test period, as *Weekly_Cases* and *Restriction_Level* increased, *Excess_Demand* began to drop. When the government removed all restrictions, *Weekly_Cases* began to increase again, resulting in a further increase in *Excess_Demand*.

- **Period 2**

Throughout the test period, as *Vaccination1* increased, *Excess_Demand* decreased, despite *Weekly_Growth_Rate* fluctuating and *Restriction_Level* remaining at 20.

Toiletries

- **Period 1**

In the middle of the test period, as *Weekly_Growth_Rate* and *Restriction_Level* increased, *Excess_Demand* began to fluctuate between 32 and 39. When the government reduced restrictions, *Excess_Demand* decreased again. Later in the period, as *Weekly_Growth_Rate* began to rise, *Restriction_Level* was increased to 60, leading to slight increase in *Excess_Demand*.

- **Period 2**

Although the *Vaccination1* variable was excluded at the modeling and forecasting stage for Period 2, vaccinations were still available during this time period and so are likely to have impacted the data. As such, the forecasting results show that despite the increase in *Weekly_Cases*, *Vaccination1* also increased and hence *Excess_Demand* decreased.

> In Period 1, as *Restriction_Level* increased due to a rise in COVID-19 cases, *Excess_Demand* likewise began to rise.
> In Period 2, *Excess_Demand* for toiletries and electronics remained stable, while that for groceries decreased. (Note: The restriction level for this period was 20 and vaccinations were available.)

3.3.2 Accuracy

The results in Tables 12, 13, and 14 were achieved when forecasting *Excess_Demand* for each retail type in each time period.

Table 12 Forecasting accuracy RMSE and MAE (mean and maximum absolute errors) and MAPE (mean absolute percentage error) for test datasets (**electronics**)

Period	Model	RMSE	MAE	Max-AE	MAPE %
1	Neural Network	14.20	8.20	41.20	12.70
2	Decision Three	9.88	9.13	14.2	29.19

Table 13 Forecasting accuracy RMSE and MAE (mean and maximum absolute errors) and MAPE (mean absolute percentage error) for test datasets (**groceries**)

Period	Model	RMSE	MAE	Max-AE	MAPE %
1	Neural Network	33.67	24.70	79.60	50.17
2	Neural Network	7.25	5.80	14.37	11.80

Table 14 Forecasting accuracy RMSE and MAE (mean and maximum absolute errors) and MAPE (mean absolute percentage error) for test datasets (**toiletries**)

Period	Model	RMSE	MAE	Max-AE	MAPE %
1	Neural Network	81.10	75.35	137.62	335.31
2	Neural Network	1.98	1.59	3.28	7.00

Table 15 Forecasting accuracy RMSE and MAE (mean and maximum absolute errors) and MAPE (mean absolute percentage error) for test datasets (**toiletries)—improved forecast**

Period	Model	RMSE	MAE	Max-AE	MAPE %
1	Neural Network	11.20	10.64	16.62	48.50
2	Neural Network	3.92	1.59	3.28	7.00

For toiletries, despite using the improved model, the initial forecasting results showed a MAPE of 335.31. To reduce this value, *Restriction_Level* was added and *Weekly_Cases* removed. This improved the accuracy, producing the results in Table 15.

3.4 Summary of Findings

3.4.1 Variable Selection Findings

An important part of this work was choosing the most appropriate variables that would produce a model that is neither overfitted nor underfitted. The variable selection methods, which considered the relationship either between target and predictors individually (ANOVA and correlation analysis) or between target and all predictors (forward stepwise selection), were intended to determine which variables are most useful for forecasting *Excess_Demand*. Analysis of the results showed that for toiletries and groceries, using the results from forward stepwise selection improved the results of predictive modeling the most. For electronics, however, using the results from forward stepwise selection did not change the predictive modeling results. Forward stepwise selection was therefore chosen as the best variable selection method for modeling the *Excess_Demand* for all three categories.

Forward stepwise selection improved the modeling results for two of the three retail types.
For the third type, it produced similar results to ANOVA and correlation analysis. As such, either method could be chosen. For consistency, forward stepwise selection was preferred.
As all variables are considered in forward stepwise selection, this method will produce a more flexible, usable model.

3.4.2 Model Selection Findings

The next important part of this work was to choose the most appropriate model for each retail type in each time period—that is, the model that could be used to forecast results with the least margin of error. This should be a model that satisfies the bias and variance trade-off, while also having the lowest RASE, RMSE, and MAE values, and hence the highest validation assessment. Analysis of the results produced the following findings:

For toiletries and groceries, the best model for both periods was a neural network.
For electronics, this model was only the best for Period 1; a decision tree was the best choice for Period 2.

3.4.3 Forecasting Findings

When forecasting *Excess_Demand* in Period 1, for groceries and toiletries the MAPE values went as high as 50%; for electronics, it remained less than 30%, generally regarded as the benchmark for accurate forecasting.
When forecasting *Excess_Demand* in Period 2, MAPE remained less than 30% for all three retail types.

4 Conclusions and Limitations

4.1 Primary Hypothesis

The primary hypothesis of this work is that the COVID-19 pandemic impacted retail supply chains. Results of the modeling analysis, as well as evidence from social media and comparisons to typical excess demand over the previous 5 years, have proved this to be unquestionably true.

4.2 Secondary Hypotheses

The secondary hypotheses of this work are as follows:

(i) Excess demand increased as number of cases increased.
(ii) Excess demand increased as greater restrictions were imposed.
(iii) Increases in vaccination levels decreased the effect of increased number of cases and restrictions on excess demand.

Building on what was learned from the in-depth analyses carried out at the modeling stage on the training and validation datasets, to investigate these hypotheses more directly a further linear regression analysis was carried out in R. This was done on the full dataset (including the training, validation, and test data) for each of the three retail areas as shown in Tables 16 and 17, with the following observations regarding the hypotheses being made.

Table 16 Excess_Demand_Search_Trend ~ Weekly_Cases_Normalised + Restriction_Level_Normalised

Period-1						
Parameter	Electronics	Std. error	Toiletries	Std. error	Groceries	Std. error
Intercept	39.88***	1.68	30.58***	2.71	52.26***	2.95
Weekly Cases	0.21**	0.06	–0.23	0.1	–0.36**	0.12
Restriction Level	0.12***	0.02	0.03	0.04	0.24***	0.04

Robust standard errors and estimation of parameters w and r, indicate statistical significant at 0 '***' 0.001 '**' 0.01 '*' 0.05 '.' 0.1 ' ' 1

Table 17 Excess_Demand_Search_Trend ~ Weekly_Cases_Normalized + Restriction_Level_Normalized + Vaccinalion_Normalised

Period-2						
Parameter	Electronics	Std. error	Toiletries	Std. error	Groceries	Std. error
Intercept	40.00***	4.66	23.97***	2.34	55.32***	4.49
Weekly Cases	0.03	0.02	0.01	0.01	0.05	0.03
Restriction Level	0.12***	0.03	0.01	0.01	0.09**	0.03
Vaccination 1	–0.21*	0.05	–0.01	0.02	–0.13**	0.05

Robust standard errors and estimation of parameters *w*, *r* and *v*, indicate statistical significant at 0 '***' 0.001 '**' 0.01 '*' 0.05 '.' 0.1 ' ' 1

Period 1: No Vaccinations Available

Period 2: Vaccinations Available

- **Electronics**
  - *Weekly_Cases* had a positive effect on *Excess_Demand*, with a one-unit increase in the former increasing the mean of the latter by 0.21. *Restriction_Level* also had a positive effect on *Excess_Demand*, with a one-unit increase in the former increasing the mean of the latter by 0.12.
- **Toiletries**
  - *Weekly_Cases* had a negative effect on *Excess_Demand*, with a one-unit increase in the former decreasing the mean of the latter by 0.23. *Restriction_Level*, however, had a positive relationship with *Excess_Demand*, with a one-unit increase in the former increasing the mean of the latter by 0.03.
- **Groceries**
  - In Period 1 (when no vaccinations were available), *Weekly_Cases* had a negative effect on *Excess_Demand*, with a one-unit increase in the former decreasing the mean of the latter by 0.36. *Restriction_Level*, however, had a positive effect on *Excess_Demand*, with a one-unit increase in the former increasing the mean of the latter by 0.24.

Electronics
Weekly_Cases had a positive effect on *Excess_Demand*, with a one-unit increase in the former increasing the mean of the latter by 0.03. *Restriction_Level* also had a positive effect on *Excess_Demand*, with a one-unit increase in the former increasing the mean of the latter by 0.12. *Vaccination1*, however, had a negative effect on *Excess_Demand*, with a one-unit increase in the former decreasing the mean of the latter by 0.21. *Vaccination1* also decreased the impact *of Restriction_Level and Weekly_Cases* on *Excess_Demand, as* the coefficient of *Vaccination1* was significantly larger than that of the other two variables (almost 2 and 7 times larger, respectively).

Toiletries
Weekly_Cases had a positive effect on *Excess_Demand*, with a one-unit increase in the former increasing the mean of *the* latter by 0.01. *Restriction_Level* also had a

positive effect on *Excess_Demand*, with a one-unit increase in the former increasing the mean of the latter by 0.01. *Vaccination1*, however, had a negative effect on *Excess_Demand*, with a one-unit increase in the former decreasing the mean of the latter by 0.01. *Vaccination1* also decreased the impact of *Restriction_Level and Weekly_Cases on Excess_Demand*, as the coefficient of *Vaccination1* was identical to that of the other two variables (and therefore negated their impact).

Groceries

In Period 2 (when vaccinations became available), *Weekly_Cases* had a positive effect on *Excess_Demand*, with a one-unit increase in the former increasing the mean of the latter by 0.05. *Restriction_Level* also had a positive effect on *Excess_Demand*, with a one-unit increase in the former increasing the mean of the latter by 0.09. *Vaccination1*, however, had a negative effect on *Excess_Demand*, with a one-unit increase in the former decreasing the mean of the latter by 0.13. *Vaccination1* also decreased the impact *of Restriction_Level and Weekly_Cases* on *Excess_Demand*, as the coefficient of *Vaccination1* was significantly larger than that of the other two variables (1.4 and 2.6 times larger, respectively).

Secondary Hypotheses Proofs

From the findings just described, the following can be observed regarding the three secondary hypotheses:

(i) Hypothesis (i) was proved to be true for all three retail areas in both time periods, except for groceries and toiletries in Period 1, though the effects were significantly lessened as vaccinations were made available.
(ii) Hypothesis (ii) was proved to be true for all three retail areas in the first half of the pandemic before vaccinations became available. Following the introduction of vaccinations, this hypothesis was proved to be false for the second half of the pandemic, as their increasing availability decreased the impact of restriction levels and weekly cases on excess demand.
(iii) Hypothesis (iii) was proved to be true, though it applies only to the second time period when vaccinations were available.

4.3 Conclusion

The results from this research show that forecasting and making supply chain decisions during a pandemic are less challenging for electronics than for toiletries and groceries, as consumers, when purchasing the items in the latter two categories, make more frequent decisions about their immediate needs. It is clear that consumer demand is affected by the public health environment of a pandemic. In the COVID-19 pandemic, when restriction levels were higher, people feared losing immediate access to products due to delivery disruption, the possibility of shortages, and the signs of panic buying and hoarding reflected on social media. As such, excess demand for key products increased. When vaccinations became available and people were less likely to become infected (and if they did, less likely to be seriously ill), excess demand decreased. It is also clear that consumers' panic buying and hoarding had a serious impact on demand for those products for which they had most immediate need, such as toiletries and groceries.

In addition to using the predictive models created in this work, the more general advice offered here to statisticians and planners in retail is to aim to ensure stock fulfillment of products related to the public's day-to-day needs, as well as of electronic products that could be used for work and/or entertainment in the early stages of any future pandemic, before the government imposes ever-increasing lockdown restrictions on the country. Retailers may then reduce their inventory levels if and when vaccinations for such a pandemic become available.

4.4 Limitations

Although this work is extensive, the understandable time and space constraints within which it was written leave room for more exploration of the topic. Further improvements could be made to the forecasting models, with more modeling techniques used, and additional models built in software packages such as Python. Despite this, extremely thorough modeling work was undertaken in this study using the techniques and packages chosen, with the end result being that the original dual focus of the work on predictive modeling and social media as outlined in the literature review (and supported by the pre-reading to prepare for it) was narrowed in practice to focus on the former. Thus, there is more scope to explore the topic and primary hypothesis of this work with additional pre-reading of more predictive modeling papers, and to further develop the ideas explored in the social media articles the literature review considered. More preliminary data preparation might also provide further insights into the data already gathered on the COVID-19 pandemic and potentially from possible primary sources such as interviews with consumers or retailers.

References

Alkahtani, M., Omair, M., Khalid, Q. S., Hussain, G., Ahmad, I., & Pruncu, C. (2021). A COVID-19 supply chain management strategy based on variable production under uncertain environment conditions. *International Journal of Environmental Research and Public Health, 18*(4). https://www.mdpi.com/1660-4601/18/4/1662

Bogards, O., & Czudaj, R. L. (2021, June). Price overreactions in the commodity futures market: An intraday analysis of the Covid-19 pandemic impact. *Resources Policy, 71*. https://www.sciencedirect.com/science/article/abs/pii/S0301420720309946

Chen, Y., Rajabifard, A., Soheil, S., Potts, K. E., Laylavi, F., Xie, Y., & Zhang, Y. (2020, September). A discussion of irrational stockpiling behaviour during crisis. *Journal of Safety Science and Resilience, 1*(1). https://www.sciencedirect.com/science/article/pii/S2666449620300037

Choi, T. M. (2021, March 5). Fighting against COVID-19: What operations research can help and the sense-and-respond framework. *Annals of Operations Research*. https://link.springer.com/article/10.1007/s10479-021-03973-w

Chowdhury, P., Paul, S. K., Kaisar, S., & Moktadir, A. (2021, April). COVID-19 pandemic related supply chain studies: A systematic review. *Transportation Research. Logistics & Transportation Review, 148*. https://www.sciencedirect.com/science/article/pii/S1366554521000478

del Rio-Chanona, R. M., Mealy, P., Pichler, A., Lafond, F., & Doyne Farmer, J. (2020). Supply and demand shocks in the COVID-19 pandemic: An industry and occupation perspective. *Oxford Review of Economic Policy, 36*(1). https://academic.oup.com/oxrep/article/36/Supplement_1/S94/5899019?login=true

Garnet, P., Doherty, B., & Heron, T. (2020, June 4). Vulnerability of the United Kingdom's food supply chains exposed by COVID-19. *Nature Food, 1*. https://www.nature.com/articles/s43016-020-0097-7

Golan, M. S., Jernegan, L. H., & Linkov, I. (2020). Trends and applications of resilience analytics in supply chain modelling: Systematic literature review in the context of the COVID-19 pandemic. *Environment Systems and Decisions*. https://link.springer.com/content/pdf/10.1007/s10669-020-09777-w.pdf. Published online 30 May 2020

Gunessee, S., & Subramanian, N. (2020, November 20). Ambiguity and its coping mechanisms in supply chains lessons from the Covid-19 pandemic and natural disasters. *International Journal of Operations & Production Management*. https://www.emerald.com/insight/content/doi/10.1108/IJOPM-07-2019-0530/full/html

Hobbs, J. E. (2020). Food supply chains during the COVID-19 pandemic. *Canadian Journal of Agricultural Economics, 68*(2). https://onlinelibrary.wiley.com/doi/full/10.1111/cjag.12237

Ishida, S. (2020). Perspectives on supply chain management in a pandemic and the post-COVID-19 era. *IEEE Engineering Management Review, 48*(3). https://ieeexplore.ieee.org/abstract/document/9169789

Ivanov, D. (2021a, April 5). Exiting the COVID-19 pandemic: After-shock risks and avoidance of disruption tails in supply chains. *Annals of Operations Research*. https://link.springer.com/article/10.1007/s10479-021-04047-7

Ivanov, D. (2021b). Supply chain viability and the COVID-19 pandemic: A conceptual and formal generalisation of four major adaptation strategies. *International Journal of Production Research, 59*(12). https://www.tandfonline.com/doi/abs/10.1080/00207543.2021.1890852

Ivanov, D., & Dolgui, A. (2021, February). OR-methods for coping with the ripple effect in supply chains during COVID-19 pandemic: Managerial insights and research implications. *International Journal of Production Economics, 232*. https://www.sciencedirect.com/science/article/pii/S0925527320302784

Kamar, A., Maalouf, N., Hitti, E., El Eid, G., Isma'eel, H., & Elhajj, I. H. (2021, February 3). Challenge of forecasting demand of medical resources and supplies during a pandemic: A comparative evaluation of three surge calculators for COVID-19. *Epidemiology & Infection, 149*(e51). https://www.cambridge.org/core/journals/epidemiology-and-infection/article/challenge-of-forecasting-demand-of-medical-resources-and-supplies-during-a-pandemic-a-comparative-evaluation-of-three-surge-calculators-for-covid19/99BF6E98712CE9A7B2299B65944B9E6E

Kirk, C. P., & Rifkin, L. S. (2020, September). I'll trade you diamonds for toilet paper: Consumer reacting, coping and adapting behaviours in the COVID-19 pandemic. *Journal of Business Research, 117*. https://www.sciencedirect.com/science/article/pii/S0148296320303271

Kumar, A. (2020, November 24). Improvement of public distribution system efficiency applying blockchain technology during pandemic outbreak (COVID-19). *Journal of Humanitarian Logistics and Supply Chain Management, 11*(1). https://www.emerald.com/insight/content/doi/10.1108/JHLSCM-06-2020-0050/full/html

Leung, J., Chung, J. Y. C., Tisdale, C., Chiu, V., Lim, C. C. W., & Chan, G. (2021, January 27). Anxiety and panic buying behaviour during COVID-19 pandemic: A qualitative analysis of toilet paper hoarding contents on Twitter. *International Journal of Environmental Research and Public Health, 18*(3). https://www.mdpi.com/1660-4601/18/3/1127

Marquez, R., Tolosa, L., & Celis, M. T. (2021, February). Understanding COVID-19 effect on the U.S. supply chain of strategic products: Important factors, current situation, and future perspective. *Artículo de Investigación. Revista Ciencia e Ingeniería, 42*(1). https://www.researchgate.net/publication/344729906_Understanding_COVID-19_effect_on_the_US_supply_chain_of_strategic_products_important_factors_current_situation_and_future_perspective

Martin-Neuninger, R., & Ruby, M. B. (2020, June 5). What does food retail research tell us about the implications of coronavirus (COVID-19) for grocery purchasing habits? *Frontiers in Psychology*. https://www.frontiersin.org/articles/10.3389/fpsyg.2020.01448/full

McMaster, M., Nettleton, C., Tom, C., Xu, B., Cao, C., & Qiao, P. (2020, August 4). Risk management: Rethinking fashion supply chain management for multinational corporations in light of the COVID-19 outbreak. *Journal of Risk and Financial Management, 13*(8). https://www.mdpi.com/1911-8074/13/8/173

Mitchell, R., Maull, R., Pearson, S., Brewer, S., & Collison, M. (2020, May 30). *The impact of COVID-19 on the UK fresh food supply chain*. Cornell University. https://arxiv.org/abs/2006.00279

Naeem, M. (2020, October 26). The role of social media to generate social proof as engaged society for stockpiling behaviour of customers during Covid-19 pandemic. *Qualitative Market Research*. https://www.emerald.com/insight/content/doi/10.1108/QMR-04-2020-0050/full/html

Naeem, M. (2021, January). Do social media platforms develop consumer panic buying during the fear of Covid-19 pandemic. *Journal of Retailing and Consumer Services, 58*. https://www.sciencedirect.com/science/article/pii/S0969698920309814

Nikolopoulos, K., Punia, S., Schaefers, A., Tsinpoulos, C., & Vasilakis, C. (2021, April 1). Forecasting and planning during a pandemic: COVID-19 growth rates, supply chain disruptions, and governmental decisions. *European Journal of Operational Research, 290*(1). https://www.sciencedirect.com/science/article/abs/pii/S0377221720306913

Pantano, E., Pizzi, G., Scarpi, D., & Dennis, C. (2020, August). Competing during a pandemic? Retailers' ups and downs during the COVID-19 outbreak. *Journal of Business Research, 116*. https://www.sciencedirect.com/science/article/pii/S0148296320303209

Panzone, L. A., Larcom, S., & She, P. W. (2021, March). Estimating the impact of the first COVID-19 lockdown on UK food retailers and the restaurant sector. *Global Food Security, 28*. https://www.sciencedirect.com/science/article/abs/pii/S2211912421000055

Pichler, A., Pangallo, M., del Rio-Chanona, R., Lafond, F., & Doyne Farmer, J. (2020, February 18). *In and out of lockdown: Propagation of supply and demand shocks in a dynamic input–output model*. Oxford University. https://papers.ssrn.com/sol3/papers.cfm?abstract_id=3788494

Punia, S., Singh, S. P., & Madaan, J. K. (2020, November). A cross-temporal hierarchical framework and deep learning for supply chain forecasting. *Computers & Industrial Engineering, 149*. https://www.sciencedirect.com/science/article/abs/pii/S0360835220305040

Queiroz, M. M., Ivanov, D., Dolgui, A., & Fosso Wamba, S. (2020, June 16). Impacts of epidemic outbreaks on supply chains: Mapping a research agenda amid the COVID-19 pandemic through a structured literature review. *Annals of Operations Research*. https://link.springer.com/article/10.1007/s10479-020-03685-7

Sayyida, S., Hartini, S., Gunawan, S., & Husin, S. N. (2021, January). The impact of the Covid-19 pandemic on retail consumer behavior. *APTSI Transactions on Management, 5*(1). https://ijc.ilearning.co/index.php/ATM/article/view/1497

Schleper, M. C., Gold, S., Trautrims, A., & Baldock, D. (2021). Pandemic-induced knowledge gaps in operations and supply chain management: COVID-19's impacts on retailing. *International Journal of Operations & Production Management, 41*(3). https://www.emerald.com/insight/content/doi/10.1108/IJOPM-12-2020-0837/full/html?utm_source=rss&utm_medium=feed&utm_campaign=rss_journalLatest#loginreload

Sharma, A., Adhikary, A., & Borah, S. B. (2020, September). Covid-19's impact on supply chain decisions: Strategic insights from NASDAQ 100 firms using Twitter data. *Journal of Business Research, 117*. https://www.sciencedirect.com/science/article/pii/S0148296320303210

Sharma, M., Luthra, S., Joshi, S., & Kumar, A. (2020, August 26). Developing a framework for enhancing survivability of sustainable supply chains during and post-COVID-19 pandemic. *International Journal of Logistics Research and Applications*. https://www.tandfonline.com/doi/full/10.1080/13675567.2020.1810213

Sharma, M., Luthra, S., Joshi, S., & Kumar, A. (2021, February 16). Accelerating retail supply chain performance against pandemic disruption: Adopting resilient strategies to mitigate the

long-term effects. *Journal of Enterprise Information Management*. https://www.emerald.com/insight/content/doi/10.1108/JEIM-07-2020-0286/full/html
Wu, B., Wang, L., Wang, S., & Zeng, Y. R. (2021, July 1). Forecasting the U.S. oil markets based on social media information during the COVID-19 pandemic. *Energy, 226*. https://www.sciencedirect.com/science/article/abs/pii/S0360544221006526
Xu, Z., Elomri, A., Kerbache, L., & El Omri, A. (2020). Impacts of COVID-19 on global supply chains: Facts and perspectives. *IEEE Engineering Management Review, 48*(3). https://ieeexplore.ieee.org/abstract/document/9174793
Zhu, G., Chou, M. C., & Tsai, C. W. (2020). Lessons learned from the COVID-19 pandemic exposing the shortcomings of current supply chain operations: A long-term prescriptive offering. *Sustainability, 12*(14). https://www.mdpi.com/2071-1050/12/14/5858

Data Sources

Weekly Restrictions

https://data.london.gov.uk/dataset/covid-19-restrictions-timeseries
Also uploaded to: https://data.gov.uk/dataset/0c8c0d09-7add-454d-84c7-a362ded66906/covid-19-restrictions-timeseries

Timeline of Restrictions

https://www.instituteforgovernment.org.uk/charts/uk-government-coronavirus-lockdowns
https://www.expressandstar.com/news/uk-news/2021/01/04/a-timeline-of-uk-lockdown-measures-since-the-pandemic-began/
https://en.wikipedia.org/wiki/Timeline_of_the_COVID-19_pandemic_in_the_United_Kingdom_(January%E2%80%93June_2020)

Weekly Cases

https://data.london.gov.uk/dataset/covid-19-restrictions-timeseries

Vaccinations

https://coronavirus.data.gov.uk/details/vaccinations

Supply Chain and SARS-CoV-2 Mitigation: Adjustments Made to Administer Six Million SARS-CoV-2 Tests in a Large Public Testing Program

Len Musielak and Ronald S. Watkins

1 Introduction

In April 2020, the global spread of SARS COVID 2 (SARS-CoV-2) and the associated Coronavirus Disease 2019 (COVID-19) had shut down economies across the globe—including activities on the campus of the University of Illinois at Urbana–Champaign (UIUC) (Butler, 2022). In the face of the pandemic, UIUC decided to go on the offensive (Peplow, 2020). Campus leaders knew that noninvasive, frequent, and extremely accurate testing of the community would allow them to resume somewhat normal activities. There was only one small problem: A noninvasive and accurate test, inexpensive enough to perform regularly, with a short enough turnaround time to allow results to be received in time to allow the campus to act, didn't exist. UIUC took that as a challenge. Within the space of a few months, UIUC researchers developed covidSHIELD assay—a saliva-based polymerase chain reaction (PCR) test that skipped the expensive and time-consuming RNA extraction stage required by other SARS-CoV-2 tests on the market (University of Illinois, 2022). With this fast, accurate (U.S. Food and Drug Administration, 2022), and inexpensive test in hand, UIUC started twice-weekly testing of the entire campus population (McGee, 2020), which drove down the positivity rate not only on campus but also in the surrounding community (Fig. 1) (Chang, 2021). The success of the SHIELD program at its Urbana–Champaign locations inspired the University of Illinois System to offer this service to other entities within the state of Illinois (Ranoa et al., 2022). With that, the SHIELD Deployment Unit of the University of Illinois System was born.

L. Musielak
SHIELD Illinois, Oak Park, IL, USA

R. S. Watkins (✉)
SHIELD Illinois, Champaign, IL, USA
e-mail: ronw@uillinois.edu

M. Moshref-Javadi, S. Seshadri (eds.), *Impacts of COVID-19 on Supply Chains*, Springer Business Cases, https://doi.org/10.1007/978-3-031-47734-8_4

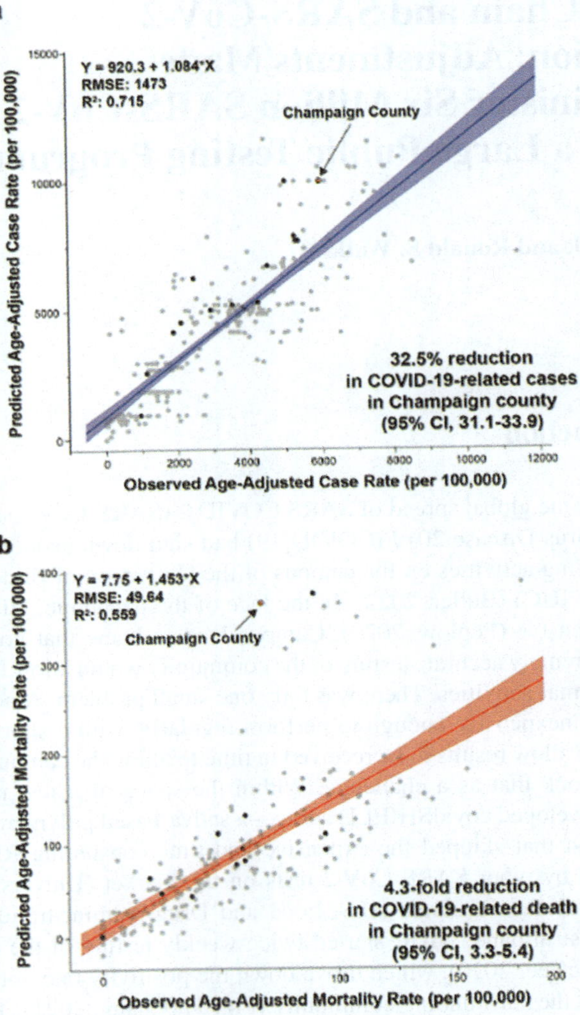

Fig. 1 Other communities without SHIELD. (**a, b**) Relationship between observed and predicted COVID-19 cases and mortality among counties with large university enrollments (student enrollment >15,000 at start of fall 2020 semester, $n = 251$). Predicted COVID-19 case and mortality rates were analyzed with a 3-week lag (to adjust for delays between exposure and outcome) using each county's social vulnerability index (SVI) and age-adjusted COVID-19 mortality, accounting for state (due to policy differences in COVID-19 management). COVID-19 human case data and SVI were provided by the Centers for Disease Control and Prevention (2021) and population data by the U.S. Census Bureau (2019). The lines indicate the fit lines for the linear regressions, with shaded areas indicating the 95% confidence intervals around the fits and circles indicating observations. Champaign County is shown in orange and other Big 10 Conference universities ($n = 16^{a}$) in black. [a]Hennepin and Ramsey counties (Minnesota) were both used for the University of Minnesota (Ranoa et al., 2022)

The initial plan for SHIELD Illinois was to act only as the "integrator." SHIELD Illinois would help laboratories prepare to run the covidSHIELD assay, to include the equipment and consumables. SHIELD Illinois would then host the technology necessary to transmit the orders to the lab, and the results back to the collecting agency. In other words, SHIELD Illinois would ensure the labs had everything needed to run the tests and the technology to make it happen. It would not collect the assays, transport them, run the laboratory, or provide customer support. The original estimate was that SHIELD Illinois would have 50 testing locations and collect 1.5 million tests in 6–12 months.

The plan to act solely in an integrator function eroded slowly over time, however. Soon SHIELD Illinois was involved in the logistics of running laboratories and collection sites, including customer support, but the estimated number of labs and locations remained constant—a few businesses and universities. But everything changed in March 2021, when the University of Illinois System signed an Intergovernmental Agreement (IGA) with the Illinois Department of Public Health (IDPH) to offer testing to every school district, all community colleges, and public universities in the state of Illinois while also running community testing sites for the general public throughout the state (Fig. 2).

As a result of the IGA, SHIELD Illinois faced an extremely challenging situation, as each aspect of building the organization was unprecedented. There was no playbook for spinning up an organization to offer testing to an entire state in just five months during a pandemic, while simultaneously coping with labor shortages and an inadequate supply chain system. The last time the United States faced a pandemic of this size—the 1918 H1N1 influenza outbreak—was the first year that American children had been mandated to attend elementary school (American Board, 2015). Most schools simply closed for two years until that pandemic was

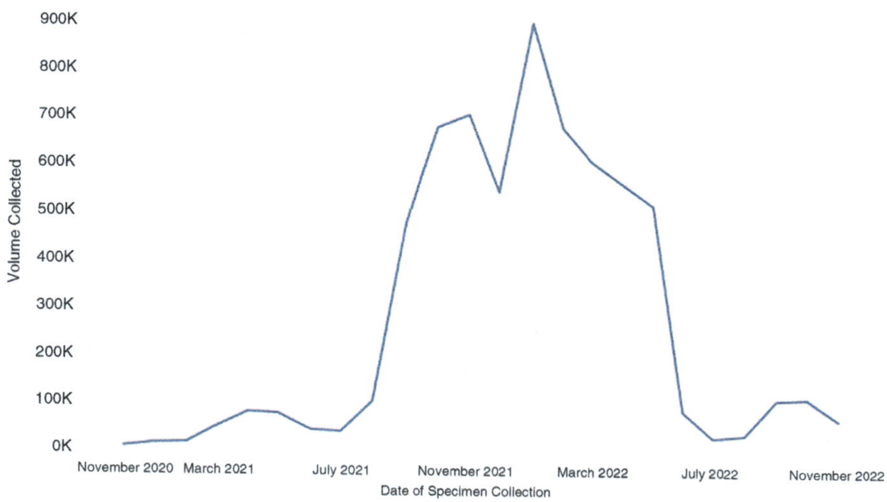

Fig. 2 Weekly testing volume performed by SHIELD Illinois

over (Markel, 2020). Of course, just closing schools for two years was not an option in 2020. SHIELD Illinois had to offer SARS-CoV-2 testing to 853 school districts covering 3977 schools with 1.9 million students (Ballotpedia, 2022). Its staff had no insight into the demand—no one knew how many districts, schools, or individuals would sign up for testing.

At the same time, SHIELD Illinois faced the same supply chain problems that everyone in the medical industry was experiencing. Staff shortages were pervasive. Personal protective equipment (PPE) was impossible to obtain. Critical supplies had ambiguous delivery schedules, with vendors stating that delivery times might range from 30 days to 9 months. From a logistics standpoint, SHIELD Illinois had no idea how to get supplies to testing sites or, more importantly, how to get specimens from testing sites to labs. Existing medical transport companies did not have either the infrastructure or the employees to provide the quantity or quality of service needed to meet the promised 28- to 48-h turnaround times. Additionally, there was a widespread labor shortage, and the availability of talent and individuals willing to work were scarce.

In the end, SHIELD Illinois would service more than 1700 sites in Illinois—including the governor's office, the state legislature, and U.S. District Court of Northern Illinois; utilize 13 labs; and, as of October 2022, perform more than 6.5 million tests (Fig. 3). Putting that in perspective, SHIELD Illinois performed 12% of all SARS-CoV-2 tests in Illinois and more tests than 24 entire states (Centers for Disease Control and Prevention, 2022). During that time, SHIELD Illinois scaled from zero units (SKUs) in inventory to 1066, issued 1683 purchase orders, built a transportation company, and even chartered a plane. How did a company of 30 scale

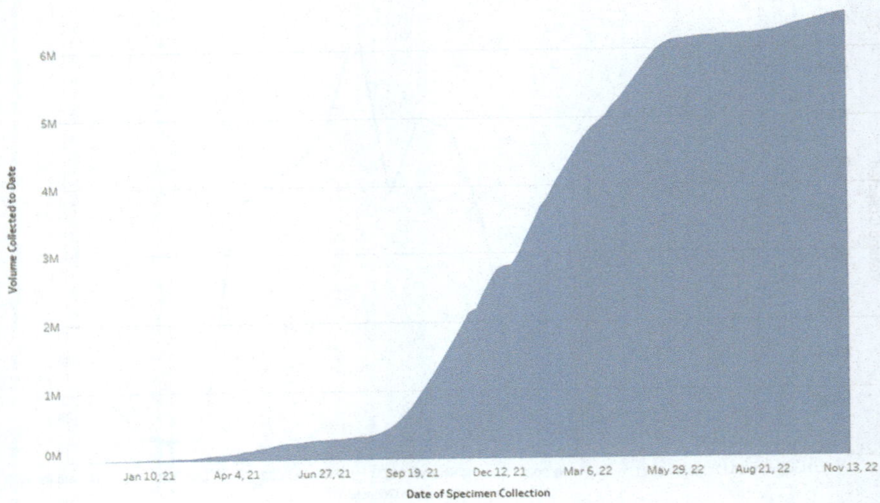

Fig. 3 Total tests performed by SHIELD Illinois

to 350 plus more than 1000 contractors? Technology integration, inventory control, and the correct mix of insourcing, outsourcing, and vendor integration.

2 Technology Integration

The first and most important step was increasing the maturity of the technology infrastructure. Like most businesses in startup mode, SHIELD Illinois began with everything managed in some sort of Microsoft Office application. The entire organization was contained in a series of Excel workbooks, SharePoint sites, and Outlook emails. Clients, deliveries, support, inventory, ordering—everything was everywhere and there was no order. There is nothing inherently wrong with Excel; it is a very powerful tool, but it does have limitations. When it became clear that the world was about to change drastically, SHIELD Illinois immediately started looking to upgrade to purpose-built applications. Specifically, the organization focused on relationship management, inventory control, and electronic health records (EHR) reporting.

2.1 Relationship Management Software

At first glance, it might not be apparent why customer relationship management (CRM) software was integral to supply chain success. However, for SHIELD Illinois at that time, it was the supply chain lifeline. With the only thing certain about the projected demand being its uncertainty, SHIELD Illinois relied on CRM software to provide client onboarding updates that drove the projections. If a school proactively reached out to SHIELD Illinois for information, 5% of the school's population estimate was added to the demand estimate. If that same school attended an online webinar, the estimate would increase to 15%. This pattern continued until the contract was signed and 100% of the population estimate was included in the overall demand estimate. The CRM software also allowed SHIELD Illinois to define and refine the population estimates. The organization not only had to project how many schools and districts would sign up for testing, but also how many students, staff, and teachers at each school would actually undergo testing. By analyzing the data provided by the CRM software, SHIELD Illinois was able to adjust the projections using a variety of factors that were found to influence adoption rates.

2.2 Inventory Management Application

Concurrently, SHIELD Illinois invested in a purpose-built inventory management and ordering system. This, too, was essential due to the ambiguity of the variables presented to SHIELD Illinois at the time. SHIELD Illinois knew it had a minimum of 7 labs and 50 collection sites to supply, but the maximum number of sites was essentially n. The ability to allow both labs and collection sites to submit their own inventory count sheets and order supplies, while giving SHIELD Illinois a macro view of how many tests they had on hand, was, and continues to be, an integral part of the supply chain success.

2.3 Reporting and Interoperability

The final upgrade to the technology infrastructure was increasing the amount of data SHIELD Illinois was able to get from the EHR and laboratory information management system (LIMS). SHIELD Illinois chose the EHR vendor, Point and Click Solutions, Inc., specifically because it knew that this company would be more willing, and able, to work with the team to design the system that was needed. Prior to its alliance with Point and Click, SHIELD Illinois had been using a larger player in the EHR space. While it had developed good products and had a plethora of integrations pre-established, SHIELD Illinois knew it would need a partner that could work with the team to build the plane while it was flying. For the LIMS, SHIELD Illinois chose to have an application custom built by the University of Illinois. Working with University Administrative Information Technology Services and the National Center for Super Computing Applications at UIUC, an end-to-end tracking system was developed that was easy to use and robust in terms of the data it captured.

This final piece, the data capture and availability, helped to balance and correct the other two technology solutions. While the CRM software told the team the estimated number of patients at each site, the EHR system could tell SHIELD Illinois how many patients actually underwent testing. The inventory management system told the team how many 96-well plates a lab said it had, and the LIMS could tell the team how many of those plates were used. This system of checks and balances would be integral in allowing the team to discover some of the other insights discussed later.

3 Inventory Control

SHIELD Illinois approached the supply chain issues during the pandemic from a different standpoint than almost every other organization. Whereas most organizations were looking at both the immediate and long-term impacts to their business,

SHIELD Illinois knew its operations would not remain a going concern. The program would end when the pandemic subsided. Furthermore, the initial funding, and the majority of the operating revenue, would come from taxpayer funds through the CARES Act appropriation. As a steward of taxpayer funds, SHIELD Illinois had a responsibility to use those funds judiciously. From a supply chain standpoint, that meant SHIELD Illinois needed to assure not only that there were enough supplies to fulfill the current demands, but also that there was no surplus of inventory leftover when the units shut down. So, while other industry players were able to get away from operating in a Lean manner in response to supply chain disruptions, SHIELD Illinois was never been able to fully abandon those concepts.

After the integration of technology, the importance of not only closely monitoring but also controlling inventory distribution was an early lesson learned, and was integral in allowing the team to successfully achieve the mission. Maintaining and controlling inventory via distribution controls, process standardization, and being comfortable with being agile allowed SHIELD Illinois to weather most of the supply chain storms unharmed.

3.1 Safety Stock

The availability of safety stock to act as a buffer allowed SHIELD Illinois to absorb and dampen supply change fluctuations. With uncertain demand and even less certain movement of materials through the supply chain, maintaining a buffer of critical supplies commensurate with projected usage and deliveries was the only way to continue operation. However, when left decentralized and unmanaged, safety stockpiles also led to some of the most severe supply shortage scares.

Early on in testing, the supply chain team approached SHIELD Illinois leadership with a problem. Collection sites were ordering more labels—insisting they were out—but there were none in inventory. This was simply impossible. At that point, SHIELD Illinois had completed only approximately one million tests and had received more than four million labels. It was not possible that these sites could be as short of labels as they claimed. This same issue was repeated with funnels, vials, racks, and other critical supplies. It would turn out that all those supplies did exist within the network—SHIELD Illinois just didn't control them.

Saliva specimens were collected at a collection site by the staff there. The collection staff might include employees of the host location ("self-collect"; e.g., a school nurse might collect specimens at an elementary school), employees of a third-party operations partner (ops partner; an external company hired by SHIELD Illinois to collect specimens at multiple locations), or SHIELD Illinois's own Field Operations (Field Ops) staff. Supplies were ordered either by the main point of contact for self-collect sites or by the main office for ops partner organizations, or picked up directly by a Field Ops team lead. When SHIELD was small, this was not a problem. Everyone ordered their supplies; everyone got their supplies. When the organization grew, however, unforeseen human factors crept into the supply chain and logistics process. Those factors finally came to a head when it was discovered that millions of labels were "missing."

A rumor had begun circulating about a shortage of certain supplies—an understandable concern, given that global supply chain disruptions were all over the news at the time. Indeed, toilet paper had become a precious resource (Fisher, 2020), and alcohol distilleries were making hand sanitizer (Schultz, 2020). When the self-collect sites, ops partners, and Field Ops teams heard that a shortage of supplies might occur, each put aside a reasonable amount of safety stock. Squirreling away a roll of labels might not seem like a big deal. Indeed, it had never been a problem before, but the increased size of the network exponentially increased the size of the problem. If each of the 1700 sites kept one roll of 1000 labels as safety stock, that would account for 2.4 million labels. Add in the number of labels left at collection sites for normal use, and it was no longer impossible for both the SHIELD warehouse and some sites to be "out" of labels or any other supply. As an organization, SHIELD Illinois had inventory available, but that inventory was just too widely distributed to be useful in this scenario.

The long-term solution to this problem was a change to the ordering and distribution process. Whereas previously SHIELD Illinois had allowed self-collect sites and ops partner organizations to order supplies directly through the inventory control system, the new process dictated that SHIELD Illinois would send weekly supply orders to a central location for each organization (e.g., school district, ops partner) automatically, with the volume based on the actual tests performed during the previous period. SHIELD Illinois would provide safety stock to cover unexpected increases in demand, but not enough that the organization could distribute the safety stock out to individual sites. It would have to remain at the central location and be used only in a true emergency. For SHIELD Field Ops, inventory was available at central SHIELD locations throughout the state, and controls were implemented to track the quantity of supplies withdrawn by each team. Catching this problem early prevented what could have been a catestropic shortage of supplies as the number of orders fulfilled by SHIELD Illinois increased exponentially in the winter of 2021–2022, as shown in Fig. 4.

3.2 *Standardization*

Another lesson that SHIELD Illinois learned early was the importance of standardization. This lesson took many forms across the organization—from the collection side, where the saliva is collected, to the labs, where it is processed.

After specimens were collected, they were placed in racks, which were sealed in bags and then placed in a plastic bin. That bin was transported to the next stage in the process, going either directly to a lab or to an intermediary distribution hub. The original standard operating procedure (SOP) for collection sites was that the site needed to provide its own bins. SHIELD gave general specifications for these containers, but sites were free to choose any vessel that met those specifications. Again,

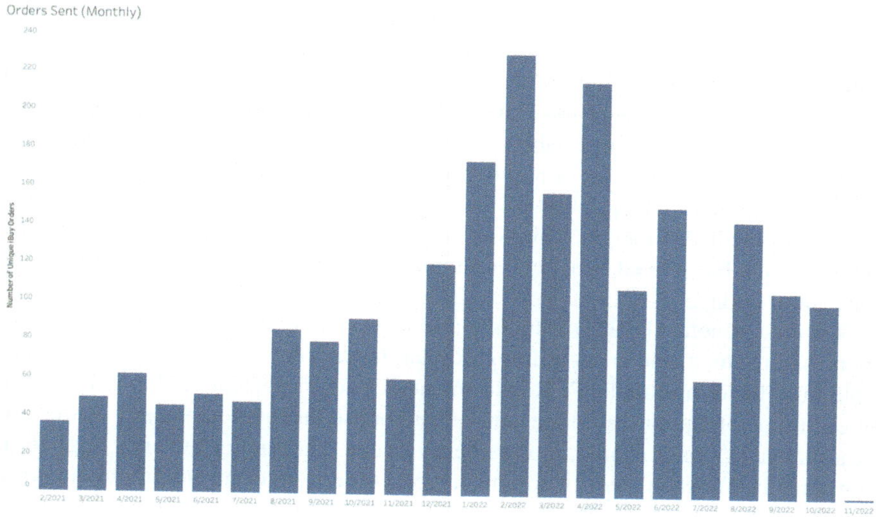

Fig. 4 Orders fulfilled by SHIELD Illinois supply chain team

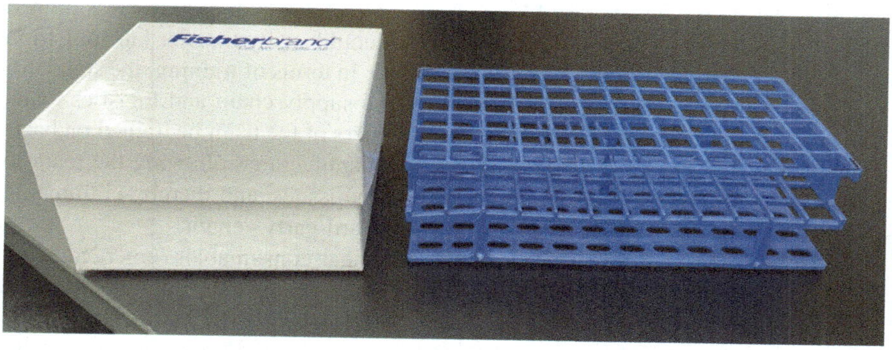

Fig. 5 Comparison of freezer box to storage rack. Photo: B. Kelly, University of Illinois

this worked perfectly fine in the early days when volumes were low and the site count was small. It became an insurmountable obstacle after things ramped up (Fig. 5). Quickly, labs were overwhelmed by empty containers waiting to be picked up. A site that tested once per week might have its bins sitting in a hallway for 7 days, while an ops partner that tested at multiple locations would have to wait for its containers to be emptied and cleaned so that it could test the next day.

Within the first six months of testing, SHIELD Illinois completely changed the SOP. The organization provided standard stackable bins to every site. When specimens were delivered to a lab or distribution hub, the courier could immediately take the corresponding number of containers that they had just deposited from the stack of emptied, cleaned, and sanitized transport vessels stacked right at the drop-off location.

The idea to standardize the specimen shipping containers should not have been new to the team, as SHIELD Illinois had been leveraging the efficiencies of standardization in the labs since they first opened. Throughout the brief history of SHIELD Illinois, anywhere from two to ten labs were operating at any one point. Regardless of whether those labs were directly owned and operated by SHIELD Illinois, pure reference labs, or a hybrid of both, one constant was the standardization of equipment. Every lab used the same water baths, ovens, robots, pipettes, PCR instruments, and so on. This was originally done to take advantage of economies of scale but proved beneficial on multiple levels beyond initially minimizing the capital outlay.

The first benefit SHIELD Illinois realized was the lower cost of backup equipment, safety stock, and cross-training. Rather than needing a backup supply of multiple fluid-handling robots, PCR instruments, or centrifuges, it could maintain one of each type of equipment in the central warehouse that could be at any of the labs in a matter of hours should an emergency occur. The same efficiency applied to consumables for each piece of equipment. A central store of pipette tips could serve multiple laboratories, as opposed to creating individual caches at each location. Furthermore, consumables could be directly transferred from one lab to another without questions of compatibility should that route be more efficient than a delivery from the central warehouse. Finally, because each lab staff member was trained on the exact same equipment, SHIELD Illinois could easily transfer lab staff from one location to another in the event of a shortage. In terms of training, the standardization of equipment also paid dividends for the supply chain and logistics team. SHIELD Illinois was able to have selected members of the team be trained on basic maintenance and troubleshooting tasks by the manufacturer, allowing the team to quickly diagnose and remedy common instrument issues, and thereby eliminating the need to wait for a service technician from a third-party vendor.

What was one of the biggest strengths, identical consumables, emerged as an Achilles' heel when a critical consumable necessary to operate the fluid handlers fell into a critical short supply across the globe. However, standardization again helped to resolve the dilemma—SHIELD Illinois had to find only one alternative product to fit every fluid handler across the network. It was able to dedicate one robot at one lab to testing and proving alternative options rather than sidelining multiple pieces of equipment across the network for this purpose.

Finally, standardization aided the supply chain team in another key area: vendor relationships. Laboratory equipment is delicate, occasionally temperamental, and maintenance intensive. Scheduling yearly preventive maintenance for one PCR instrument at one lab is time consuming but doable. Scheduling yearly maintenance for 30 PCR instruments, 40 fluid handlers, and 30 pipettes at 10 labs spread across a 400-mile by 200-mile area of the state would be on the verge of impossible—unless each type of equipment is the same make and model from the same manufacturer. It was not easy, but the standardization of equipment made the task possible.

3.3 Agility

Despite all the benefits that standardization provides, it is important to remain agile and creative when it comes to problem solving. Renowned computer scientist Rear Admiral Grace Murray Hopper is quoted as saying, "The most dangerous phrase in the language is 'We've always done it this way'" (Industry Insights, 2020). That statement could have been the motto of the operations organization at SHIELD Illinois. Standardization is important, but getting the job done is more important. At one point, the organization was running critically low on the 72-well racks used to ship specimens from the collection sites to the labs. As with the label issue discussed previously, this shortage should not have been possible based on the number of racks purchased previously and the number of specimens processed each day. However, it did happen, and the problem needed to be remedied immediately. The supply chain team explored every option to get additional racks, including medical suppliers, Amazon, and eBay. SHIELD Illinois even had a member of the Field Ops team who was a 3D printing hobbyist explore printing new racks. Nothing worked, and the supplies kept dwindling.

It was a member of the science team who finally found the "missing" racks. They were right in the lab all along. At that time, positive specimens were held at –80 °C (–112 °F) until they were collected by the Department of Public Health for variant identification. When that pickup schedule slowed, it meant that SHIELD Illinois had thousands of racks out of circulation in deep freezers at each lab. Until this point, SHIELD Illinois had never stored specimen vials in anything except racks. It had always been done that way, and team members assumed there was a reason it had to be done that way. However, when faced with a major shortage of a critical item, someone finally asked the question—and it turned out there was no reason that racks were needed for storage. Within days, every rack in every freezer was replaced with a disposable vial storage box, and the supply of transport racks was back up and running. This change had the added benefit of increasing the freezer capacity (another constraint), as the boxes allowed SHIELD Illinois to store more specimens in a smaller area. If no one had asked that one question, the operation would have ground to a halt.

The same type of outside-the-box, "do we have to do this" thinking was at the core of many of the innovations that occurred in and around SHIELD Illinois. It drove UIUC researchers to first try producing an assay that skipped the time-consuming and expensive RNA extraction step (University of Illinois, 2022). It led to the move to change the covidSHIELD process from requiring heat treatment in water to performing the same treatment in an oven. From large issues to small, refusing to accept the thinking that "the way things have been done is the way that they must be done" was the driving force behind what made the impossible possible.

4 Off-Shoring/On-Shoring, Insourcing/Outsourcing, and Vendor Integration

The balance between insourcing and outsourcing has never been more critical (Jaekel, 2020). This balance was integral to minimizing, if not negating, many supply chain issues in the SHIELD Illinois operation. However, it was the relationship SHIELD Illinois struck up with the vendors that truly made the difference.

As discussed earlier, when SHIELD Illinois was first imagined, the plan was to outsource everything. The organization would train collection sites and pair them with a third-party reference lab that SHIELD Illinois had trained to perform the covidSHIELD assay. Like collections and labs, medical transportation was another operational aspect that SHIELD Illinois eventually decided to insource. The tight turnaround times and large volumes were beyond what existing couriers could provide. At the program's height, SHIELD Illinois operated a fleet of 40 vehicles across a 200-mile by 400-mile coverage zone. In addition, during peak demand experienced as the Delta variant swept across the state, SHIELD Illinois chartered an airplane that flew specimens from Chicago to Kentucky for processing at an affiliated lab outside of Lexington. Insourcing these operational areas was the first of many decisions SHIELD Illinois made to insource aspects of the operation that it had originally planned to contract out to other parties. As discussed previously, SHIELD Illinois insourced the development of the Laboratory Information Management System to a University of Illinois unit. Customer success, level 2 technical support, and data management were all eventually insourced.

In some cases, a hybrid of insourcing and outsourcing was chosen. That was eventually the case with collection site management. SHIELD Illinois originally planned to outsource this function before deciding to insource it. However, when demand for testing skyrocketed, the organization contracted with third-party vendors to augment the staffing due to a lack of resources. Production of specimen labels was another hybrid insource/outsource solution. Original production was in-house until demand spiked and overwhelmed those capabilities. At that point, SHIELD Illinois outsourced production to a professional print shop. However, it maintained the production ability and used it for emergency orders, custom labels, and other times when a small quantity was needed in a quick turnaround time.

Another hybrid arrangement involved warehouse services. The main warehouse for SHEILD Illinois was operated by a third party in Peoria, Illinois. Within the first few months of the program, it became apparent that SHIELD Illinois would need more accessible warehousing facilities closer to the main areas of operations. At that point, it created two satellite facilities in Darien and Champaign–Urbana, Illinois. These facilities were fed by the main warehouse and held a cache of the most used consumables for easy, convenient pick-up and delivery. The main warehouse was still where most of the inventory was held, maintained, and protected by a third-party warehouse provider, but SHIELD Illinois operated the satellite warehouses to facilitate the most urgent needs.

Deciding to outsource is not the end, but only a beginning. For outsourcing to be successful, SHIELD Illinois found it was necessary to forge extremely close ties with each outsourced vendor. This was essential not only to have visibility into how its business practices could impact the business's exposure to potential supply chain issues (i.e., whether the U.S.-based manufacturer was dependent on, or actually off-shoring production to, an international plant), but also to understand issues that the vendor was facing in real time and that SHIELD Illinois might be able to resolve. The level of integration with each vendor differed depending on many factors, but at the very least the supply chain team had weekly in-depth meetings with representatives from each vendor to get updates, provide feedback, and strategically plan future needs. At one such meeting, SHIELD Illinois discovered that manufacturing of critical collection vials was being held up by the vendor's inability to source raw polypropylene. The SHIELD Illinois team was able to work through their individual personal networks to find someone who could source the necessary materials. This process repeated itself multiple times, with SHIELD Illinois sourcing everything from staffing to complete industrial HVAC units, to enable the vendors to keep the projects running on time and on budget. Its close relationships with the vendors allowed SHIELD Illinois to understand the problems they were facing and help them to fix those issues before they derailed the operation.

5 Summary

SHIELD Illinois can by no means claim victory in every supply chain battle it fought. Early on, the attempt to find alternatives to PPE needed for the lab led SHIELD Illinois to purchase a large quantity of rubber gowns. As one can imagine, rubber gowns are in no way comfortable, cause massive amounts of sweating, and were deemed unacceptable by the lab team. A decision to place an order for three million vials with a turnaround time of 6–9 months backfired when the supply chain suddenly freed up and the vials were delivered 1 month after the order was placed. SHIELD Illinois was wrong about a lot of things. It thought it would not run the collection sites and labs, but eventually wound up doing just that. It estimated it would have 50 testing sites, but ended up with more than 1700. It estimated it would do 1.5 million tests in 6 months, but performed 4 million. Finally, SHIELD Illinois thought this program might last 6 months, but it is now past the second year.

Acknowledgment We would like to thank the entire SHIELD Illinois team for their hard work and dedication in the face of incredible odds and our families for their support through the long nights and missed weekends—especially, my operations partner, Rhiannon Clifton, my wife, Katie, and my children, Betty and Lucy.

References

American Board. (2015, July 1). 11 facts about the history of education in America. Retrieved November 18, 2022, from https://www.americanboard.org/blog/11-facts-about-the-history-of-education-in-america/#:~:text=By%201918%2C%20every%20state%20required,became%20widespread%20by%20the%201930s.

Ballotpedia. (2022, November 19). Public education in Illinois. https://ballotpedia.org/Public_education_in_Illinois.

Butler, R. (2022, January 12). The story behind the race to test for COVID-19 at the University of Illinois. *CU-CitizenAccess*. Retrieved November 22, 2022, from https://cu-citizenaccess.org/2022/01/the-race-to-test-for-covid-19-at-the-university-of-illinois/.

Centers for Disease Control and Prevention. (2022, November 17). United States COVID-19 cases, deaths, and laboratory testing (NAATs) by state, territory, and jurisdiction. https://covid.cdc.gov/covid-data-tracker/#cases_totaltests.

Chang, K. (2021, August 22). Good, but not great: Taking stock of a Big Ten university's Covid plan. *The New York Times*. Retrieved November 22, 2022, from https://www.nytimes.com/2021/08/22/health/university-illinois-covid.html.

Fisher, M. (2020, April 7). Flushing out the true cause of the global toilet paper shortage amid coronavirus pandemic. *The Washington Post*. Retrieved November 22, 2022, from https://www.washingtonpost.com/national/coronavirus-toilet-paper-shortage-panic/2020/04/07/1fd30e92-75b5-11ea-87da-77a8136c1a6d_story.html.

Industry Insights. (2020, February 11). We've always done it this way. Retrieved November 22, 2022, from https://www.audienceview.com/library/weve-always-done-it-this-way/#:~:text=But%20I%20did%20recently%20stumble,United%20States%20Navy%20rear%20admiral.

Jaekel, B. (2020). COVID-19 pressures the supply chain to rethink outsourcing. *Supply and Demand Chain Executive*. Retrieved November 11, 2022, from https://www.sdcexec.com/warehousing/article/21139180/covid19-pressures-the-supply-chain-to-rethink-outsourcing.

Markel, H. (2020, July 13). Analysis: Why some schools stayed open during the 1918 flu pandemic. Retrieved November 18, 2022, from https://www.pbs.org/newshour/health/analysis-why-some-schools-stayed-open-during-the-1918-flu-pandemic.

McGee, K. (2020, August 4). University of Illinois to require twice weekly COVID-19 testing in Urbana–Champaign. *NPR-WBEZ*. Retrieved November 11, 2022, from https://www.npr.org/local/309/2020/08/04/898935688/university-of-illinois-to-require-twice-weekly-c-o-v-i-d-19-testing-in-urbana-champaign.

Peplow, M. (2020, November 1). How one university built a COVID-19 screening system. *Chemical and Engineering News*. Retrieved November 22, 2022, from https://cen.acs.org/biological-chemistry/infectious-disease/one-university-built-COVID-19/98/i42.

Ranoa, D. R. E., Holland, R. L., Alnaji, F. G., Green, K. J., Wang, L., Fredrickson, R. L., Wang, T., Wong, G. N., Uelmen, J., Maslov, S., Weiner, Z. J., Tkachenko, A. V., Zhang, H., Liu, Z., Ibrahim, A., Patel, S. J., Paul, J. M., Vance, N. P., Gulick, J. G., … Burke, M. D. (2022). Mitigation of SARS-CoV-2 transmission at a large public university. *Nature Communication, 13*(1), 3207. https://doi.org/10.1038/s41467-022-30833-3.

Schultz, E. J. (2020, April 7). How Malort got into the hand-sanitizer business. *Crain's Chicago Business*. Retrieved November 22, 2022, from https://www.chicagobusiness.com/consumer-products/how-malort-got-hand-sanitizer-business?adobe_mc=MCMID%3D16581457172023975429202802999535104058%7CMCORGID%3D138FFF2554E6E7220A4C98C6%2540AdobeOrg%7CTS%3D1669136424&CSAuthResp=1%3A%3A951914%3A359%3A24%3Asucc.

University of Illinois. (2022, November 22). covidSHIELD. https://www.uillinois.edu/covidshield

U.S. Food and Drug Administration. (2022). Accelerated Emergency Use Authorization (EUA) summary: covidSHIELD assay (University of Illinois, Office of the Vice President for Economic Development and Innovation) for in vitro diagnostic use Rx only For use under Emergency Use Authorization (EUA) only. Retrieved November 22, 2022, from https://www.fda.gov/media/146317/download.

The Role of Technologies in Supply Chain Efficiency and Resiliency

Mehmet Eren Ahsen and Mohammad Moshref-Javadi

1 Introduction

Even before the onset of the COVID-19 pandemic, transformative technologies such as artificial intelligence (AI), blockchain, and robotics were increasingly being adopted in supply chains. Numerous enterprises explored the potential advantages of these technologies and invested in them to enhance their supply chain operations and achieve a competitive advantage. For example, a survey conducted by McKinsey in 2019 found that 58% of the companies surveyed reported having implemented AI in at least one of their functions (Balakrishnan et al., 2020). According to a 2018 survey by PWC, 84% of the 600 supply chain executives surveyed said that they were working on a blockchain-related project, and a quarter of those executives reported a blockchain implementation pilot in progress (10%) or fully live (15%) (PwC, 2018). The pandemic further emphasized the important role of technology in global supply chains and further increased the adoption of various technologies in the supply chain industry. With lockdowns and travel restrictions in place, businesses had to rapidly adjust their supply chain strategies to maintain continuity,

Mohammad Moshref-Javadi contributed equally with all other contributors.

M. E. Ahsen (✉)
Department of Business Administration, Gies College of Business, University of Illinois at Urbana-Champaign, Champaign, IL, USA

Department of Biomedical and Translational Sciences, Carle Illinois School of Medicine, University of Illinois at Urbana-Champaign, Urbana, IL, USA
e-mail: ahsen@illinois.edu

M. Moshref-Javadi
Department of Business Administration, Gies College of Business, University of Illinois at Urbana-Champaign, Champaign, IL, USA

M. Moshref-Javadi, S. Seshadri (eds.), *Impacts of COVID-19 on Supply Chains*, Springer Business Cases, https://doi.org/10.1007/978-3-031-47734-8_5

mitigate risks, and adapt to new market conditions. According to the findings of the 2023 MHI Annual Industry Report, a significant 74% of supply chain leaders are boosting their investments in supply chain technology and innovation (MHI, 2023). Moreover, 90% of these leaders plan to allocate more than $1 million, marking a notable 24% increase compared to the previous year (MHI, 2023). Additionally, 36% of respondents are planning to spend over $10 million, which reflects a substantial 19% increase compared to previous findings (MHI, 2023).

The primary focus of this chapter is to highlight the potential advantages and actual benefits observed during the pandemic of the following cutting-edge technologies: AI, blockchain, augmented reality, autonomous driving and drones, robotics, digital twin, and advanced planning and scheduling. We will briefly explain each individual technology and its potential uses in supply chain management, followed by examples of various companies' uses of these technologies to cope with the COVID-19 pandemic.

AI and machine learning have shown great promise in optimizing supply chain planning and forecasting. AI technologies such as predictive analytics, machine learning, and natural language processing became essential for businesses to gain insights into customer demand, optimize inventory, and enhance supply chain visibility. By analyzing historical data and identifying patterns and trends, machine learning technologies can help businesses make more accurate predictions about demand, optimize inventory levels, and streamline their supply chain operations. According to a 2022 PWC survey, 52% percent of companies accelerated their AI adoption plans because of the COVID-19 crisis and 86%, say that AI is becoming a "mainstream technology" at their company in 2021 (PwC, 2021).

Blockchain technology initially gained tremendous traction in the financial sector, and it is now recognized as having significant potential in supply chain management (SCM) as well. The distributed and transparent nature of blockchain can offer several benefits to the supply chain. With its inherent features, blockchain has the potential to enhance transparency, traceability, security, and efficiency across the supply chain ecosystem. By creating an immutable ledger of transactions, blockchain can help to ensure that transactions are transparent, secure, and efficient. This technology provides a decentralized and tamper-proof platform that enables all parties involved in the supply chain to track the movement of goods and exchange information securely and transparently. For example, in the food industry, blockchain can be used to track the origin of food products from the farm to the table and provide consumers with information about the quality, safety, and environmental impact of the food they are consuming. According to a report by MarketsandMarkets, the global blockchain in the supply chain market is projected to reach $3.31 billion by 2026, at a CAGR of 87.0% during the forecast period of 2021–2026 (MarketsandMarkets, 2023).

Augmented reality (AR) can be used in supply chain management to improve efficiency and accuracy in various ways. By overlaying digital information on real-world objects, AR can help to provide real-time updates on the location and status of products, enabling businesses to better monitor and manage inventory. AR can also be used to facilitate remote collaboration and training. For instance, workers in different locations can use AR to communicate and collaborate on tasks, reducing the need for physical travel and improving operational efficiency. This proved to be extremely useful when social distancing measures were put in place during the pandemic. Additionally, augmented reality can be used for quality control and inspection, enabling workers to identify defects and errors in real time and make corrections promptly. A survey conducted by DHL in 2019 revealed that 23% of logistics companies surveyed were already using augmented reality or virtual reality technologies, and 29% were planning to adopt these technologies in the next 3 years (DHL, 2022).

Drones and robotics have also become increasingly popular in supply chain management, particularly for making last-mile deliveries. Drones and robots can help businesses overcome some of the logistical and operational challenges they face. For instance, drones can be used for contactless delivery, allowing businesses to maintain social distancing while fulfilling customer orders. Robotics can be used to automate tasks that require close human interaction, such as packing and sorting. One of the main advantages of drone and robot usage is that they can operate continuously without breaks, reducing reliance on human labor and helping businesses maintain the required level of productivity. Using these technologies can help businesses respond more quickly and efficiently to changes in demand, thereby improving customer satisfaction and loyalty.

Autonomous driving has shown great promise in improving the efficiency and safety of logistics operations. By reducing the need for human drivers, businesses can potentially reduce costs and improve delivery times. According to a 2018 report by McKinsey, autonomous vehicles have the potential to reduce transportation costs by up to 45%, as they can operate 24/7 without rest breaks and optimize routes for fuel efficiency, leading to potential cost savings in supply chain transportation (Chottani et al., 2018).

Finally, digital twin technology and advanced planning and scheduling (APS) can be used to create digital replicas of physical assets and simulate supply chain scenarios in real time. This has helped businesses to optimize their operations and improve decision-making, even in the face of unprecedented disruptions like those caused by the pandemic. In January 2020, the market for digital twins was valued at $3.8 billion, and it is projected that the market will reach a value of $35.8 billion by 2025 (Deloitte, 2020a).

The rest of this chapter is organized as follows. In Sect. 2, we will briefly describe a framework for how SCM will transform in the post-pandemic world. In Sect. 3 we will first briefly talk about the importance and potential of digitization of supply chain, which enables the adaption of most of the technologies we will discuss. Then we will discuss each technology in its subsection, where we delve into its features and explore relevant use cases by companies. We conclude the chapter in Sect. 4 by discussing some challenges facing technology adoption in supply chain management and some future research directions.

2 Digitization of Supply Chain

Digitization of supply chains refers to the process of using digital technologies to streamline and optimize supply chain management which involves digitizing supply chain processes and operations using technologies such as cloud computing, and AI. Digitization of supply chains is transforming the way that companies manage their supply chains, enabling them to become more efficient, agile, and responsive to customer needs. The 2023 Digital Trends in Supply Chain Survey revealed that a significant majority of respondents, at 86%, believe that supply chain resilience is achievable through digitization and technology (PwC, 2023). In response to this, these respondents plan to invest more in technology to improve their ability to identify, track, and measure supply chain risk. Among others, digitization of the supply chain involves the following processes (Aamer et al., 2023):

- Data collection and analysis: Digital technologies such as Internet of Things (IoT) sensors and RFID tags can collect real-time data on the location, condition, and status of goods as they move through the supply chain. This data can be analyzed using AI to identify patterns and trends that can help optimize supply chain operations.
- Automation: Digitization of supply chains involves automating repetitive and manual supply chain processes such as order processing, inventory management, and invoicing. This can help reduce errors, save time and money, and free up resources for more value-added activities. As we discuss in the next section, NLP and AI can chime in for this purpose.
- Collaboration and communication: Digital platforms can facilitate collaboration and communication between suppliers, manufacturers, and customers, enabling real-time sharing of information and improving supply chain visibility.
- Supply chain visibility: Digitization of supply chains enables real-time tracking of inventory and shipments, providing greater visibility and transparency across the supply chain. This can help companies identify potential disruptions and respond quickly to minimize their impact.

The most important spillover effect of the digitization of supply chains is the creation of vast amounts of data that can be leveraged by various technologies (DDC FPO, 2023). This data can be analyzed to identify patterns and trends, enabling companies to optimize their supply chain processes and improve overall efficiency. Furthermore, this data can be used to feed advanced technologies such as AI and ML, enabling more accurate demand forecasting, better inventory management, and improved supply chain risk management. Additionally, the data generated by digitization can be used to improve collaboration and communication between supply chain partners, leading to enhanced visibility and coordination across the supply chain.

One of the key enablers of data collection in the digitization of supply chains is the use of IoT sensors. IoT sensors and devices can be used to gather real-time data on a variety of aspects of the supply chain, including inventory levels, shipment status, and environmental conditions. Some example uses of IoT in supply chain are:

- Inventory management: IoT sensors can be used to track inventory levels in real-time, providing insights into stock levels, expiration dates, and other important data points. This can help companies optimize their inventory management processes, reduce the risk of stockouts, and improve overall efficiency.
- Asset tracking: IoT devices can be attached to vehicles, containers, and other assets, providing real-time visibility into their location and condition. This can help companies track the movement of goods throughout the supply chain, identify potential delays or disruptions, and optimize their transportation processes.
- Condition monitoring: IoT sensors can be used to monitor the condition of products during transportation, tracking temperature, humidity, and other environmental factors. This can help companies identify potential issues with product quality and take corrective action before products are delivered to customers.
- Supply chain visibility: By collecting real-time data from IoT sensors and devices, companies can gain greater visibility into their supply chain operations, enabling them to identify inefficiencies, optimize processes, and improve overall performance.

Digitization of supply chains involves the use of technologies that we will discuss in the next section. For example, blockchain technology plays a significant role in digitizing supply chains. Blockchain is a distributed ledger technology that allows data to be securely and transparently stored and shared among different parties in the supply chain network. By digitizing supply chains, companies create vast amounts of data that can be used by some of the technologies that will be described in the next section. For example, AI can use be used to analyze historical sales data, market trends, and other factors to forecast future demand for products. This helps companies optimize inventory levels and reduce the risk of stockouts or overstocking.

Although digitization of the supply chain is essential and promises numerous benefits, several challenges must be overcome to utilize its benefits to the fullest. According to a PWC survey, the lack of digital skills among employees (80%) and the availability of data and digital tools (73%) were the most commonly cited challenges to integrating Environmental, Social, and Governance (ESG) into company supply chains (PwC, 2023). Another challenge is the cost of incorporating digital technologies, which can be a huge barrier for small and medium-sized businesses that may not have the resources to invest in new infrastructure or software.

3 Use of Technologies in Mitigating the Effects of COVID-19

In this section, we describe various technologies along with real examples of how they can help with supply chain efficiency and resiliency.

3.1 *Artificial Intelligence*

Artificial intelligence can enhance supply chain operations by gathering and analyzing data from various sources to provide thorough insights into processes and operations. AI-driven supply chain solutions utilize predictive analytics and big data analysis to forecast risks and demand, providing recommendations and actions for various business functions.

Machine learning (ML), as a subset of AI, enables the identification of patterns in supply chain data and the discovery of key factors while continuously learning and improving. This capability allows supply chain managers to respond promptly with the most effective workflows and operational strategies. Several companies use AI to enhance supply chain efficiency. For example, C3 AI is a provider of Enterprise AI software, helping organizations to speed up their digital transformation (Kennedy, 2022). C3 AI's Inventory Optimization enables manufacturers to actively monitor their inventory levels in real-time, encompassing purchased parts, components, and finished goods. It leverages data from production orders, purchase orders, and supplier deliveries to continuously learn and generate stocking recommendations and other insights.

During the pandemic, Amazon encountered several obstacles in its supply chain, including high demand for essential products, logistical disruptions, and a constrained workforce. Therefore, the company needed to enhance its inventory management, expedite deliveries, and reduce expenses to fulfill customers' expectations. To tackle these challenges, Amazon utilized AI and ML algorithms to study customer behavior, predict demand, and optimize its logistics network for faster deliveries and lower costs. Amazon integrated various automation technologies, such as robots and drones, to enhance its warehouse and delivery operations. Using AI and ML, Amazon achieved notable improvements in its supply chain performance and customer experience during the pandemic. Forbes reports that Amazon's adoption of these technologies resulted in a 24% reduction in inventory carrying costs and a 35% reduction in out-of-stock items. Furthermore, the company achieved a 40% reduction in delivery time and a 5–15% improvement in overall productivity (IBM, 2022a).

Walmart faced two major challenges in managing its supply chain during the pandemic. First, it was difficult for the company to meet the evolving needs of customers and maintain sufficient stock levels. Second, with the closure of physical stores, there was a surge in online sales, which put pressure on its supply chain, causing delayed deliveries and out-of-stock items. In the early stages of the pandemic, Walmart experienced high demand for essential items such as face masks and hand sanitizer, resulting in stock shortages in some of its stores (Palmer, 2022). To address the supply chain challenges posed by the pandemic, Walmart implemented AI and ML technologies to monitor inventory levels, anticipate demand, and enhance supply chain operations. By using predictive analytics, Walmart was able to predict demand for essential items and restock them accordingly. For instance, the company used ML algorithms to analyze past sales data, social media trends, and other external factors to forecast demand for face masks and hand sanitizers (Silverstien, 2020). Walmart experienced a 10% increase in online sales and a 15% reduction in out-of-stock items during the pandemic, which allowed them to maintain adequate inventory levels and meet the changing needs of consumers through the use of predictive analytics and inventory optimization tools (ProjectPro, 2023). Furthermore, the deployment of chatbots and virtual assistants driven by AI led to a 10% decrease in customer inquiries and a 30% increase in customer satisfaction (Statista, 2020).

Throughout the pandemic, Johnson & Johnson encountered numerous obstacles in their supply chain, including disruptions in the supply of raw materials, transportation, and logistics. Moreover, the company had to contend with a shortage of essential medical items such as masks and gloves, leading to delays in deliveries. The organization also faced challenges with medication research and clinical trials, resulting in prolonged development time and increased expenses due to complicated processes. To tackle these issues, Johnson & Johnson used AI and ML to streamline their medication development and supply chain management procedures. The drug discovery process was also accelerated by AI and ML, which helped to identify potential drug candidates and screen them for safety and efficacy. ML was employed to optimize clinical trials, allowing for more effective study design, including the identification of acceptable objectives, eligible patient demographics, and more efficient research methods. The utilization of AI and ML technologies allowed Johnson & Johnson to make substantial improvements to their medication research and supply chain processes. By integrating AI and ML into drug discovery and clinical trials, the company was able to decrease development time by 30% and reduce expenses by 50% (IBM, 2022b). Furthermore, Johnson & Johnson experienced a 25% increase in supply chain productivity and a 15% decrease in inventory storage costs. Analysis time was also reduced by 35%, which contributed to further operational efficiencies (Phipps & Rusin, 2021).

Pfizer encountered a notable hurdle in the prompt and efficient development of a COVID-19 vaccine. Furthermore, the company had to ensure the effective management of its supply chain to meet the surge in demand for its products. Pfizer's manufacturing plants and distribution channels were running at maximum capacity, and any supply chain inefficiencies or delays could result in product shortages or delivery delays, adversely affecting public health. To expedite the development of COVID-19 vaccines, Pfizer leveraged AI and ML to analyze a vast pool of potential vaccine ingredients and identify the most viable ones. In addition, AI and ML were applied to enhance supply chain management, encompassing demand forecasting, inventory optimization, and logistics management. The integration of chatbots and virtual assistants powered by AI enabled Pfizer to provide precise information about their products to customers and handle their inquiries. By utilizing these technologies, Pfizer accelerated vaccine development and efficiently managed its supply chain, guaranteeing a timely and sufficient supply of critical drugs and vaccines during the pandemic. As reported by Fortune, Pfizer utilized AI and ML to examine thousands of potential vaccine ingredients, resulting in the development of a highly effective COVID-19 vaccine (Sharma et al., 2022). Pfizer's AI and ML-powered supply chain management was also successful, resulting in a 20% reduction in manufacturing time and a 30% decrease in supply chain expenses (Pfizer, 2021).

The pandemic created unprecedented demand for vaccines worldwide, and companies such as Moderna faced supply chain challenges such as raw material shortages, transportation delays, and logistical complexities in ensuring timely and equitable distribution of the vaccine doses. The vaccine development process also required rigorous clinical trials and regulatory approvals, which were time-consuming and expensive. Moderna used AI and ML to enhance its production and distribution processes and speed up the development of its mRNA-based COVID-19 vaccine. The company also implemented AI-powered chatbots to help clients with their inquiries and provide accurate information about its products. Specifically, Moderna utilized AI and ML to address these challenges by automating and optimizing several aspects of its supply chain such as demand forecasting, inventory management, and distribution planning. It also employed AI algorithms to speed up the vaccine development process by analyzing vast amounts of data to identify the most promising mRNA sequences for the vaccine. For instance, the company used an AI platform developed by Google Cloud to analyze data from over 60,000 COVID-19 cases and identify the best mRNA sequences for the vaccine (Afeyan, 2022). According to a report by Supply and Demand Chain Executive, the company reduced the manufacturing time of its COVID-19 vaccine by 30% by using AI and automation in its production process (Earl, 2021). The vaccine also received emergency use authorization from the FDA just 11 months after the pandemic's outbreak, which is record time for vaccine development. The company's AI-powered chatbots also improved customer engagement and reduced response times, leading to increased customer satisfaction.

3.2 *Blockchain*

Blockchain is a distributed ledger technology that enables the recording of transactions in a tamper-proof and verifiable way among multiple parties. In the supply chain, blockchain has the potential to increase trust, transparency, efficiency, security, and sustainability. Innovations driven by blockchain technology in the supply chain have the potential to provide substantial business value by enhancing transparency, mitigating risk, and optimizing efficiency and overall supply chain management (Deloitte, 2020b). The utilization of blockchain technology in supply chains can enhance communication and collaboration among all parties involved. By sharing databases among multiple parties, blockchain can eliminate the requirement for intermediaries to authenticate, document, or arrange these transactions, as stated in a report by shipping and logistics company DHL (Glover, 2022).

As a result of the COVID-19 outbreak, Walmart's supply chain faced significant difficulties, including transportation issues, a labor shortage, and abnormally high demand for products such as food and household essentials (Akilo, 2018). The lack of real-time visibility into inventory and shipment monitoring made it difficult for the business to respond quickly to changing consumer requirements and supply chain disruptions (Shetty, 2021). To solve these challenges, Walmart collaborated with IBM to create the IBM Food Trust, a supply chain solution based on blockchain technology. With the aid of this technology, Walmart and its suppliers can track the origin, quality, and safety of food products in real-time, providing customers with greater confidence and transparency about the products they purchase. The implementation of blockchain technology has resulted in several benefits for the supply chain, including increased efficiency, reduced risk of fraud, and enhanced product visibility and tracking. During the pandemic, Walmart was able to rapidly adapt to the changing needs of its customers by leveraging the capabilities of blockchain technology to enhance the transparency and efficiency of its supply chain (Shetty, 2021). The implementation of the IBM Food Trust platform has had a substantial impact on Walmart's supply chain management, enabling the corporation to attain higher levels of transparency and traceability in its food supply chain. According to a World Economic Forum report, Walmart utilized the blockchain-based network to decrease the time required to trace the origin of a food item from 7 days to a mere 2.2 s (Glover, 2022). Additionally, the platform has helped Walmart to promptly detect and address potential food safety concerns, decreasing the risk of foodborne illnesses and elevating consumer trust in the quality of the brand's products.

Schneider Electric encountered supply chain challenges during the pandemic such as restricted access to labor, interruptions in global logistics, and scarcities of raw materials and components. In response, the company has allocated more than $100 million to enhance the resilience of its regional supply chains and has added 100 new suppliers (MarketScreener, 2021; SE-News, 2021). Although there is no indication that Schneider Electric implemented blockchain technology to overcome pandemic-related supply chain issues, the corporation has employed digitization to create an expanded supply chain that facilitates transparency and traceability (Tricoire, 2020). The integration has fostered cooperation and trust between manufacturers and suppliers, eradicating barriers and boosting circularity (Yeeles, 2020). Schneider Electric has been recognized for its supply chain excellence, ranking #4 in Gartner's 2020 Global Supply Chain Top 25 companies, and #1 in Europe's Top 15 companies. In addition, Schneider Electric was named the winner of the 2022 Supply Chain Award for Process or Technology Innovation, thanks to its self-healing supply chain platform driven by adaptive machine learning, which saved over 100 million EUR (Gartner, 2022).

UPS experienced supply chain problems as a result of border restrictions, quarantine regulations, and a lack of labor. Due to these interruptions, deliveries were delayed, there were stockouts, and logistics expenses increased. UPS turned to blockchain technology as a solution to address the supply chain challenges caused by the pandemic. To promote supply chain transparency across all industries, UPS joined the Blockchain in Trucking Alliance (BiTA) in November 2018. In collaboration with other logistics firms and technology providers within BiTA, UPS developed the Trucker Connect blockchain-based network. The Trucker Connect platform is a peer-to-peer network that enables shippers, carriers, and brokers to communicate and transact directly, without intermediaries, improving supply chain transparency (Sharma, 2020). In addition to Trucker Connect, UPS also employs blockchain-based solutions for its customs brokerage business, allowing clients to manage their customs clearance obligations more effectively and transparently. Through this technology, UPS was able to expedite customs clearance, reduce costs, and improve supply chain visibility and communication. During the outbreak, UPS's supply chain operations were significantly impacted by their implementation of blockchain technology. UPS was able to decrease the need for middlemen and boost transparency by using Trucker Connect, which led to cost savings and quicker delivery times.

One of the supply chain problems that IBM faced during the pandemic was the lack of transparency and visibility in the supply chain. With disruptions in global supply chains due to the pandemic, it became difficult to track the movement of goods and ensure their safety. This led to supply-demand imbalances, delays in delivery, and increased costs for businesses. IBM addressed these challenges by utilizing its blockchain-based platform, TradeLens. The platform was designed to provide complete visibility and transparency throughout the supply chain by utilizing blockchain technology. TradeLens is a global supply chain management platform that offers real-time information on the movement of goods, including their location, status, and condition, to supply chain stakeholders such as shippers, freight forwarders, and customs officials. This provides companies with better insights to forecast demand, manage their supply chains, and respond to disruptions in a timely manner (IBM, 2023a). The utilization of blockchain technology by IBM resulted in up to 25% savings on supply chain costs for companies (IBM, 2023a). Moreover, it increased supply chain efficiency by reducing paperwork and manual processes, resulting in faster and more accurate transaction processing. According to a recent IBM news release, the TradeLens platform has processed over 30 million shipping events and onboarded more than 200 users since its inception in 2018 (Akilo, 2018), the TradeLens platform has processed over 30 million shipping events and onboarded more than 200 users since its inception in 2018.

Maersk faced a significant challenge in managing its supply chain during the COVID-19 pandemic. Global supply chains were severely disrupted by the pandemic, with shipments delayed or canceled and supply chains collapsing. Because of the pandemic, there was a sharp fall in demand for commodities, which resulted in lower freight rates and lower firm profitability (Naidu & Halpin, 2022). Maersk integrated TradeLens, a blockchain-based platform developed in collaboration with IBM, to manage its supply chain. The platform provides end-to-end visibility and transparency by utilizing blockchain technology. It digitalizes all supply chain processes, including customs clearance, paperwork, and container tracking, enabling Maersk to function more efficiently and reduce expenses. Additionally, the platform aids in the rapid identification and resolution of supply chain issues, reducing downtime and costs (IBM, 2023b). Maersk was able to respond quickly to supply chain challenges during the pandemic with TradeLens, which provided real-time visibility into the movement of goods. The platform also helped the company reduce manual tasks, minimizing the risk of errors and delays. With TradeLens, Maersk had access to a unified source of truth for its supply chain data, allowing for more informed decision-making and streamlined operations. By providing real-time visibility into the movement of goods, the platform has also helped Maersk enhance its customer service. According to a study by the World Economic Forum, TradeLens has enabled Maersk to reduce the time required for processing import and export documentation by up to 40%, and the time required for customs clearance by up to 50% (Maersk, 2021).

Coca-Cola's supply chain was disrupted by manufacturing plant closures and logistical issues. In several markets, the corporation encountered a shortage of raw materials, packaging materials, and completed goods. To enhance the visibility and resilience of their supply chain, Coca-Cola adopted blockchain technology. To keep track of their bottling supply chain, the company partnered with SAP to establish a digital ledger based on blockchain. By providing real-time data on the supply chain, the software enables Coca-Cola to monitor inventory levels, identify bottlenecks, and improve logistics. The technology allows the company to verify the authenticity and origin of raw materials, guaranteeing ethical and sustainable supply. The adoption of blockchain technology by Coca-Cola has had a significant impact on the company. The technology has enabled greater transparency, traceability, and efficiency in its supply chain operations. Coca-Cola has been able to reduce the time required to reconcile its supply chain data by 50%, leading to faster decision-making and increased collaboration with suppliers, according to a report by Business Insider (Business-Insider, 2019). By eliminating unnecessary processes and improving inventory management, the technology has helped Coca-Cola streamline its operations and reduce costs.

3.3 *Augmented and Virtual Reality Technology*

Augmented reality (AR) is a technology that overlays digital information on top of the real-world environment, enhancing the user's experience of reality. It is often achieved through a mobile device, smart glasses, or a head-mounted display that uses sensors and cameras to capture and display digital information.

Nestlé encountered challenges in its supply chain and experienced supply-demand imbalances during the pandemic. The restrictions on travel made it difficult for Nestlé to provide on-site support to its production and research and development (RD) sites as well as connect with suppliers (Nestle, 2020). The pandemic caused a surge in demand for specific products, exacerbating the existing supply-demand imbalances (Sweeney, 2022). Nestlé used AR technology to provide remote support to its production and RD sites and connect with suppliers (Meenu, 2021). The company used smart glasses, 360-degree cameras, and 3D software to assist complex projects in its worldwide branches. AR helped in increasing efficiency, as smart glasses allowed workers to take a heads-up approach to their tasks, and information required to do their jobs was readily available (ASCM, 2018). AR also helped in reducing travel and related costs, as remote support was provided. AR helped Nestlé cut down on travel and its associated expenses (Nestle, 2020). Nestlé has committed an investment of $2 billion to fast-track its sustainable packaging program with the aim of reducing the use of virgin plastics by one-third before 2025 (Procureconeast, 2021).

One of the key challenges Warby Parker faced was the need to improve their supply chain management to meet customer demand. The company needed to ensure that they had the right inventory at the right time to fulfill orders, maintaining high levels of control within their supply chain to ensure the highest quality at the fastest speed (Plex DemandCaster, 2014). The pandemic created new challenges for the company, as it needed to adapt to changing customer behavior and supply chain disruptions. Warby Parker implemented AR technology to address supply chain challenges and fulfill customer demand. The company introduced an AR feature on its app that enables customers to virtually try on frames using computer-generated images projected onto real-world imagery (Holley, 2019). This initiative led to a decrease in the number of returns resulting from poorly fitting frames, reducing waste and improving inventory management (Marr, 2019a). The AR feature provided customers with a distinctive and customized shopping experience, which boosted sales and enhanced customer satisfaction (Marr, 2019b). The company also leveraged AI to personalize product recommendations, thereby enhancing the overall shopping experience. AR and personalized recommendations had a positive impact on Warby Parker's sales and revenue. In 2021, the company reported a 23% increase in revenue, with online sales up 36% and in-store sales up 4% (Warby-Parker, 2022). The company's online sales were particularly strong during the pandemic, as more customers shifted to online shopping. AR also helped to reduce the number of returns, which helped to reduce costs and increase profitability (Marr, 2019b).

L'Oréal was facing significant operational impacts due to e-commerce and changing order profiles, as the volume of orders had increased but the lines per order had decreased (Rahn, 2017). This posed a challenge for L'Oréal's supply chain management and logistics, which had to process a large volume of orders in a short amount of time. L'Oréal used AR to improve its e-commerce operations and supply chain management. By leveraging this technology, L'Oréal was able to provide customers with virtual try-on experiences for its products, which helped to increase customer engagement and drive sales. L'Oréal also implemented smart factories and agile production lines that enabled them to process dozens of different product formats in a very short amount of time. L'Oréal experienced a significant surge in online sales, which can be attributed to the effective use of AR, live-streaming services, and cloud software. The demand for augmented reality technology is expected to continue to rise in the coming years, partially due to increased adoption by certain sectors (Castellanos, 2021; CIO, 2021). In collaboration with Perfect Corp., L'Oréal launched a global partnership aimed at integrating the company's makeup products into the YouCam Makeup augmented reality app. Through this partnership, millions of beauty enthusiasts can virtually test L'Oréal products, explore new items, and purchase them directly through the app or in physical stores (L'Oreal, 2021).

3.4 Drone and Robotics Technology

Drone technology has been gaining popularity in recent years and is being utilized in various industries, including logistics and supply chain management. Drones have the potential to revolutionize the way supply chains operate by providing efficient and reliable delivery options, enhancing inventory management, and increasing overall supply chain visibility.

The combination of the COVID-19 pandemic and worsening climate change has strained supply chains past their breaking point, leading to unprecedented disruptions, delays, and shortages (Fu, 2021). Moreover, supply and demand imbalances created significant issues for companies. For instance, during the Covid-19 pandemic, there was an unforeseen surge in demand for products like toilet paper and cleaning supplies, which led to widespread shortages (AWS, 2021). Amazon has been exploring the use of drone technology to improve its supply chain operations and address supply and demand issues. For example, Amazon has implemented drone-based logistics networks to increase supply chain resiliency and efficiency (Fu, 2021). Additionally, Amazon has been using AI-driven predictive forecasting to respond quickly to unforeseen demand signals and increase production, which can help to prevent supply chain disruptions and shortages (Forbes, 2021). The utilization of drone technology in Amazon's supply chain operations can have a significant positive effect by improving efficiency and lowering costs through faster delivery times and reducing reliance on conventional delivery methods (Sweeney, 2022). Moreover, the implementation of predictive forecasting has allowed Amazon to optimize inventory management, resulting in cost savings and revenue growth (Riaz, 2021).

Zipline International, Inc. is a for-profit California-based startup that used the world's first commercial drone delivery service in partnership with the Government of Rwanda in October 2016. The company revolutionized the delivery of medical supplies to the last mile, starting with routine and emergency deliveries of blood in Rwanda, while adding value to multiple layers of the country's health supply chain (Doe, 2017). The COVID-19 pandemic and worsening climate change result in significant supply chain disruptions and inefficiencies. Chaos and confusion have become the order of the day, with global supply chains struggling to keep pace with the sudden changes in demand and disruptions in transportation networks (Goel, 2021a). Zipline's drone technology helped solve supply chain issues by providing a reliable and efficient method of delivering medical supplies to remote and hard-to-reach areas. By bypassing traditional transportation networks, drones helped Zipline save money on fuel costs and reduced delivery times, resulting in improved supply chain efficiency. Drone delivery also reduced the need for physical contact between people, making it an ideal solution during the pandemic (SpendEdge, 2021). Since its inception, Zipline's drone technology has made a significant impact on the company's operations by delivering more than 1 million doses of vaccines, blood, and crucial medical supplies to over 2500 health facilities in Rwanda (Goel, 2021a). Zipline's drone delivery service has drastically reduced delivery times from several hours to mere minutes, with an average delivery time of 30 min from order placement to delivery. This service has also enhanced the reliability of medical supply deliveries, with 99.8% of Zipline's deliveries arriving at their destination on time and in full (Goel, 2021b). Additionally, during the pandemic, Zipline's drone delivery service played a crucial role in supplying essential medical supplies to remote and hard-to-reach regions while minimizing the risk of transmission (Ackerman, 2020).

Last-mile delivery has always been a problem for logistics companies. Traditional methods of delivering goods are not always efficient, especially when it comes to time and cost. For example, during the pandemic, Wing faced supply chain issues due to restrictions on movement, causing delays in the delivery of essential items such as medical supplies and groceries. Wing was able to deliver essential items such as food, medicines, and other necessities to households within minutes using drones. This technology helped Wing overcome the supply chain issues faced during the pandemic. According to a study by the University of Virginia, the delivery time using drones was 5–12 min faster than traditional delivery methods (SpendEdge, 2021). Moreover, drone delivery saves fuel costs and reduces emissions caused by traditional delivery methods, contributing to the environment's betterment. A report by Goldman Sachs stated that the global drone industry's value would reach $100 billion by 2020, indicating the potential of this technology (HBR, 2020).

During the pandemic, Unilever faced several challenges in their supply chain operations, including disruptions in transportation, production, and distribution. For example, in India, the company faced challenges in distributing its products due to the lockdown restrictions, resulting in a decrease in demand for their products. Additionally, there were issues with maintaining the availability of raw materials due to disruptions in the supply chain caused by the pandemic. To tackle the supply chain challenges brought on by the pandemic, Unilever adopted robotics and automation technology. The company employed autonomous robots to handle routine tasks such as packaging and sorting in their warehouses and distribution centers, allowing their employees to focus on more intricate tasks. Furthermore, Unilever utilized machine learning algorithms to enhance their inventory management, enabling them to respond to changes in demand more efficiently. They leveraged artificial intelligence to examine data on consumer buying behavior and adjust production and distribution accordingly (Unilever, 2022). The implementation helped the company to streamline its supply chain operations and improve its response to the pandemic. Unilever's use of AI and automation helped the company to avoid significant supply chain disruptions during the pandemic and resulted in a 10% increase in sales in Q2 2020 (Goel, 2021a). Additionally, Unilever's supply chain was recognized as one of the top 25 global supply chains by Gartner for the fourth consecutive year in 2022 (Unilever, 2022).

3.5 *Autonomous Driving Technology*

Autonomous driving technology, also known as self-driving or driverless technology, is a rapidly advancing field that involves vehicles capable of sensing their environment and operating without human input. The technology relies on a combination of sensors, cameras, and other high-tech devices to perceive, think, and act like a human driver, allowing the vehicle to make decisions and safely navigate roads. Autonomous driving technology has many potential applications in the field of supply chain management. For example, autonomous trucks could help address global supply chain challenges caused by driver shortages. With older drivers retiring and fewer young drivers entering the field, the increased use of technology could attract younger drivers to the industry. Additionally, self-driving vehicles could potentially improve safety and reduce transportation costs by eliminating the need for human drivers.

The pandemic created supply chain challenges worldwide due to lockdowns, border restrictions, and workforce disruptions. According to the International Road Transport Union, European companies were expected to face a 17% shortfall in drivers in 2021 due to driver shortages as older drivers retired and younger drivers were not attracted to the industry (Bateman, 2021). The implementation of autonomous delivery vehicles, such as those developed by Waymo Via, can offer a solution to supply chain difficulties by reducing the dependence on human drivers and enhancing efficiency. To illustrate, Waymo Via collaborated with UPS to extend their existing 2-year partnership to incorporate deliveries facilitated by Waymo's self-driving trucks in Texas. This initiative helped UPS to expand its delivery capacity and mitigate driver shortage risks, ultimately decreasing delivery expenses. Furthermore, Waymo Via joined forces with global logistics provider C.H. Robinson to explore the practical use of autonomous driving technology in trucking and local delivery, thereby minimizing delivery costs and augmenting efficiency (Robison, 2022). The partnership aims to "drive down delivery costs, reduce supply chain waste, and improve carbon emissions," indicating the potential for cost savings and environmental benefits (Robison, 2022). Additionally, Waymo Via's autonomous delivery vehicles are designed to improve efficiency and reduce costs by eliminating the need for human drivers, which could lead to significant cost savings for companies in the long term.

As a result of supply chain disruptions during the pandemic, many companies faced difficulties in meeting their customers' demands due to the reduced workforce and transportation challenges. For instance, many US retailers struggled to keep their shelves stocked with essential goods, leading to long wait times for customers. Aurora's self-driving technology can assist logistics fleets in expanding their operations to keep up with the growing demand for delivery services. The technology reduces the dependence on human drivers, allowing for uninterrupted 24/7 operation, resulting in faster and more effective delivery of goods. Additionally, autonomous trucks can transport goods between warehouses, decreasing human contact and lowering the possibility of COVID-19 transmission (Aurora-Innovation, 2023).

According to a study conducted in 2017, automated trucks could reduce the demand for drivers by as much as 50–70% in the US and Europe by 2030, with 4.4 million of the 6.4 million professional drivers affected (Hawkins, 2021). This could help address the shortage of drivers that the industry is currently facing. Additionally, autonomous trucks can operate around the clock, increasing the efficiency of the supply chain and reducing costs associated with human drivers (Aurora-Innovation, 2023).

The pandemic highlighted the need for social distancing and contactless deliveries, which can be challenging for traditional delivery methods (UNC, 2019). TuSimple's autonomous delivery vehicle technology offers a solution to the challenges faced by logistics companies during the pandemic. Their technology enables fully autonomous long-haul deliveries, reducing the need for human drivers and minimizing the risk of COVID-19 exposure. Autonomous vehicles can operate 24/7, increasing delivery capacity and reducing delivery times, which is especially critical during periods of high demand (Heilweil, 2020). For nearly 3 years, TuSimple has collaborated with UPS to expand its Autonomous Freight Network and has covered over 160,000 autonomous miles (Fuller & Stinson, 2021). Integrating autonomous vehicles into the logistics industry can reduce delivery lead times by 40% and elevate truck utilization from 29 to 78% (Burnette & Eshel, 2022). These advancements can considerably benefit the business models of logistics enterprises.

To address the driver shortage and improve delivery efficiency, DHL Supply Chain, a member of Embark's Partner Development Program, intends to integrate Embark's autonomous technology into its fleet starting in 2024 (Business-Wire-News, 2021). According to Embark Trucks, their self-driving software can lead to a 10% improvement in fuel efficiency, a 300% increase in yearly per-truck revenue, and a 40% decrease in delivery time (Business-Wire-News, 2021). Although it is still too early to fully gauge the impact of autonomous delivery vehicles, they could help alleviate global supply chain issues and the shortage of drivers. It is estimated that by 2030, autonomous trucks will make up 10% of the world's truck fleet (Bateman, 2021).

The supply chain was hampered during the COVID-19 pandemic by traffic and labor-related delays, resulting in delivery delays and an increase in transportation costs. For instance, a lack of drivers and a rise in the demand for home delivery services significantly disrupted the food industry's supply chain (Winston, 2021). By reducing labor-related and congestion delays, autonomous delivery vehicles such as self-driving trucks have helped address supply chain issues. PlusAI's self-driving trucks operated smoothly in congested shipping lanes and near the shore, mitigating the risk of accidents and enhancing delivery times. PlusAI accomplished its first Level 4 autonomous coast-to-coast delivery in under 3 days, a task that would have taken much longer with a human driver (Forde, 2019). A Deloitte analysis claims that integrating autonomous robots into the supply chain can significantly increase productivity and efficiency while lowering labor costs (Smith, 2021). An estimated $250 million in revenue was anticipated to be made from AI in 2022 (Smith, 2021).

3.6 *Digital Twin Technology*

Digital twin technology refers to a virtual model or a digital replica of a physical object or system. It involves creating a computer-based simulation of a real-world object, process, or system, which can be used to visualize, monitor, and analyze the performance of the real-world counterpart. This technology allows for the creation of a digital twin that can be used for predictive maintenance, testing, and optimization of systems or processes without affecting the actual physical object (IBM, 2023c). It also involves the use of interconnected devices and objects equipped with sensors and unique identifiers, allowing them to transmit and receive digital data. These connected devices collect data and communicate with a central system, which AI can analyze and use to make informed decisions and automate workflows and processes throughout the supply chain.

PepsiCo faced difficulties in production planning and logistics due to the pandemic's uncertainties. It was a challenge to manage production, distribution, and inventory levels in such an environment, given that the pandemic's duration and severity were unknown (PepsiCo, 2021). Digital twin technology was employed by PepsiCo to create a digital twin model of their entire supply chain to optimize operations and manage potential disruptions in the supply chain and take preventive measures to mitigate them (PepsiCo, 2021). Real-time data and insights provided by the digital twin technology enabled PepsiCo to adjust its production schedules in response to fluctuating market demands and supply chain constraints. Furthermore, it facilitated the optimization of inventory levels throughout the supply chain, thus reducing the likelihood of stockouts or overstocking. These improvements led to cost savings for PepsiCo and enhanced customer satisfaction. Finally, the digital twin model acted as a single source of truth and improved collaboration among different teams and functions involved in the supply chain, thereby streamlining communication and decision-making across the organization (Olavsrud, 2021). According to PepsiCo, the implementation of digital twin technology resulted in cost savings of more than $80 million in operational expenses, achieved through reduced inventory levels, optimized production and logistics planning, and improved collaboration across the organization (PepsiCo, 2021). In Q4 2021, PepsiCo's financial results showed a net revenue growth of 4.8% compared to the previous year, attributed to strong demand for its snacks and beverages in the US and other regions (Maloney, 2020).

GE encountered difficulties in monitoring and optimizing its supply chain assets and inventory levels, making it challenging to identify potential disruptions and take proactive measures to mitigate them. This challenge became even more pressing during the pandemic, which created supply-demand imbalances and affected the entire supply chain. The pandemic led to an unprecedented surge in demand for essential goods such as personal protective equipment (PPE) kits, ventilators, and medicines, and companies were struggling to keep up with the increased demand while ensuring the safety of their employees and maintaining their operations (Boff, 2017). GE leveraged digital twin technology to optimize their supply chain operations by monitoring and managing their assets and inventory levels. The technology involves creating a virtual replica of a physical asset that uses real-time data and advanced analytics to simulate its behavior and performance. By implementing a digital twin model of their supply chain operations, GE could monitor their assets in real time and detect potential disruptions proactively. The digital twin model also enabled GE to simulate various scenarios and optimize their operations to enhance their performance. During the pandemic, GE utilized the digital twin model to optimize the production of ventilators, resulting in a 50% increase in their production capacity (General-Electrics, 2022a). GE reported that their implementation of digital twin technology resulted in a 30% reduction in lead times and a 25% increase in productivity (General-Electrics, 2022b). Colin Parris, GE Digital's Senior Vice President and Chief Technology Officer, stated that from 2016 to 2017, GE created more than 1.2 million digital twins, which generated roughly $600 billion in value for the company and its clients (Jarrell, 2021). In addition, GE's ADMS, GIS, and AEMS technologies aided grid operators in creating a Network Digital Twin that provides a comprehensive view of the entire network of assets, based on actual operational data. This technology helped reduce costs by up to 30% (General-Electrics, 2022b).

Over 350,000 Volvo trucks have been equipped with IoT sensors that allow the Swedish automaker to monitor the trucks' condition and collect data for analysis and troubleshooting purposes. Thanks to the combination of IoT and AI, Volvo Trucks has been able to reduce diagnostic time by 70% and truck repair time by 25%, resulting in more efficient and proactive maintenance that leads to increased uptime and reduced costs associated with service interruptions (SumatoSoft, 2022).

DHL partnered with a company to create a specialized sensor that discreetly tracks roller cages within and between their facilities. The sensors were designed with low power consumption in mind and have a battery life of up to 15 years. The collected data is accessible to operators through a cloud-based management portal, allowing them to reduce losses resulting from shrinkage (SumatoSoft, 2022). Another IoT initiative implemented by DHL resulted in a 40% reduction in energy costs. The company uses a smart HVAC system that can adjust temperature settings in real-time based on predicted weather conditions, building occupancy, and business activity, all while maintaining the desired temperature range.

3.7 *Big Data Analytics and Advanced Planning and Scheduling Technology*

Advanced planning and scheduling (APS) technology is a comprehensive software solution that assists organizations in optimizing resources, managing risks, and minimizing costs in their production environments. By utilizing advanced mathematical algorithms, APS software analyzes and calculates optimal production schedules, taking into account various constraints based on business rules. In a supply chain context, APS can provide decision-making support for overtime, order prioritization, split production batches, due date negotiation, and order processing, thereby helping to resolve supply chain issues and supply-demand problems. By creating detailed production schedules, allocating resources, and monitoring progress against targets, APS enables planners to identify potential bottlenecks and manage risks. Furthermore, APS helps organizations use their capacity efficiently and reduce inventory levels by building production schedules around customer demand and supply chain constraints.

Due to factors such as the COVID-19 pandemic, natural disasters, and supply chain disruptions, Toyota has been experiencing a scarcity of vital components, including semiconductors, batteries, and other essential parts. For instance, following the 2011 earthquake in Japan, Toyota's primary plant ceased operations for 3 months, and the company anticipated that the procurement of over 1200 parts and materials would be impacted (Reuters, 2021; Shirouzu, 2021). Recently, Toyota had to reduce production and halt operations at some of its factories due to the global chip shortage and an earthquake in Japan (BBC, 2022). Toyota implemented APS to optimize its supply chain processes, enabling it to better cope with disruptions caused by the pandemic. APS helped Toyota improve its production efficiency and responsiveness to changing demand patterns by providing real-time data and analytics. During the pandemic, Toyota used APS to monitor and adjust its production schedules based on changes in consumer demand, ensuring that the right products were available at the right time (Davis, 2021) The utilization of APS technology has had a significant impact on Toyota's business, resulting in improved production efficiency and reduced costs. Toyota was able to achieve a 50% reduction in planning time, 95% accuracy in delivery dates, and a 30% decrease in inventory levels by using APS (Davis, 2021). According to a report by the Wall Street Journal, Toyota's effective supply chain management enabled it to outperform General Motors in the US for the first time (Mclain, 2021). Furthermore, Toyota's implementation of APS during the pandemic enabled the company to weather the disruptions caused by the pandemic and maintain its position as one of the largest automakers globally (Ismail, 2021).

Procter & Gamble faced supply chain issues and demand-supply imbalances during the pandemic, dealing with disruptions in transportation, shipping, and production, which led to inventory shortages, stockouts, and decreased service levels. For example, at the onset of the pandemic, the company faced a shortage of hand sanitizer due to the sudden increase in demand (Zimmerman, 2021). To address supply chain challenges and enhance demand-supply planning, Procter & Gamble employed APS, collaborating with Microsoft and Google to leverage their technology platforms and concentrate on three primary objectives: improving supply chain visibility, enhancing demand forecasting, and increasing planning agility (Barsky, 2021). The technology enabled the company to monitor real-time demand and supply data to adjust production and logistics plans quickly, use predictive analytics to forecast demand and optimize inventory levels, collaborate with suppliers, distributors, and retailers to ensure the availability of products and reduce lead times, and improve agility in responding to unexpected disruptions and changes in consumer behavior (Banker, 2019). Procter & Gamble's implementation of APS aided the company in enhancing its supply chain resilience and adapting to the challenges presented by the pandemic. The company's emphasis on demand-driven planning through digital forecasting and operations integration facilitated better sensing and responding to demand, leading to increased sales and revenue (ST, 2017). Additionally, the study emphasized the importance of a highly integrated supply chain process in achieving sustainable growth opportunities (ST, 2017). Moreover, Procter & Gamble's CEO revealed that the company's advanced supply chain capabilities had resulted in a "significant improvement" in service levels and customer satisfaction during the pandemic (Barsky, 2021).

Pfizer needed to rapidly scale up their manufacturing capabilities to meet the unprecedented demand for COVID-19 vaccines worldwide. Additionally, they needed to manage the complex logistics of distributing the vaccines globally while also ensuring the vaccines remained effective during transportation and storage. These challenges were further complicated by the urgency of the situation, as people around the world were counting on Pfizer to quickly deliver a safe and effective vaccine. Pfizer leveraged advanced planning and scheduling technology to manage its supply chain during the pandemic. This technology enabled Pfizer to optimize its production schedules and plan for future demand more precisely, mitigating potential supply shortages. Furthermore, it facilitated more efficient inventory management, guaranteeing the availability of necessary materials and supplies for vaccine production and distribution. Although it is challenging to credit Pfizer's accomplishments during the pandemic entirely to their adoption of APS, it is evident that this technology significantly aided them in surmounting the significant supply chain difficulties they confronted. As of February 2023, Pfizer has delivered more than 3.5 billion doses of their COVID-19 vaccine worldwide (Pfizer, 2023). Furthermore, Pfizer announced revenues of $22.2 billion for the first quarter of 2021, mainly driven by sales of their COVID-19 vaccine (Young, 2022).

Johnson & Johnson had to ensure that its supply chain kept running smoothly to meet the increased demand for its products, including medical devices, consumer health products, and pharmaceuticals. The company faced issues with supply and demand, and the lack of visibility in its supply chain led to delays in shipments and stockouts of essential products. Johnson & Johnson used APS to tackle supply chain issues triggered by the pandemic (Brody, 2020). The company utilized Smart Glasses equipped with remote access functionality, GPS-enabled Track-and-Trace sensors, and data crawlers to collect and index enormous amounts of data based on predefined criteria. By doing so, Johnson & Johnson gained visibility in its supply chain and monitored inventory levels, demand, and supply in real-time. Consequently, the company was able to identify bottlenecks and supply chain disruptions and react promptly. Furthermore, Johnson & Johnson employed an intelligence-based call routing system and auto-answer technology to enhance customer satisfaction (Shapiro, 2021). Johnson & Johnson's utilization of advanced technology resulted in a 6.4% increase in customer satisfaction score from 2017 to 2020, with the score rising from 85.5 to 91.9% (Shapiro, 2021). The improved customer experience was attributed to the company's implementation of advanced technology. Additionally,

Johnson & Johnson's supply chain technology efforts were recognized by industry experts in 2020, receiving accolades from Fast Company's Best Workplaces for Innovators and Interbrand's Best Global Brands for their COVID-19 response efforts (JNJ, 2023).

With an increase in demand for essential goods such as medical supplies and food, UPS also had to manage a surge in e-commerce orders as people shifted to online shopping. These challenges resulted in supply-demand imbalances, delivery delays, and a need for greater visibility and control over their supply chain (UPS, 2022). UPS implemented several advanced packaging solutions technologies to address supply chain issues during the pandemic. One of the technologies they used was the UPS My Choice for Business platform, which allowed customers to receive delivery alerts, reroute packages, and provide specific instructions for deliveries. This helped UPS manage delivery volumes and minimize contact between drivers and customers. Another technology they used was the UPS WorldShip platform, which allowed shippers to access real-time data and track shipments across their supply chain. This helped improve visibility and control over their supply chain (Blasquez, 2021). The implementation of advanced packaging solutions technologies helped UPS manage supply-demand imbalances and delivery delays and improve visibility and control over their supply chain during the pandemic. This helped them meet customer expectations and maintain business continuity. According to their Q2 2021 earnings report, UPS reported a 13% increase in revenue in their US domestic package segment, which was driven by higher demand for residential deliveries due to the pandemic (Blasquez, 2021).

John Deere encountered supply chain issues and supply-demand problems that resulted in production delays, reduced inventory levels, and increased shipping costs. The global supply chain was disrupted by the pandemic, leading to a shortage of raw materials and transportation difficulties for finished goods. To tackle the supply chain problems it faced, John Deere utilized Precision Agriculture technology and analytics. The company employed its data analysis expertise to improve its production processes and supply chain. One example of this is John Deere's use of JDLink Modems, which connected its machines and facilitated rapid data transfer. This technology enabled the company to monitor its equipment's performance and maintenance requirements remotely. Furthermore, John Deere's Intelligent Solutions Group introduced innovative technology solutions and procedures to the agriculture division's four equipment groups (Williams, 2019). John Deere was able to overcome the supply chain issues it faced during the pandemic, resulting in the company announcing record profits in November 2021 (Scrum-Inc., 2022). The technology also proved to be beneficial to farmers, as it allowed them to efficiently manage and monitor their farm operations with greater accuracy, leading to improved productivity. John Deere's innovative solutions enable its customers to make informed decisions and perform their work more efficiently and effectively through advanced technology (John-Deere, 2023).

4 Conclusions and Future Research

In this chapter, we discussed several cutting-edge technologies and their potential impacts on the optimization of supply chains. Furthermore, we illustrated the crucial and significant impact of these technologies on supply chains during times of unprecedented disruptions, such as the recent global COVID-19 pandemic. The pandemic necessitated accelerating the adoption of these technologies in SCM, but their benefits extend far beyond the pandemic response. Table 1 presents a summary of the discussed supply chain technologies and their benefits.

Although there is great potential in the use of technology in supply chains, there are still considerable challenges that need to be addressed before fully realizing the potential of technology to improve supply chain efficiency, transparency, resilience, and sustainability. One of the key challenges facing supply chain technology adoption is the lack of interoperability between different systems and platforms. Many companies have invested in proprietary technology solutions that are not easily integrated with newer systems, which can create information silos and hinder collaboration across the supply chain. This challenge also affects the short-term return on investment (ROI) of adopting these technologies. Companies need to assess the ROI of adopting a technology and justify the costs associated with implementation, training, and maintenance. Budget constraints and uncertainty around the potential benefits of a technology can hinder its adoption.

The complexity of supply chains is another significant challenge that requires a collaborative approach to technology adoption. To optimize supply chain performance, it is essential for all parties involved, including suppliers, manufacturers,

Table 1 Summary of supply chain technologies and their benefits

Technology	Applications and benefits
Artificial intelligence and machine learning	Accurate demand forecasting; enhanced predictive maintenance; improved route optimization; enhanced quality control; efficient supply chain risk management
Blockchain	End-to-end tracking in supply chain, enhance food safety; promote ethical and sustainable sourcing; enable fast and secured financial transactions; efficient communication and collaboration; increase security and visibility
Virtual and augmented reality	Enhanced warehouse operations; improved inventory management; streamlined transportation; enhanced customer experience
Robotics and drone technology	Faster deliveries; efficient inventory management; efficient last-mile delivery; improved sustainability; enhanced supply chain visibility
Self-driving vehicles	Efficient resource (labor, vehicle, budget) usage; improved delivery routes; efficient inventory management
Digital twin	Simulation of physical systems to visualize; monitor, and analyze; efficient analytics; improved inventory management; enhanced supply chain risk management
Big data analytics and advanced planning	Enhanced production and scheduling efficiency; optimized supply chain processes; improved disruption management

distributors, and customers, to embrace the technology solutions being implemented. Companies must prioritize collaboration and communication with all stakeholders throughout the technology adoption process to address this challenge. This includes engaging suppliers and other partners early in the planning process, communicating the benefits and expected outcomes of the technology solutions being implemented, and providing training and support to ensure that all parties can effectively utilize the technology.

Another challenge associated with most of the above-mentioned technologies is data quality and security. New technologies in supply chains rely heavily on data, and ensuring data quality, accuracy, and security is crucial. Ensuring data quality is essential to ensure that the data used in supply chain processes is accurate, reliable, and consistent. Poor data quality can lead to inaccurate forecasting, suboptimal inventory management, and inefficient decision-making. Data integrity issues can arise from data entry errors, data duplication, inconsistent data formats, or data integration challenges when adopting new technologies.

In addition to data quality, data security is another significant concern in SCM. The increasing reliance on digital technologies and data-driven processes in supply chains exposes organizations to potential data breaches, cyber-attacks, and data theft. The sensitive nature of supply chain data, such as customer information, pricing data, intellectual property, and trade secrets, makes it imperative to have robust data security measures in place to protect against unauthorized access, data leaks, and other security breaches. Supply chains also involve multiple stakeholders, including suppliers, logistics providers, customers, and other partners, who may have access to sensitive data. Ensuring secure data sharing and collaboration across the supply chain ecosystem can be challenging, as it requires establishing trust, implementing strong authentication measures, and encrypting data during transmission and storage.

Acknowledgments We would like to thank Harish Singi for his invaluable assistance in the preparation of this paper. His diligent research has significantly enriched the quality of our work. We also would like to thank Dr. Ujjal Mukherjee for his insightful comments on improving the quality of this chapter.

References

Aamer, A., Sahara, C. R., & Al-Awlaqi, M. A. (2023). Digitalization of the supply chain: transformation factors. *Journal of Science and Technology Policy Management, 14*(4).

Ackerman, E. (2020). Autonomous drone networks are a faster route to sustainable supply chains. https://spectrum.ieee.org/zipline-long-distance-delivery-covid19-supplies

Afeyan, N. (2022). AI puts Moderna within striking distance of beating COVID-19—Digital, Data, and Design Institute at Harvard. https://d3.harvard.edu/ai-puts-moderna-within-striking-distance-of-beating-covid-19/

Akilo, D. (2018). Blockchain platforms to solve supply chain problems—Business Blockchain HQ. https://businessblockchainhq.com/business-blockchain-news/blockchain-supply-chain-platforms

ASCM. (2018). Five ways augmented reality enhances supply chain management. https://www.ascm.org/ascm-insights/five-ways-augmented-reality-enhances-supply-chain-management/

Aurora-Innovation. (2023). Moving us towards a self-driving future. https://aurora.tech/

AWS. (2021). Amazon Web Services BrandVoice: Predicting the future of demand: How Amazon is reinventing forecasting with machine learning. https://www.forbes.com/sites/amazonwebservices/2021/12/03/predicting-the-future-of-demand-how-amazon-is-reinventing-forecasting-with-machine-learning/

Balakrishnan, T., Chui, M., Hall, B., & Henke, N. (2020). The state of AI in 2020. https://www.mckinsey.com/capabilities/quantumblack/our-insights/global-survey-the-state-of-ai-in-2020

Banker, S. (2019). Procter & Gamble embraces continuous planning and execution. https://www.forbes.com/sites/stevebanker/2019/11/05/procter%2D%2Dgamble-embraces-continuous-planning-and-execution/

Barsky, N. (2021). Procter & Gamble's tech spending boosts supply chain resilience. https://www.forbes.com/sites/noahbarsky/2021/10/26/procter-gamble-tech-spending-boosts-supply-chain-resilience/

Bateman, K. (2021). Could autonomous trucks be the answer to the global supply chain crisis? https://www.weforum.org/agenda/2021/11/can-autonomous-trucks-fix-supply-chain/

BBC. (2022). Global chip shortage: Toyota profits fall as production hit. https://www.bbc.com/news/business-60313571

Blasquez, P. (2021). UPS meets logistical challenges amidst pandemic, discusses future of supply chain and e-commerce. https://dallasinnovates.com/ups-meets-logistical-challenges-amidst-pandemic-discusses-future-of-supply-chain-and-e-commerce/

Boff, L. (2017). GE's CMO on digital transformation. https://deloitte.wsj.com/articles/ges-cmo-on-digital-transformation-1485752539

Brody, B. (2020). 4 high-tech tools Johnson & Johnson is using to get products to you during the pandemic. https://www.jnj.com/innovation/johnson-johnson-supply-chain-technology-during-coronavirus

Burnette, D., & Eshel, P. (2022). The surprising benefits of self-driving trucks. https://www.weforum.org/agenda/2020/03/self-driving-trucks-will-change-the-world-more-than-you-might-think/

Business-Insider. (2019). Coca-Cola bottlers and SAP are scaling a major blockchain project poised to remake a 21 billion dollar a year supply-chain operation. It's one example of the still nascent tech's promise. https://www.businessinsider.com/coca-cola-bottlers-sap-scaling-up-a-major-blockchain-project-2019-10

Business-Wire-News. (2021). DHL supply chain partners with autonomous software leader embark to deploy fleet starting in 2024. https://www.businesswire.com/news/home/20211028005341/en/DHL-Supply-Chain-Partners-with-Autonomous-Software-Leader-Embark-to-Deploy-Fleet-Starting-in

Castellanos, S. (2021). Augmented reality gets pandemic boost. https://www.wsj.com/articles/augmented-reality-gets-pandemic-boost-11611866795.

Chottani, A., Hastings, G., Murnane, J., & Neuhaus, F. (2018). Distraction or disruption? Autonomous trucks gain ground in US logistics. McKinsey & Company. https://www.mckinsey.com/industries/travel-logistics-and-infrastructure/our-insights/distraction-or-disruption-autonomous-trucks-gain-ground-in-us-logistics

CIO. (2021). L'Oréal supercharges ecommerce with digital techL'Oréal supercharges ecommerce with digital tech. https://www.cio.com/article/188822/loreal-supercharges-ecommerce-with-digital-tech.html

Davis, R. (2021). How Toyota steered clear of the chip shortage mess. https://www.bloomberg.com/news/articles/2021-04-07/how-toyota-s-supply-chain-helped-it-weather-the-chip-shortage

DDC FPO. (2023). What is supply chain digitization and why does it matter? Retrieved 2023, from https://www.ddcfpo.com/freight-process-insights/what-is-supply-chain-digitization-and-why-does-it-matter.

Deloitte. (2020a). Digital twin applications: Bridging the physical and digital. https://www2.deloitte.com/us/en/insights/focus/tech-trends/2020/digital-twin-applications-bridging-the-physical-and-digital.html

Deloitte. (2020b). Using blockchain to drive supply chain transparency. https://www2.deloitte.com/us/en/pages/operations/articles/blockchain-supply-chain-innovation.html

DHL. (2022). Augmented and extended reality. https://www.dhl.com/us-en/home/insights-and-innovation/thought-leadership/trend-reports/augmented-and-extended-reality.html

Doe, J. (2017). Zipline: drones that can save lives and revolutionize supply chains—Technology and operations management. https://d3.harvard.edu/platform-rctom/submission/zipline-drones-that-can-save-lives-and-revolutionize-supply-chains/

Earl, C. (2021). How automated contract management is a critical link in the COVID-19 vaccine supply chain. https://www.sdcexec.com/sourcing-procurement/article/21391923/agiloft-how-automated-contract-management-is-a-critical-link-in-the-covid19-vaccine-supply-chain

Forbes. (2021). Amazon Web Services BrandVoice: Predicting the future of demand: How Amazon is reinventing forecasting with machine learning. https://www.forbes.com/sites/amazonwebservices/2021/12/03/predicting-the-future-of-demand-how-amazon-is-reinventing-forecasting-with-machine-learning/?sh=579007501b6b

Forde, M. (2019). Plus.ai autonomous truck completes coast-to-coast delivery in 3 days. https://www.supplychaindive.com/news/plusai-autonomous-truck-completes-coast-to-coast-delivery-in-3-days/568729/

Fu, E. (2021). Autonomous drone networks are a faster route to sustainable supply chains. https://www.weforum.org/agenda/2021/11/drone-delivery-supply-chains/

Fuller, S. L., & Stinson, J. (2021). TuSimple readies autonomous runs to UPS hubs in Florida, North Carolina. https://www.supplychaindive.com/news/TuSimple-UPS-autonomous-uptime/609445/

Gartner. (2022). Supply Chain Award Winner 2022: Schneider Electric. https://www.gartner.com/en/supply-chain/trends/supply-chain-award-winner-2022-schneider-electric

General-Electrics. (2022a). Digital twin creation. https://www.ge.com/research/offering/digital-twin-creation

General-Electrics. (2022b). Digital twins highlighted in analyst ranking report. https://www.ge.com/digital/applications/digital-twin

Glover, E. (2022). 5 uses of blockchain in the supply chain. https://builtin.com/blockchain/blockchain-in-supply-chain

Goel, A. (2021a). How technology can help with Covid-19 supply chain disruptions. https://www.forbes.com/sites/forbesbusinessdevelopmentcouncil/2021/01/28/how-technology-can-help-with-covid-19-supply-chain-disruptions/

Goel, A. (2021b). Autonomous drone networks are a faster route to sustainable supply chains. https://www.weforum.org/agenda/2021/11/drone-delivery-supply-chains/

Hawkins, A. J. (2021). Volvo and Aurora team up on fully autonomous trucks for North America. https://www.theverge.com/2021/3/30/22358005/volvo-aurora-autonomous-truck-partnership

HBR. (2020). Four ways technology can enhance your supply chain. https://hbr.org/sponsored/2020/11/four-ways-technology-can-enhance-your-supply-chain

Heilweil, R. (2020). Networks of self-driving trucks are becoming a reality in the US. https://www.vox.com/recode/2020/7/1/21308539/self-driving-autonomous-trucks-ups-freight-network

Holley, P. (2019). Warby Parker's latest tool lets shoppers try on glasses using augmented reality. https://www.washingtonpost.com/technology/2019/02/04/warby-parkers-latest-tool-lets-shoppers-try-glasses-using-augmented-reality/

IBM. (2022a). IBM Watson Health is now Merative. https://www.ibm.com/watson-health/merative-divestiture

IBM. (2022b). AI drives business success. IBM Watson powers AI for you. https://www.ibm.com/watson

IBM. (2023a). IBM Institute for Business Value—Research, reports, and insights. https://www.ibm.com/thought-leadership/institute-business-value/en-us

IBM. (2023b). IBM Blockchain—Enterprise blockchain solutions and services. https://www.ibm.com/blockchain
IBM. (2023c). What is a digital twin. https://www.ibm.com/topics/what-is-a-digital-twin
Ismail, A. (2021). Toyota prepared for the chip shortage years ago. Why didn't anyone else? https://jalopnik.com/toyota-prepared-for-the-chip-shortage-years-ago-why-di-1846641653
Jarrell, M. (2021). Artificial intelligence and digital twins at General Electric. https://emerj.com/ai-sector-overviews/ai-at-general-electric/
JNJ. (2023). Supply chain. https://www.jnj.com/tag/supply-chain
John-Deere. (2023). John Deere technology and innovation. https://www.deere.com/en/our-company/innovation/
Kennedy, L. (2022). C3 AI and Google Cloud partner to optimize supply chains with enterprise AI. https://www.businesswire.com/news/home/20220614005469/en/C3-AI-and-Google-Cloud-Partner-to-Optimize-Supply-Chains-with-Enterprise-AI
L'Oreal. (2021). Augmented reality is revolutionising the beauty experience. http://www.loreal--finance.com/en/annual-report-2017/digital/augmented-reality-beauty-experience
Maersk. (2021). How blockchain technology is beefing up supply chain visibility. https://www.maersk.com/news/articles/2021/07/27/how-blockchain-technology-is-beefing-up
Maloney, J. (2020). PepsiCo sales snap back from pandemic. https://www.wsj.com/articles/pepsico-sales-rise-as-beverage-segment-improves-11601550380
MarketsandMarkets. (2023). Blockchain supply chain market by offering (platform, services), application (payment & settlement, product traceability, smart contracts, governance, risk & compliance management), user (small & medium-sized enterprises (SMEs), large enterprises), vertical, and region—global forecast to 2026. https://www.marketsandmarkets.com/Market-Reports/blockchain-supply-chain-market-90851499.html
MarketScreener. (2021). Schneider Electric: Our supply chain message to our U.S. partners and distributors. https://www.marketscreener.com/quote/stock/SCHNEIDER-ELECTRIC-SE-4699/news/Schneider-Electric-Our-supply-chain-message-to-our-U-S-partners-and-distributors-37197046
Marr, B. (2019a). How is Warby Parker using artificial intelligence and augmented reality to change retail? https://www.linkedin.com/pulse/how-warby-parker-using-artificial-intelligence-augmented-bernard-marr
Marr, B. (2019b). The fascinating ways Warby Parker uses artificial intelligence and AR to change retail. https://www.forbes.com/sites/bernardmarr/2019/04/18/the-fascinating-ways-warby-parker-uses-artificial-intelligence-and-ar-to-change-retail/
Mclain, S. (2021). Toyota's chip supply helps it beat General Motors for the first time. https://www.wsj.com/articles/toyotas-chip-supply-helps-it-beat-general-motors-for-the-first-time-11625569943
Meenu, E. G. (2021). Nestle: Driving innovation through AI and other Disruptive Tech. https://www.analyticsinsight.net/nestle-driving-innovation-through-ai-and-other-disruptive-tech/
MHI. (2023). MHI Annual Industry Report 2023. https://www.mhi.org/publications/report
Naidu, R., & Halpin, P. (2022). Maersk sees no let up in surging cost of shipping goods. https://www.reuters.com/business/maersk-sees-no-let-up-surging-cost-shipping-goods-2022-06-22/
Nestle. (2020). Nestle speeds up factory support with augmented reality. https://www.nestle.com/media/news/nestle-factory-support-augmented-reality/
Olavsrud, T. (2021). PepsiCo tackles supply chain with data. https://www.pepsico.com/our-stories/press-release/pepsico-announces-strategic-end-to-end-transformation-pep-pepsico-positive09152021
Palmer, A. (2022). Amazon, Walmart and others battle price gouging on coronavirus-related products. https://www.cnbc.com/2020/03/03/amazon-walmart-e-retailers-battle-price-gouging-on-coronavirus-products.html
PepsiCo. (2021). Press release: PepsiCo announces strategic end-to-end transformation: pep+ (PepsiCo Positive). https://www.pepsico.com/our-stories/press-release/pepsico-announces-strategic-end-to-end-transformation-pep-pepsico-positive09152021

Pfizer. (2021). Environmental, social & governance report. https://www.pfizer.com/sites/default/files/investors/financial reports/annual reports/2021/files/Pfizer_ESG_Report.pdf
Pfizer. (2023). Global manufacturing, supply & distribution. https://www.pfizer.com/products/how-drugs-are-made/global-supply
Phipps, P., & Rusin, G. (2021). Johnson & Johnson reduces analysis time by 35 percent with their data science platform using Amazon EFS—Amazon Web Services. https://aws.amazon.com/blogs/storage/johnson-johnson-reduces-analysis-time-by-35-with-data-science-platform/
Plex DemandCaster. (2014). Demand-Caster: Warby Parker aligns business objectives with supply chain management to drive growth. https://www.demandcaster.com/blog/warby-parker-aligns-business-objectives-with-supply-chain-management-to-drive-growth/
Procureconeast. (2021). How Nestle maintained a "robust" supply chain in 2020 and prepared itself for the future. https://procureconeast.wbresearch.com/blog/how-nestle-maintained-a-robust-supply-chain-in-2020-and-prepared-itself-for-the-future
ProjectPro. (2023). How big data analysis helped increase Walmart's sales turnover? https://www.projectpro.io/article/how-big-data-analysis-helped-increase-walmarts-sales-turnover/109
PwC. (2018). Blockchain Initiatives by PwC Jamaica. https://www.pwc.com/jm/en/press-room/blockchain-initiatives.html
PwC. (2021). PwC US tech effect: AI business survey. Retrieved 2022, from https://www.pwc.com/us/en/tech-effect/ai-analytics/ai-business-survey.html.
PwC. (2023). 2023 digital supply chain survey. https://www.pwc.com/us/en/services/consulting/business-transformation/digital-supply-chain-survey.html
Rahn, D. (2017). L'Oréal: A gorgeous supply chain makeover. https://d3.harvard.edu/platform-rctom/submission/loreal-a-gorgeous-supply-chain-makeover/
Reuters. (2021). Why Toyota had a big pile of chips when semiconductor shortage dealt others a bad hand. https://www.autoblog.com/2021/03/09/toyota-how-it-avoided-semiconductor-shortage/
Riaz, O. (2021). Council post: Amazon Inventory Management: Solutions to common problems. https://www.forbes.com/sites/forbesagencycouncil/2021/11/15/amazon-inventory-management-solutions-to-common-problems/
Robison, C. H. (2022). C.H. Robinson and Waymo VIA Enter Strategic Partnership. https://www.chrobinson.com/en-us/newsroom/press-releases/2022/02-16-22_chrobinson_and_waymo_enter_partnership/
Scrum-Inc. (2022). Adaptive and resilient supply chain management: How John Deere uses scrum to create supply chain solutions in the midst of disruption. https://www.scruminc.com/john-deere-scrum-supply-chain-solutions/
SE-News. (2021, December 16). A message to customers and partners. https://www.se.com/us/en/about-us/press/news/global-2021/update-covid-19.jsp
Shapiro, M. (2021). How Johnson & Johnson's innovative supply chain technology is helping transform how we work—And live. https://www.jnj.com/innovation/how-johnson-johnsons-innovative-supply-chain-technology-is-helping-transform-how-we-work-and-live
Sharma, A., Virmani, T., Pathak, V., Sharma, A., Pathak, K., Kumar, G., & Pathak, D. (2022). Artificial intelligence-based data-driven strategy to accelerate research, development, and clinical trials of covid vaccine. *BioMed Research International*. https://doi.org/10.1155/2022/7205241
Sharma, T. K. (2020). Top companies using blockchain to increase supply chain management. https://www.blockchain-council.org/blockchain/top-companies-using-blockchain-to-increase-supply-chain-management/
Shetty, S. (2021). How does blockchain solutions help in overcoming supply chain challenges? https://www.researchdive.com/blog/how-does-blockchain-solutions-help-in-overcoming-supply-chain-challenges
Shirouzu, N. (2021). How Toyota thrives when the chips are down. https://www.reuters.com/article/us-japan-fukushima-anniversary-toyota-in-idUSKBN2B1005
Silverstien, S. (2020). The state of AI in 2020. https://www.supplychaindive.com/news/walmart-grocery-AI-demand-operations/585424/

Smith, J. (2021). Plus's SPAC merger marks autonomous trucking shift to public markets. https://www.wsj.com/articles/pluss-spac-merger-marks-autonomous-trucking-shift-to-public-markets-11620640801

SpendEdge. (2021). Everything that is wrong with drone technology in supply chain. https://www.spendedge.com/blogs/problems-drone-technology-supply-chain

ST. (2017). P&G: End-to-end supply chain model. https://d3.harvard.edu/platform-rctom/submission/pg-end-to-end-supply-chain-model/

Statista. (2020). Statista: Supermarket consumer satisfaction—Walmart U.S. https://www.statista.com/statistics/819713/supermarket-consumer-satisfaction-walmart-us/

SumatoSoft. (2022). IoT supply chain: Real-life use cases & challenges. https://sumatosoft.com/blog/iot-supply-chain

Sweeney, E. (2022). The big challenges for supply chains in 2022. World Economic Forum. https://www.weforum.org/agenda/2022/01/challenges-supply-chains-covid19-2022/

Tricoire, J. (2020). The supply chain of tomorrow. https://blog.se.com/energy-management-energy-efficiency/2020/08/04/the-supply-chain-of-tomorrow/

UNC. (2019). Autonomous driving affecting supply chain management. https://online.uncp.edu/articles/mba/autonomous-driving-affect-supply-chain.aspx

Unilever. (2022). Unilever supply chain in Gartner 'Masters' category fourth year running. https://www.unilever.com/news/news-search/2022/unilever-supply-chain-in-gartner-masters-category-fourth-year-running/

UPS. (2022). Fall 2022 supply chain virtual connect. https://www.ups.com/us/en/supplychain/insights/ups-supply-chain-virtual-connect-october-5-2022.page?

Warby-Parker. (2022). Annual report 2021. https://s28.q4cdn.com/987131352/files/doc_financials/2021/annual/Warby-Parker-Annual-Report-2021.pdf

Williams, C. (2019). Farm to data table: John Deere and data in precision agriculture. https://d3.harvard.edu/platform-digit/submission/farm-to-data-table-john-deere-and-data-in-precision-agriculture/

Winston, C. (2021). The answer to America's supply-chain woes lies in automation. https://www.barrons.com/articles/supply-chain-crisis-autonomous-vehicles-solution-51635367731

Yeeles, M. (2020). Schneider Electric: Building the supply chain of tomorrow. https://supplychaindigital.com/digital-supply-chain/schneider-electric-building-supply-chain-tomorrow

Young, L. (2022). Covid-19 vaccine rollout carries lessons for pharma supply chains, says Pfizer executive. https://www.wsj.com/articles/covid-19-vaccine-rollout-carries-lessons-for-pharma-supply-chains-says-pfizer-executive-11664017202

Zimmerman, S. (2021). P&G shifts suppliers, product formulas to avoid supply chain issues. https://www.supplychaindive.com/news/procter-gamble-alternate-suppliers-reformulate-products/608625/

The manufacturer's authorised representative in the EU is Springer Nature Customer Service Centre GmbH, Europaplatz 3, 69115 Heidelberg, Germany. If you have any concerns regarding our products, please contact ProductSafety@springernature.com

Printed and bound by CPI Group (UK) Ltd, Croydon, CR0 4YY

02/10/2026

02226885-0004